# International Tribunals and Human Security

# International Tribunals and Human Security

James Meernik

ROWMAN & LITTLEFIELD
*Lanham • Boulder • New York • London*

Published by Rowman & Littlefield
A wholly owned subsidiary of The Rowman & Littlefield Publishing Group, Inc.
4501 Forbes Boulevard, Suite 200, Lanham, Maryland 20706
www.rowman.com

Unit A, Whitacre Mews, 26-34 Stannary Street, London SE11 4AB



British Library Cataloguing in Publication Information Available

**Library of Congress Cataloging-in-Publication Data**
Names: Meernik, James David, author.
Title: International tribunals and human security / James Meernik.
Description: Lanham, Maryland : Rowman & Littlefield, 2016. | Includes bibliographical references and index.
Identifiers: LCCN 2016025194 (print) | LCCN 2016025480 (ebook) | ISBN 9781442269668 (cloth : alk. paper) | ISBN 9781442269675 (pbk. : alk. paper) | ISBN 9781442269682 (Electronic)
Subjects: LCSH: International criminal courts. | Humanitarian law—International cooperation. | Human rights.
Classification: LCC KZ7230 .M44 2016 (print) | LCC KZ7230 (ebook) | DDC 345/.01—dc23
LC record available at https://lccn.loc.gov/2016025194

∞™ The paper used in this publication meets the minimum requirements of American National Standard for Information Sciences—Permanence of Paper for Printed Library Materials, ANSI/NISO Z39.48-1992.

Printed in the United States of America

# Contents

## *Chapter 1*

# Introduction

If you have ever seen documentary or old newsreel footage of the concentration camps of Nazi Germany, you know what horrible things humans can do to one another. The scope of Nazi Germany's and Imperial Japan's war crimes during World War II was of a magnitude that the world had never before witnessed. The scale of those atrocities was unique, but their occurrence was, unfortunately, not. There were earlier atrocities, such as the German massacre of the Herero and Nama people from 1904 to 1907 and the genocide of the Armenian population by the Ottoman Empire during World War I. More recently, tens and hundreds of thousands of innocent people have been killed in places like Bosnia-Herzegovina, Burundi, Cambodia, Rwanda, and Iraq. The difference now is that we have come to expect some sort of international response to these tragedies. "Never again" has been the battle cry since the Holocaust of World War II. "No impunity for war criminals" has been the clarion call of this generation that has created multiple war crimes tribunals and now an International Criminal Court to prosecute and punish the political and military organizers of massive human rights crimes. But have these efforts worked? Do international courts and tribunals succeed in apprehending and prosecuting the political and military leaders who organize large-scale human rights violations? Most importantly of all, has this effort at providing international justice actually improved human security? We will delve into these questions to examine the work of the tribunals, what they have accomplished, and where they have fallen short.

The evolution of international justice over the last one hundred years is one of a doggedly persistent idealism whose reach often exceeds its grasp. The revelation of the horrors that have befallen a people in some faraway land produces revulsion and outrage among those of us living in nations that have moved beyond such violence. The clamor of voices demanding a response has grown ever louder. Throughout the twentieth century, these reactions have inspired attempts to pin the blame on the criminal masterminds. International outrage has led diplomats and scholars to devise and enlarge international law to criminalize the seemingly endless ways humans have dreamed up to abuse and eliminate their fellow species members. The twentieth century has seen both the greatest levels of human rights abuses in history and the most far-reaching efforts to hold those responsible accountable to the law.

My purpose in this book is to examine *whether international justice, and specifically the international criminal tribunals, has advanced the cause of human security*. The astute reader will notice that I did not claim that I would answer this question because there is no one true answer on which everyone can agree. Instead, I will review what we do know. We actually know quite a bit from a surge of research in recent years. At this point, perhaps more than a few of you let out a groan at the thought of plowing through a long, tedious account of who researched what. My goal, however, is not to take you on a tour of all the books and articles on international justice and human rights. Instead, I want to tell you about the most important and interesting findings that will allow you to make sense of what we can expect of international justice. We will talk about some of this research, but we will also explore the data on international justice and human security, as well as some of the history of this subject.

This book is about international justice and human security. It concerns a term—*human security*—that has come into parlance as a lens or perspective through which we seek to understand the dangers of the world as experienced by people the world over. When we speak of human security, we speak of the living conditions of individuals and whether such conditions—that is, people's existence—can be considered safe and stable or dangerous and uncertain. A human security focus is a focus on people and the problems they face regardless of national boundaries. It emphasizes humans, not nations, to understand these threats. Human security is actually more than just a frame of reference. It is the thing that we study. It is the subject of our analysis. Human *security* is a particular set of conditions or types of existence in which humans live. Human security exists when individuals can live without threats of violence to their personal and bodily integrity and can live in conditions that are conducive to basic human needs. By personal integrity, we mean the physical and psychological health of the individual (Poe and Tate 1994). Actions by public actors, such as governments that torture, can certainly jeopardize human security. The behaviors of private actors, such as rebel armies that destroy villages, also threaten human security. These actions create innumerable problems for people, especially when government security forces or criminal gangs make daily existence a continual battle for safety.

We limit our attention to those threats to human security that endanger the human right to personal integrity. Most obviously, these involve actual or imminent threats to one's ability to survive in the present. Governments that systematically round up entire villages to coerce their loyalty under threat of execution create such harm. Under such conditions, people do not live in a state of human security; instead, they live in a constant state of fear or danger. Human security is freedom from such violence and the pervasive fear it creates. While human security can be threatened by other economic, social, and environmental forces in the world, our focus will be on whether international justice has advanced or harmed human security as measured by justice, human rights, and peace. Let's begin with a brief account of the strange and unexpected journey that international justice has been on since World War II.

## INTERNATIONAL JUSTICE EMERGES FROM HIBERNATION

International law and international justice were catapulted to prominence after the defeat of the Axis powers in World War II. The Axis crimes, especially the Nazi genocide of the Jews and their systematic massacre of political opponents, homosexuals, Roma, and anyone else they deemed insufficiently Aryan, led to the creation of the first international tribunal—the Nuremberg Tribunal. It was a triumph of dispassionate justice over emotional revenge. As Robert Jackson, U.S. Supreme Court Justice and Chief Prosecutor for the Allies, proclaimed in his opening address on November 10, 1945,

> That four great nations, flushed with victory and stung with injury stay the hand of vengeance and voluntarily submit their captive enemies to the judgment of the law is one of the most significant tributes that Power has ever paid to Reason.

A similar tribunal was created to deal with the Japanese war criminals—the Tokyo Tribunal. While both tribunals faced accusations that they were little more than "victor's justice" (in the sense that to the victor go the spoils of dealing with the defeated enemy) cloaked in judicial robes, the tribunals did set many important precedents. They helped define what came to be known as "crimes against humanity," which are those atrocities committed typically against civilians during war and even during times of peace by governments that feel threatened by their own people or those they conquer. They established the principle that a superior is responsible for the crimes of his subordinate. Prior to these tribunals, presidents, prime ministers, and generals would claim they were not personally liable for any crimes their forces may have committed. Rather, they would argue that the "state" was responsible. The irony of such claims was that while every government employee was part of the "state," no one person *was* the state and could be held responsible for what the state did. All could hide behind this abstract wall of impunity. Thus, one of the most important accomplishments of these first two tribunals was to show that there can be more effective strategies for confronting massive atrocities than simply accepting that states can do whatever they wish (Bass 2002).

Flush with the victory of which Justice Jackson spoke, the work of the victorious allies and the international legal community did not stop there. The world drew up and ratified the Geneva Conventions on War Crimes in 1949 and the Convention on the Prevention and Punishment of the Crime of Genocide, which entered into force in January 1951. The Geneva Conventions, comprising four conventions and three later, additional protocols, set out a series of standards governing the conduct of war. The four conventions detail how the wounded and sick on the battlefield and at sea are to be taken care of, how prisoners of war are to be treated, and the proper conduct toward civilian populations during wartime. The additional protocols to these conventions provide further information on these standards, but also extend many of these rules to apply in civil or intrastate wars. Prior to these protocols, political and military leaders had insisted that they had the right as leaders of sovereign states to do whatever they needed to do in order to deal with domestic unrest and rebellion. All too often, such excuses simply served to cover up human rights abuses and allow leaders, as well as the rebels they were fighting, to escape blame. Taken together, the Geneva Conventions and Protocols made clear that the ill-treatment of POWs and civilian populations was abhorrent and illegal. More importantly for the future protection of human rights, they established practices that all states are supposed to honor, even if some did so more in the breach.

The Genocide Convention outlaws what has come to be called the "crime of crimes." Hitler's Holocaust against the Jews and his efforts to exterminate other populations in Europe were the latest in a sad history of systematic efforts to eliminate what the Genocide Convention refers to as "national, ethnical, racial or religious" groups. A Polish refugee, Rafael Lemkin, coined the term *genocide* and worked doggedly to see the Genocide Convention become law. The Genocide Convention not only indicates which types of groups enjoy protection, it also lists the types of actions (e.g., killing, forcibly transferring children) that are considered to be international crimes. The convention provides that individuals, not "states," are to be held responsible and that these persons must demonstrate a special intent to commit genocide. They must be deliberately seeking to commit acts of genocide against one of the protected groups. The Genocide Convention does set a fairly high bar of proof that is required before someone can be convicted of committing this crime of crimes. And interestingly, it also stipulated that the convention's signatory states should also take steps to prevent and punish the crime. We will return to this question of prevention later to see just what role these tribunals have played in deterring such crimes.

Unfortunately, those heady days of international justice did not last long. The Cold War struggle between the Soviet Union and the West led by the United States ensured that nearly every dispute in the world was viewed as an opportunity for gain on one side or loss for the other. Notions of justice rarely intruded into such considerations. Neither side was willing to accept the establishment of any new international tribunal. The United States and the USSR grounded their arguments in the name of noninterference in the internal affairs of nations—the sacrosanct notion of state sovereignty. At the same time, they also feared that if international justice was given the teeth necessary to prosecute those responsible for the many and horrific human rights crimes of the era (such as the Chinese Cultural Revolution and the vast machinery of repression used by the Soviet Union, to say nothing of the crimes committed by various and sundry dictators around the world allied to both sides), it would be used for political and not judicial purposes. Certainly there were small victories. The issue of human rights rose to assume a very prominent place on the global agenda with the formation of organizations like Amnesty International and Human Rights Watch. It took the end of the Cold War and the disintegration of the Soviet Union, however, to usher in a new era of international justice. Unfortunately, the disintegration of the bipolar world order also eroded the balance of power and loosened the political restraints that helped prevent many conflicts from occurring. The advance of human rights was accompanied by an uglier, darker side as well.

First and most prominently, the collapse of communism in Yugoslavia in the late 1980s hastened the demise of that state and helped create the first of the post–Cold War humanitarian disasters that led to renewed calls for international justice (Bass 2002). Yugoslavia had always been an artificial creation of disparate peoples and without the binding agent of communist dictatorship to hold them together, the centripetal forces of nationalism and bigotry broke apart the state. Leaders like Slobodan Milošević of Serbia and Franjo Tuđman of Croatia sought to make their societies more ethnically pure and expand their territory. A series of wars throughout the 1990s ensued, which I will describe below, but the end result in most cases was horrific crimes against humanity, war crimes, and genocide as these leaders pursued their violent dreams of ethnic supremacy. A scant few years later, the Rwandan genocide erupted in 1994. That nation had also weathered years of tension between the Hutu majority and Tutsi minority that occasionally flared up into systematic killings. The Hutu government, not unlike the Nazis before them, determined that they required a final solution to rid themselves of the ethnic minority—the Tutsi—they feared sought their downfall. The Rwandan genocide claimed the lives of roughly 800,000 people, who were systematically slaughtered in just a few months.

There was, unfortunately, no shortage of such atrocities in the post–Cold War period. Iraq under Saddam Hussein continued its brutal treatment of its Shiite and Kurdish populations. The government of North Korea perpetuated famines that killed hundreds of thousands and maintained its own brutal gulag for anyone who questioned the "worker's paradise" led by the Kim family. The Yugoslav and Rwanda atrocities, however, through a combination of media attention, the guilt of the international community for failure to take any meaningful action to stop these atrocities, and a rare display of United Nations Security Council consensus, led to the creation of the International Criminal Tribunal for the Former Yugoslavia (ICTY) and the International Criminal Tribunal for Rwanda (ICTR). These were the first international tribunals since World War II. Just like the early years after that war, the skies parted for ever so brief a moment and made possible a triumph for international justice and human rights. But this time, international justice secured its beachhead and refused to retreat back into the fringes of world politics.

## THE REBIRTH OF INTERNATIONAL CRIMINAL JUSTICE AND THE INTERNATIONAL CRIMINAL TRIBUNAL FOR THE FORMER YUGOSLAVIA

The rebirth of international justice begins with the establishment of the ICTY. The ICTY was created in May 1993 by the United Nations Security Council using its Chapter VII powers to maintain international peace and security. The wars of the former Yugoslavia had begun after it became clear that the ideological and political glue holding the nation together had eroded severely during the 1980s, due to economic problems, the rise of nationalist leaders like Franjo Tuđman and Slobodan Milošević, and the fall of the Berlin Wall. When the Yugoslav republic of Croatia declared its independence in June 1991, the national government and army offered strong resistance. Serbs in Croatia, especially in border regions with Serbia where they lived in large numbers, declared their own micro states and sought to drive out the Croatian population to create ethnically pure or "cleansed" areas they could dominate or even merge into a "greater" Serbia. For the rest of 1991, fighting raged in these areas until peace was established in January 1992.

It wasn't long before the next war of secession started in Bosnia-Herzegovina in April 1992 when that Yugoslav republic declared its independence over the fierce objections of its Serbian population. The Muslim, or Bosniak and Croatian, populations of Bosnia feared domination and discrimination by the Serb-led national government in Belgrade if they remained in Yugoslavia, while the Bosnian Serbs either dreamed of creating their own micro state or joining up with a greater Serbia. Fighting began in many areas of Bosnia-Herzegovina that were either in the eastern part of the country and close to Serbia or where there were sizeable Serb populations. Once again the ethnic cleansing that had been witnessed in Croatia was repeated, but with even greater levels of violence as Serb forces sought to drive out Bosniaks and Croats from areas they wished to make ethnically pure. Pictures of starving and emaciated prisoners in Serb-run concentration camps and the shelling and sniping in the capital city of Bosnia, Sarajevo, provoked international outrage and UN investigations.

Despite substantial evidence of such atrocities, there was little stomach among the dominant powers in Europe, principally Great Britain, France, and Germany, as well as the United Nations Security Council, to resort to military force to compel an end to the war. Nonetheless, given the evidence of war crimes and crimes against humanity in Croatia and Bosnia-Herzegovina detailed by the UN-authorized Commission of Experts and the enormous international outcry over the appearance of concentration camps on European soil for the first time since World War II, some type of response was necessary. Hence, in May 1993 the UN Security Council authorized the creation of the International Criminal Tribunal for the Former Yugoslavia to investigate and prosecute allegations of war crimes, crimes against humanity, and genocide.[1] Because the governments that supported the tribunal's creation had also failed to stop these atrocities, there were perhaps heightened expectations that international justice would provide the just deserts for those who were responsible. Especially coming on the heels of the end of the Cold War, there was a sense that the world was entering a new era and that war criminals could now be properly punished (Scharf 1997).

But if the cries for international justice for the victims of the Yugoslav wars were powerful enough to demand an international response, it was not at all clear just how far the UN and the ICTY's principal advocates in Europe and the United States were prepared to go to provide the tribunal with the kind of support it would need to succeed. I will not attempt to relate a comprehensive history of the ICTY here. There are many excellent histories of the ICTY (such as Kerr 2007 and Schabas 2006) that can give the reader a more in-depth historical account of the evolution of the ICTY. Instead, my purpose is to describe those parts of its legal and political development that will help us understand its impact on human security. Indeed, I will follow the same pattern as I describe the birth of the other ad hoc tribunals and provide the essential details and set the stage for evaluating the tribunals' effectiveness in promoting human security.

The ICTY was, and still is, a novel experiment. No international criminal tribunal had been created since World War II. No tribunal had ever been created in the midst of ongoing fighting. No tribunal had been created that involved one set of actors (in this case the United Nations, and especially the United States, Great Britain, and France) sitting in judgment of the actions taken during a war involving another set of actors (the states of the former Yugoslavia). The World War II tribunals involved the victors sitting in judgment of the losers. And while international law had continued progressing incrementally during the years since the Nuremberg and Tokyo tribunals, as I described earlier, the law had not been applied internationally. There was little "institutional memory" for the ICTY to build upon. Despite such challenges, there was no shortage of voices hailing the ICTY as the harbinger of a new dawn in the protection of human rights.

The French representative on the Security Council proclaimed, "France is pleased, therefore, that the initiative that it took this past February has led to such a resounding expression by the United Nations of our common resolve not to tolerate infamy and to assert the rule of law. My country hopes that this message will be understood by all and that it will help silence the guns on the territory of the former Yugoslavia." The U.S. representative, Madeleine Albright, declared, "Truth is the cornerstone of the rule of law, and it will point towards individuals, not peoples, as perpetrators of war crimes. And it is only the truth that can cleanse the ethnic and religious hatreds and begin the healing process." As evidenced by the Japanese representative's statement, members of the Security Council were aware of the challenges that would lie ahead for the new institution: "Thirdly, cooperation and assistance on the part of the States concerned is essential to guarantee the smooth functioning of the Tribunal. If there is any politically misguided effort to block such cooperation, our exercise could be seriously hampered." And to conclude, we return to the words of the U.S. representative: "Finally, of this we are certain: the Tribunal must succeed, for the sake of the victims and for the credibility of international law in this new era."[2]

To return to the ICTY and to understand its role in the history of international justice, we must first briefly review what it does and how it functions. The ICTY has jurisdiction over 1) grave breaches of the Geneva Conventions of 1949; 2) violations of the laws and customs of war; 3) violations of the

1948 Genocide Convention; and 4) crimes against humanity that occurred in the former Yugoslavia since 1991. The ICTY, like its sister tribunals (ICTR, Special Court for Sierra Leone and the ICC), is divided into three branches—the Trial Chambers, the Office of the Prosecutor (OTP) and the Registry. The judges sit in panels of three that hear cases brought forward in a largely adversarial proceeding. Attorneys from both sides square off in a legal contest that is very much like any criminal trial, although the crimes and the stakes are much larger. Judges are elected to their positions by the United Nations General Assembly for terms of four years and can be reelected. There have also been numerous temporary or *ad litem* judges who are also elected by the UN General Assembly, but serve in only one trial. The common Appeals Chamber of the ICTY and ICTR consists of seven judges, with five coming from the ICTY and two from the ICTR. When appeals arise from the ICTY, five of these judges make up what is officially known as the Appeals Chamber of the ICTY. The same process occurs with regard to the ICTR. The judges develop their Rules of Procedure and Evidence, which have been revised numerous times since the ICTY opened its doors. These rules govern everything, including the questioning of suspects, the development of indictments, guilty pleas, the production of evidence, the testimonial process, judgments, sentencing, and appellate procedures.

Trials at the ICTY, ICTR, and SCSL are strongly influenced by the adversarial process, such as we use in the United States and in other former British colonies in which the prosecution and the defense call witnesses, present exhibits, offer theories, and contest the evidence of the other side. Trials may take several months to several years, as some involve as few as one person who pleads guilty while others involve multiple defendants vigorously contesting all of the charges against them. At the conclusion of these trials, the trial chamber judges review the evidence and assess its value. They must also determine what type of liability individuals may be found guilty of, such as principal or superior liability (Boas, Bischoff, and Reid 2011). Principal liability takes place when an individual is involved in physically carrying out offenses under international law, such as pulling the trigger that murders an innocent civilian or committing sexual assault. There have been relatively few such cases at the tribunals because these courts focus on those who hold the greatest criminal responsibility for violations of international law. Superior liability occurs when a commanding officer or political leader is held responsible for the actions of his subordinates. Superiors may be held responsible either for failing to take measures to stop violations of international law or for failing to punish subordinates who commit crimes. Individuals can also be charged with aiding and abetting the commission of international crimes and other forms of lesser liability. In addition to determining what type of liability the accused demonstrates, the judges must also determine if the factual evidence proves that the accused committed the crimes charged and whether he or she had the necessary intent. Some crimes, like genocide, require that individuals have a specific intent or desire to achieve some goal, such as seeking to destroy a religious or national group.

The judgments handed down by the tribunals explain and analyze an often enormous record of evidence and conclude with a disposition that formally announces the verdicts and the sentences for those found guilty. Verdicts are issued on each count, although most sentences reflect the totality of the guilty conduct and do not provide a specific penalty for each proven charge. The judgments also indicate whether any of the three judges disagreed with the majority. The votes of two judges are required to convict an individual on any charge.

The Office of the Prosecutor (OTP) selects, manages, and presents cases at trial and may also appeal verdicts and sentences. There is not an "official" office of defense at the tribunals, but the defense falls under the supervision of the Registry—the administrative arm of the tribunals. Most defendants plead poverty and thus the cost of defense is paid for by the tribunal. In addition, the tribunal develops a list of approved attorneys from which defendants may select. The Registry manages the entire administrative apparatus of the tribunal and is responsible for overseeing many diverse operations, including detention, translation, document management, witness services and protection, and outreach. The chief prosecutor at the ad hoc tribunals is elected by the UN Security Council for a four-year renewable term (at the ICC it is a single nine-year term and the chief prosecutor is elected by the Assembly of States Parties), while the registrar, who leads the Registry, is selected by the Secretary General of the United Nations General Assembly for a renewable term of four years (the registrar of the SCSL serves a three-year term, while at the ICC the registrar is elected by the judges, serves a five-year term, and is eligible for reelection once).

The ultimate conclusion of the work of the ICTY, like all tribunals, is the verdict and punishment for the guilty. The ICTY, which is now in its final phase and concluding its remaining trials, indicted 161 persons for war crimes, crimes against humanity, and genocide. At the time of writing, of those 161 individuals charged, 80 have been found guilty, 19 were acquitted, 36 had their indictments withdrawn or proceedings terminated (due to the death of the defendant), 13 were transferred for domestic prosecution in the former Yugoslavia, and 12 are involved in ongoing proceedings.[3] The sentences for the guilty have ranged from a few years in some cases to a lifetime sentence for others. Those found guilty serve their sentences in the prison systems of those nations that have reached incarceration agreements with the tribunals.[4]

Now that you know the basic operations of the tribunal, let's talk about just how it works in practice. The principal function of any judicial body is to dispense justice—justice for the larger community it serves, justice for the victims and those directly affected by the crime, and justice for those accused of committing crimes. According to the United Nations Security Council Resolution creating the ICTY, having established that crimes had been committed in the former Yugoslavia, the ICTY is designed "to take effective measures to bring to justice the persons who are responsible for them."[5] Justice for the larger global community and for the victims requires the apprehension of those suspected of committing violations of international humanitarian law.

The ability of these tribunals to function and thrive, however, was not expressly provided for by the United Nations in the case of the ad hoc tribunals (ICTY, ICTR, and SCSL) or the states parties in the case of the ICC. While they have mostly been amply supported with financial resources, political support from the international community to carry out their mission in conflict zones and against recalcitrant leaders suspected of committing crimes has often not been available. All of the tribunals have, at one time or another, faced challenges in apprehending suspects, finding witnesses willing to testify, and gathering evidence. Instead, the tribunals have been forced to develop these abilities gradually, with great reliance on the major powers (e.g., the United States, Great Britain, France, and other European states), but with inconsistent levels of cooperation from the nations involved in the conflicts that fell under the jurisdiction of the tribunals. The history of the ICTY in dealing with these issues is emblematic of the struggles faced by all the tribunals.

After the great fanfare involved in the birth of the ICTY, the challenges of building an international tribunal from scratch were quite daunting. The ICTY had to not only obtain and build the machinery of justice—everything from courtrooms, detention facilities, translation, witness support, and budgets to personnel—judges had to develop their own Rules of Procedure and Evidence to guide their proceedings. While the ICTY was governed by its UN Security Council Statute, that document, much like a constitution, left most of the details of international justice to the judges and other ICTY officials to work out. Those matters that could be resolved internally, like Rules of Procedure and Evidence, presented practical hurdles to be overcome, but did not typically require exceptional international commitment and support. Yet creating and administering international justice means little if there are no trials to be held. And the only way trials would be held would be if someone arrested those 161 individuals indicted by the ICTY. While it is possible to look back now and admire that there are no longer any suspected war criminals sought by the ICTY still at large, the early days of the tribunal's history certainly gave no indication that such a record of success was a foregone conclusion. Indeed, the international community behaved as if its work was finished when the ICTY was created. But there was one thing that this international justice enterprise was missing that all national courts have on which to rely, and that is a set of governmental officials who will arrest those individuals charged with crimes. The ICTY, like all the other tribunals, was given no police force, no organization like the U.S. Federal Bureau of Investigation to arrest suspects. Instead, it would have to *persuade* others to do this most essential task.

The apprehension of suspects is the most complex of all the requirements for a functioning international criminal tribunal. When the ICTY began its operations, there was no group of suspects awaiting transfer to The Hague from jails in the former Yugoslavia. Many of those who planned, organized, and executed international crimes in the former Yugoslavia were still in positions of power or leading normal lives. Indeed, fighting in Bosnia was still ongoing when the tribunal was created and only ended in the summer of 1995.[6] Even after the war ended, many suspected violators of international law lived open lives without much evident fear. Oddly enough, one individual, Dražen Erdemović, who later pleaded guilty to being part of an execution squad at Srebrenica, had confessed to his crimes already and was looking for a court willing to formally charge him. The ICTY took his case. The Office of the Prosecutor also took on the case of another individual, Duško Tadić, who had been arrested in Germany, but who was only indicted after the ICTY was asked by the German government if it wished to try him. How did it happen then that the ICTY, like the ICTR, was finally able to turn things around and hold trials for those individuals, especially the powerful ones, they indicted?

One of the chief reasons why the tribunals succeeded against the odds was that the world's major powers, mostly the usual troika of the United States, Great Britain, and France, realized it was in their best interests for the tribunals to gain custody of these suspects not just for legal reasons, but for political and military ones as well (Akhavan 2001; Meernik 2013). In the former Yugoslavia, and particularly Bosnia-Herzegovina, these three nations deployed thousands of peacekeeping troops in 1996 to protect the hard-won gains of the Dayton Peace Accords that ended the Bosnian war. These countries at first had no wish to use their military forces to execute arrest warrants for suspected war criminals. Their militaries did not look upon this as a proper military function and all the parties were afraid that if the peacekeeping forces began trying to arrest suspects, that this would lead to more violence and instability. Political leaders in the West also seemed reluctant to use their other forms of power to force local leaders and officials to turn over suspects. This reluctance by the United States, Great Britain, and France to utilize all the power and influence at their disposal only changed when they began to understand that the peace they kept might never firmly take root unless those who sought to undermine it, many of whom were suspected war criminals, were removed from the scene and brought to justice. Toward the end of the 1990s and early in the new millennium, pressure was placed on all the governments of the region to surrender suspects or face the economic consequences. Those who complied were rewarded with international aid, loans, and the prospect of closer ties with the European Union for their efforts. This change of heart and tactics paved the way for the trials that ultimately became the legacy of the ICTY. Let's take a look at the history of the other tribunals now.

## RWANDA AND THE INTERNATIONAL CRIMINAL TRIBUNAL FOR RWANDA

The Rwandan genocide of 1994 was an effort by extremists from the Hutu ethnic group in the governing political party of Rwanda, the National Republican Movement for Democracy and Development, to eliminate people from the Tutsi ethnic group from politics and from the nation of Rwanda located in the center of Africa. The ethnic animosity between the Hutus and Tutsis had flared off and on again since Rwanda's independence from Belgium in 1962. When Rwanda was a part of the Belgian colonial empire, the Belgians had governed through the Tutsi minority, believing them to be more capable of leadership. While the Tutsis tended to be cattle herders and the Hutus farmers, there were few noticeable differences in ethnicity, religion, and culture between the two groups. Indeed, the Belgians began the process of requiring ethnic identification cards to clearly distinguish between the two groups. But as the winds of change began to blow through Africa in the 1960s and the old colonial powers decided to give up their empires and let their former charges rule themselves, the Belgians determined that majority rule was the appropriate strategy, instead of Tutsi favoritism. So when elections were held in Rwanda in 1960, the Hutus, given their 84 percent majority, easily eclipsed their Tutsi rivals. For the next thirty years, Hutu-dominated governments ruled with an iron fist and passed a series of restrictive laws that made life difficult for the Tutsis and systematically discriminated against them in government positions, education, and politics. Occasionally these policies flared into violence and the government would engage in human rights atrocities that would leave hundreds dead and cause frightened Tutsis to flee into neighboring countries like Uganda and the Congo (Prunier 1995).

In 1990, an antigovernment insurgency group based in Uganda, the Rwandan Patriotic Army, which was mostly Tutsi, launched an invasion of Rwanda from its base in southwest Uganda. While initially the rebel army did not fare well against the Hutu-dominated army, over time it began to pose enough of a threat to the government to bring about peace talks in the Tanzanian city of Arusha. It was after a particularly important summit in April 1994 in Arusha meant to ensure that the Hutus would create a more inclusive government that would bring in more Tutsi voices that the Rwandan president's plane was shot down as it returned to the Rwandan capital city of Kigali. This incident ignited the genocide that led to the deaths of approximately 800,000 Tutsis in the span of about 100 days. The genocide only ended when the Rwandan Patriotic Army defeated the Hutu army in early July 1994 and caused the Hutu extremist government to collapse and flee into exile to Zaire, as it was then called, and other nations in the region.

The International Criminal Tribunal for Rwanda was authorized by the United Nations Security Council shortly thereafter in November 1994. Having created the ICTY only some months ago, the Security Council used the ICTY blueprint with some minor modifications and established the ICTR in Arusha, Tanzania. The ICTR's statute shared most of the same provisions with the ICTY's and differed only in a few important respects. The chief prosecutor for the ICTR was to be the same chief prosecutor for the ICTY—she was to divide her time between managing and leading trials on two continents involving two different conflicts (later the ICTR was given its own prosecutor). The ICTR's statute also limited its legal jurisdiction to crimes involving genocide, crimes against humanity, and those war crimes that were illegal under international law when pertaining to internal or civil wars. Because not all international war crimes are illegal when committed during a civil war, the ICTR's jurisdiction was more limited than the ICTY's. In practice this meant very little because the violations of international law committed in Rwanda almost all pertained to the campaign of genocide. No one escaped international justice because of such legal details. Otherwise, the ICTR was set up just like the ICTY, with a trial chambers section, an Office of the Prosecution, and its own Registry to manage the administration of the tribunal.

The ICTR, like the ICTY, at first found it difficult to hold trials, as many suspects had scattered throughout Africa and into Europe. And again, it was not until the major powers placed economic and political pressure on the nations where these suspects were hiding to turn them over that the ICTR became a viable tool for prosecuting those most responsible for the Rwandan genocide. The ICTR secured its first conviction, and the first conviction by an international tribunal of an individual for genocide, in September 1998, when the mayor of a small community in Rwanda, Jean-Paul Akayesu, was found guilty and sentenced to life imprisonment for helping to organize the genocidal violence in the town of Taba. Altogether, the ICTR indicted ninety-three individuals for genocide, crimes against humanity, and war crimes, and of those sixty-one were found guilty and sentenced, fourteen were acquitted, and the remainder either died before completion of their trial, had their case referred to prosecution in Rwanda, the case ended in some other manner, or the individual is still at large.[7] Having completed nearly all of the trials and appeals for almost all of those indicated, the ICTR is now currently shuttering its doors. The international trials for the Rwandan genocide have ended. Only a handful of suspects are still at large. Both the ICTY and the ICTR, as ad hoc tribunals, were designed to live a finite life span. And that is precisely what has happened. Any remaining issues that the tribunals must address, such as appeals of judgments and sentences, will be handled by a new hybrid institution called the Mechanism for the International Criminal Tribunals (MICT). It will basically keep the lights on until these last appeals are exhausted and there is no more business for these courts. At that point, the experiment with these temporary tribunals will come to an end.

## THE SPECIAL COURT FOR SIERRA LEONE

The Special Court for Sierra Leone grew out of another complex and violent civil war whose methods were so bloody and egregious that they demanded some sort of international condemnation. Sierra Leone is a small, poor country in the west of Africa that had been a British colony. Its civil war began in 1991 when the forces of the Revolutionary United Front (RUF) began attacking the Sierra Leonean government and seizing towns along the border with Liberia. Despite elections, one military coup after another, and failed efforts to stop the civil war, the violence continued throughout the 1990s. In part, the war was fueled by the blood diamond trade in which the RUF and other factions would force people in areas of the country under their control to scour the rivers and the earth for the gem. The profits from the sale of the diamonds allowed the rebels to support their insurgency and also provided a reason for their existence—to continue to enrich the rebel elite. The leadership of the rebel movement and its supporters, especially the president of the neighboring nation of Liberia, Charles Taylor, grew rich from the proceeds of this valuable and relatively easily exportable resource. In 1998, to stem the tide of violence and restore peace, Nigeria led a force of West African troops in an attempt to stop the fighting and stabilize the country. But after a triumphant entry into the Sierra Leonean capital of Freetown in February 1998, the rebels of the RUF struck back and seized parts of the capital from the West African peacekeeping force. The violence and its trademark tactic of amputation to terrorize and coerce the population continued.

Yet another peace accord was reached in the summer of 1999 and later that year UN troops began to arrive to keep the peace, even as the West African peacekeeping force continued to do battle in the countryside. When the UN and West African forces proved incapable of fending off the Revolutionary United Front and the other militia groups that sprang up to protect their people or to get rich off the blood diamond trade, in 2000 the British government sent in a military force to rescue British citizens and others trapped in the melee and to help stabilize the situation. After the British troops finished their tour of duty, elections were held once again, and the Sierra Leonean army was sufficiently trained to keep the peace, the war was finally declared over (see Kelsall 2009).

The awful violence of the civil war, international attention to the blood diamond trade, amputations, and rampant use of child soldiers demanded that there be some sort of international response. The Special Court for Sierra Leone (SCSL) was a hybrid court that was created as a result of an agreement between the United Nations General Assembly and the government of Sierra Leone. The ICTY and the ICTR, established by the UN Security Council and the governments of the former Yugoslavia and Rwanda, had very little say in the running of the tribunals. In contrast, the Special Court for Sierra Leone was intended to better reflect the interests of Sierra Leone and hence the court differed from its sister institutions in several notable ways. First and most important symbolically, the SCSL was headquartered in Freetown, the capital of Sierra Leone, unlike the other two tribunals that were deliberately located at a distance from their conflicts. For the ICTY and the ICTR, that distance was intended to help ensure the objectivity and independence of the court from the scenes of the crimes and the tense political situations that might jeopardize the security of the tribunals. By the time the SCSL was established, however, such fears were deemed mostly groundless, while the cost in public acceptance of the tribunals located hundreds of miles away had undermined the tribunals' legitimacy. Second, the SCSL was to be staffed by both an international cadre of judges, attorneys, and administrators and a local contingent, unlike the ICTY and ICTR, whose judges and prosecutors were international. Again, the desire to preserve a reputation for neutrality and impartiality had led to the decision to keep the citizens of the former Yugoslavia and Rwanda out of sensitive positions in the Office of the Prosecution and especially the Trial Chambers. Legally, such strategies made sense because they made the tribunals less susceptible to charges of favoring one side in a civil war over another. But again, the lack of connection between the people in whose name the tribunals were providing justice and the tribunals themselves made public awareness and support of the ICTY and ICTR much more difficult and politically complicated.

The SCSL was expressly designed to try those who held the most responsibility for the horrific violence and crimes committed during the civil war. In fact, the prosecutorial strategy of trying those senior leaders on all sides of the war resulted in a more focused and smaller caseload than the ICTY and ICTR, whose trials involved senior and mid-level suspects, as well as some number of fairly low-level soldiers and concentration camp guards. The SCSL held jurisdiction over crimes against humanity, war crimes as they pertained to intrastate wars, and other violations of Sierra Leonean law. The chief prosecutor brought charges against the RUF, as well as other rebel leaders and supporters, including Liberian president Charles Taylor. Ten persons were tried, although one died before his trial was completed. The other nine individuals, including President Taylor, who was tried in The Hague, Netherlands, because of security concerns in Sierra Leone, were convicted and sentenced to terms of incarceration ranging from fifteen to fifty-two years. The Special Court for Sierra Leone has now officially closed its proceedings.

## THE INTERNATIONAL CRIMINAL COURT

The international tribunals we have discussed so far have all been ad hoc—each had a particular duty and jurisdiction and each was expected to conclude its affairs and then close up shop. Not so with the International Criminal Court (ICC). It is a permanent court with a worldwide jurisdiction. Yet its worldwide jurisdiction does not mean it can investigate conflicts in every single country on the planet. There are a set of requirements that must be met before the ICC can begin doing its detective work in a particular state and then indicting those whom the prosecution suspects of wrongdoing. Understanding how the ICC takes jurisdiction of a case is the key to understanding the court's potential and its strengths, as well as its weaknesses.

The ICC was the product of a diplomatic conference in Rome that wrote the treaty that was eventually ratified by the requisite number of nations to become a reality in July 2002 (the Rome Statute). The statements of support at the time of the Rome conference give some indication of the great expectations the ICC has faced. The UN Secretary General remarked that "the breakthrough achieved should not be underestimated, but should be recognized as a genuine step forward in safeguarding human rights and the rule of law." From the summary records of the Rome proceedings we learn that the representative of the European Union asserted that "the European Union had always been committed to the creation of a permanent judicial institution which would make the world a more just, safer and more peaceful place, and had always affirmed that the Statute of the International Criminal Court must be generally acceptable if it was to become effective." According to the conference proceedings, "Mr. Westdickenberg (Germany) said that a strong, effective and independent international criminal court would certainly be established. The world would hear the signal that heinous crimes like genocide, crimes against humanity, war crimes and the crime of aggression would no longer go unpunished." There were many more comments made about the treaty, and although most were generally supportive, there were a fair number that found fault with, among other issues, the powers of the prosecutor, the lack of a crime of aggression, a fear of interference in the internal affairs of states by the UN Security Council, and the lack of a method for registering reservations about the treaty. And while the conference ended on a high note amid renewed optimism about the prospects for international justice, it is also clear that the concerns expressed at the conclusion of the conference foreshadowed many of the ICC's most pressing problems.

The Rome Statute provides that the ICC has jurisdiction over situations in which 1) the state in which an alleged crime takes place is a party to the treaty; 2) the suspect(s) is a national of a state that is a party to the treaty; or 3) the case is referred to it by the United Nations Security Council. In addition to referral by the Security Council, the mechanisms by which the court may begin a case occur when 1) states that have ratified the Treaty of Rome refer situations meeting the first or second criteria above or 2) the prosecutor initiates an investigation on her own initiative (the Latin term for this is *proprio motu*, or on his or her own initiative) that meets at least one of the first two criteria above. Perhaps the most critical and controversial of the ICC's powers is the authority of the prosecutor to launch his or her own investigations with judicial approval. This opens up the possibility that any one of the 120-plus states party to the treaty could be investigated and those most responsible for violations of the relevant international law brought before the ICC. Furthermore, the UN Security Council's power to refer cases to the ICC makes it theoretically possible that any state in the world could be investigated. Surely, if any tribunal could advance human security it would be the powerful ICC. To understand the struggles that the ICC faces today as it seeks to achieve the level of effectiveness of the ad hoc tribunals, we need to explore the process that allows the ICC to take jurisdiction.

First and foremost, it is important to understand that the ICC was not meant to be a court of first resort—a court that would be the first to get involved in investigating allegations of violations of international law. Instead, the framers of the Rome Statute understood that for the ICC to be effective it would not be possible to investigate every human rights atrocity everywhere—it would quickly exhaust its resources and overwhelm its staff. There are still just too many threats to human security in the world today. Instead, the ICC was designed not to be a court of first resort, but rather a court of last resort. States were expected to use their own laws, courts, and people to investigate suspected violations of international law. The ICC would become involved in investigating human rights abuses after a nation's own courts proved to be unable or unwilling to investigate. This requirement was also intended to reassure states that they need not fear an international court peering into their business all the time. Nonetheless, some states, especially large and powerful nations like the United States, Russia, and China, have refused to sign the ICC treaty because they fear the ICC will still investigate their militaries when they are deployed overseas or their security forces that are used internally to keep order. President Bill Clinton did sign the ICC treaty in 2000, but his successor, President George W. Bush, "unsigned" the treaty in 2002 because he was so afraid that the world would gang up on the big, bad United States. So what has actually happened?

Interestingly, the ICC prosecutor has launched only one investigation at the time of writing on her own authority—a case involving the deaths of several thousand people in Kenya in election-related ethnic violence in 2007 and 2008. The fear of the great powers like the United States that a rogue ICC prosecutor would become involved in conflicts where they had substantial interests or seek politicized investigations of these countries has so far proved unfounded (Bosco 2014). In fact, most of the cases currently before the ICC have been referred to it by state parties seeking investigation of alleged crimes committed on their own territory. The government of Uganda sought ICC investigation of Joseph Kony's Lord's Resistance Army (LRA) for its campaign of terror in northern Uganda. The Democratic Republic of Congo sought and received ICC investigation of human rights atrocities committed in the far eastern region of its territory (some of these human rights abuses were committed by the former Rwandan militias that committed the 1994 Rwandan genocide and then fled over the border to the Congo). Indeed, even nonstate parties have utilized this method, such as the Ivory Coast, which requested the ICC investigate allegations against its former president.

Why would these states be interested in having the ICC launch an investigation on their own territory? The ICC is actually only supposed to become involved in situations in which the country itself is either unable or unwilling to investigate and prosecute.[8] This was supposed to be another check on the power of the prosecutor to avoid interference in the internal affairs of states. But for states lacking the will and the means to investigate, the ICC could provide a critical fallback option. That is basically what has happened with the several cases in which states have sought ICC involvement. They lack the capacity to prosecute suspected war criminals, principally because they have failed to capture them. They may be hoping that the ICC can bring to bear the greater resources of the international community to find these individuals and prosecute them. Unfortunately, regardless of the merits of prosecuting these warlords and their henchmen, the ICC has focused its energies on situations in which others, and not the ICC, have set the agenda. In some places like Uganda, the ICC has had to deal with a government that runs hot and cold on international investigations (Clark 2010). When Uganda believes it can reach a peace agreement with the Lord's Resistance Army on its own, it would prefer the ICC to butt out. When Joseph Kony and the LRA disappear back into the wilderness of central Africa, then outside assistance is more readily sought. Many fear the ICC has become a political pawn or tool in these internal battles and has been diverted from focusing its attention on the world's worst human rights atrocities.

That leaves us with the third route by which the ICC can take jurisdiction: Security Council referral. So far the ICC has received two cases via this route—one involving allegations of genocide in Darfur, Sudan, and the other involving the civil war that ousted Muamar Khadafy from Libya. In both cases, none of the permanent five members of the Security Council had a clear stake in these conflicts and so let the ICC take jurisdiction. Because no major power had a special interest in these conflicts, however, they also did not have a compelling reason to throw their political muscle and international influence into making sure the ICC was able to gain access to the evidence and suspects necessary to effectively prosecute a case.[9] Not surprisingly, these cases have languished and little has been done to provide justice. The paradox in the UN Security Council referral to the ICC is that when the permanent five members do not have a stake in a conflict and are thus more likely to refer cases, they have no particular reason to help the ICC. When one of the permanent five does have a strong interest in a conflict situation, it is more likely to veto referral of the case in order to protect an ally. For example, there is support from many quarters for an ICC investigation into the long-running and brutal civil war in Syria, but it is clear that the Syrian government's ally Russia would veto any such referral. Security Council referral has not proven to be the best strategy by which the ICC can mount an effective investigation. So where does this leave us? How does and how will the ICC function and mount effective prosecutions?

Thus far, we have seen that there are significant problems associated with each of the three mechanisms by which the ICC can take jurisdiction (*proprio motu*, state request, and United Nations Security Council referral): none has developed as envisioned or feared (Bosco 2014). The ICC faces the same challenges faced by the ad hoc tribunals—it must function as an independent judicial institution, but operate in an environment in which it is a dependent political institution. None of these tribunals can conduct their business without the support of powerful states, but neither can they behave like just another extension of the influence of these actors. The ICC must convince powerful states to use the kind of political and economic pressures that were so effective on behalf of the ICTY and ICTR to support its investigations into politically delicate and militarily dangerous conflict zones and apprehend those suspected of being most responsible for violations of international law. The trick is to have just enough support from the major powers so that the tribunals can carry out their mission without having so much interest from the major powers that they become the meddlers into what are appropriately judicial affairs. The remainder of the book will assess the successes and failures of the tribunals in advancing human security given these substantial challenges. I do not focus on the other ad hoc tribunals such as the East Timor Special Panels for Serious Crimes, the Extraordinary Chambers in the Courts of Cambodia, and the Special Tribunal for Lebanon because their work has been characterized by numerous problems involving apprehending suspects, completing trials, and publishing their records. They have not compiled the actual and documentary records necessary to investigate their impact.

## CONCLUSION

Now that the reader has been introduced to the three principal ad hoc tribunals and the permanent ICC, we can begin to evaluate just how successful they have been at advancing human security. Their principal mission has been and always will be to provide justice—justice for the victims of violations of international law, justice for the international community whose laws have been violated, and justice for the accused. These are no ordinary courts, however. They must be judged on the expectations of the international community that designed them. These expectations go considerably beyond simply holding trials and pronouncing verdicts, as necessary and valuable as those duties may be. If their job performance evaluations were strictly limited to what transpired in the courtroom, then could we really justify the time and expense it takes to hold such trials? We might be better off letting national courts handle these trials and saving the money to help rebuild the nations that have been affected by wars and violence.

That is not the case, however. The United Nations and the states that signed the Rome Statute that created these tribunals expect a broader impact across humanity. Let's return again to the words of Robert Jackson, the U.S. chief prosecutor at the Nuremberg Tribunal. He understood and articulated so very well the hopes for these international courts when he stated the following in his opening address:

> The wrongs which we seek to condemn and punish have been so calculated, so malignant and so devastating that civilization cannot tolerate their being ignored because it cannot survive their being repeated.

The world has a vital interest in and responsibility for holding such trials. If we ignore these horrific human rights abuses then we signal that these crimes do not matter and the criminals who commit them can be left free to perpetrate even more atrocities. If laws are to mean anything then they must be enforced and used in the service of humankind. Because these international crimes are so terrible, the international tribunals are intended to provide more than just justice—they also exist to help ensure that such crimes are not repeated and that the cause of peace is advanced in both the nations affected and the wider world. These are the bigger goals that justify the time and expense of running an international tribunal. These are the bigger goals that explain why we must evaluate how well the tribunals have performed in advancing human security. Let's review each of these three principal goals and the plan of this book.

## CHAPTER 2: VERDICTS, PUNISHMENTS, AND JUSTICE

To assess the impact of the four tribunals, we must begin and end with the founding documents that describe their goals. The United Nations, or the nations that have signed the Rome Statute in the case of the International Criminal Court, state what exactly are their expectations and the mandates of these courts. I will evaluate their impact based on these objectives that are found in the UN resolutions and the Rome Statute that authorized their creation. We will briefly review what these goals are below, but save a more in-depth examination of these objectives for each of the chapters. We begin with the most fundamental purpose of all that motivates their creation—providing justice. Each of the tribunals is given a mandate to provide justice. The resolution authorizing the creation of the ICTY asserts that the United Nations Security Council is "determined to put an end to such crimes and to take effective measures to bring to justice the persons who are responsible for them" and that "the establishment of an international tribunal and the prosecution of persons responsible for the above-mentioned violations of international humanitarian law will contribute to ensuring that such violations are halted and effectively redressed."[10] The resolution establishing the ICTR contains almost identical language.[11] While the Security Council did not create the Special Court for

Sierra Leone, it did pass a resolution asking the Secretary General to work with the government of Sierra Leone to create such a court. The resolution acknowledges the "importance of compliance with international humanitarian law" and that "persons who commit or authorize serious violations of international humanitarian law are individually responsible and accountable for those violations."[12] Similarly, the ICC treaty provides that "the most serious crimes of concern to the international community as a whole must not go unpunished and that their effective prosecution must be ensured by taking measures at the national level and by enhancing international cooperation." The last sentence of the preamble to the ICC treaty proclaims that the states parties are "resolved to guarantee lasting respect for and the enforcement of international justice."[13]

While the wording of each of the resolutions may vary somewhat, they essentially proclaim that these international courts are to provide justice and see that wrongs are righted. Justice is a both a means and an end. The prosecution of alleged violations of international law through trials in international courtrooms provides the process that is governed by the Rules of Procedure and Evidence of each tribunal. If the process of justice is unbiased and in accordance with international human rights standards for fair trials, it should, in theory, be assessed as "just." And part of chapter 2 is concerned with whether the process of justice meets such standards. However, the outcomes of such trials matter equally. At the heart of international criminal justice are the trials of suspected war criminals and those who violate international law. And the final conclusion of these trials and the most visible output of the tribunals are their verdicts and sentences. Fair trials that ensure that all the relevant evidence and testimony are heard in court and that produce impartial verdicts and fix appropriate punishments to the guilty can aid in the social and political reconstruction of the affected societies. But have the trials at the tribunals resulted in verdicts and punishments that are impartial, appropriate, and just?

The aim of chapter 2 is to analyze the selection of cases that have been prosecuted at the tribunals as well as the verdicts and sentences they hand down to evaluate the quality of their justice. We will look at whether the choice of conflicts and suspects to investigate and prosecute could be considered fair and impartial or biased and politically motivated. I will examine whether these trials can be viewed as just from the perspective of the defendants by analyzing their procedural fairness. Are suspected violators of international law and their attorneys equipped to mount a vigorous defense or have the tribunals, in effect, stacked the deck against them? Is there any evidence of bias in the pronouncements of guilt and the severity of sentences? I use both legal, textual analysis of the rules and procedures of the international courts and data on verdicts and sentences to make these assessments.

As I argued earlier, however, we must look beyond the justice provided in the courtroom and examine whether the justice these trials embody has advanced or diminished human security. At the heart of this debate is whether these courts have been fair and neutral in the selection of individuals to prosecute.

## CHAPTER 3: INTERNATIONAL TRIBUNALS AND HUMAN RIGHTS

The founding documents of the tribunals provide that they shall aid in the establishment of peace and help ensure that the human rights violations at issue in these conflicts do not occur again. In the ICTY and ICTR resolutions, the Security Council found that the wars in the former Yugoslavia and Rwanda constituted threats to "international peace and security" and the Security Council is "determined to put an end to such crimes." The ICTR is also supposed to enable the "process of national reconciliation."[14] The Security Council resolution authorizing the Secretary General to work with the government of Sierra Leone to establish the Special Court for Sierra Leone stipulates that the "situation in Sierra Leone continues to constitute a threat to international peace and security in the region" and that it is "deeply concerned" about the "prevailing situation of impunity."[15] The ICC treaty preamble recognizes that its signatories are "mindful that during this century millions of children, women and men have been victims of unimaginable atrocities that deeply shock the conscience of humanity," while they also recognize "that such grave crimes threaten the peace, security and well-being of the world." Therefore, these states are "determined to put an end to impunity for the perpetrators of these crimes and thus to contribute to the prevention of such crimes."[16]

The tribunals are intended to facilitate peace and the prevention of human rights atrocities and violations of international law. I assess the performance of these courts in achieving these objectives in chapters 3 and 4. I focus on the courts' contributions to improvements in human rights in the nations over which they exercise jurisdiction in chapter 3 and assess their accomplishments in advancing peace in chapter 4. Specifically, in chapter 3 I analyze the human rights records of the countries that have been subject to the tribunals using extensive data on human rights that scholars have been collecting for many years. It is critical that we always look to see how well these tribunals have achieved their broad objectives to determine if there is an "added value" to holding international criminal trials. Have international tribunals advanced the cause of human security and human rights? Have human rights conditions in the countries targeted by the international tribunals improved since those courts began their judicial enterprise? Or are these courts too distant and far removed from the conflict scene and contemporary political developments in these societies? These are the questions we will explore.

## CHAPTER 4: INTERNATIONAL TRIBUNALS AND PEACE

The fourth chapter concerns whether tribunals have advanced the cause of peace. Ending violence and promoting peace and reconciliation are perhaps the tribunals' most vital goals, but also the ones over which those institutions exercise the least control. The intention of those who created all four tribunals was that by trying and punishing those who commit violations of international law, the world would help deter future atrocities. In addition, the individualization of guilt is intended to lessen the perceived need felt by members of affected communities to attribute guilt to all members of ethnic and other groups whose leaders organized and committed atrocities. By making clear that only *some* are guilty and that the individuals most responsible were the political and military leaders, the tribunals are intended to lessen the need for retribution aimed at all members of the group. These are some of the most fundamental purposes of justice, but also the most intangible. This chapter sets out the full scope of these arguments and makes use of a wide variety of data on civil wars, international conflicts, and other such data to determine if the use of tribunals is associated with more peace and stability in the nations over which they exercise jurisdiction. Or, as some scholars argue, are these tribunals more apt to interfere in military matters or political decisions that would be better left to local participants or international actors to confront? In this chapter I assess where international justice has or has not worked in helping to bring and sustain peace. I analyze whether the nations that are subject to international tribunals are more or less likely to remain peaceful than other nations that have not been targeted with such international investigations and trials.

## CHAPTER 5: INTERNATIONAL TRIBUNALS AND LEGITIMACY

For any system of criminal justice to function effectively it must enjoy some degree of legitimacy from those in whose name it provides justice. But while such legitimacy in domestic criminal justice systems within advanced democracies tends to run quite high, what of the legitimacy of international institutions among those living in the states subjected to their authority? Do the citizens of these nations, such as Bosnia, Croatia, Serbia, Rwanda, Sierra Leone, Uganda, Kenya, and so on accept the justice as provided to them by these international tribunals? Or do they view such efforts as meddling and an intrusion on their sovereignty? Arguably, support among the publics in the affected countries is one of the most critical types of success necessary for these institutions to gain legitimacy and facilitate the realization of their more far-reaching objectives, such as promoting deterrence, peace, and reconciliation. As deGuzman (2012, 268) writes, "the globalization of communications increasingly means that an institution's legitimacy depends on the opinions of ordinary citizens around the world." However, scholars have pointed to many potential deficiencies in international courts, such as their "democracy deficit" (Drumbl 2007), a legalistic method of dispute resolution that privileges justice over peace (Snyder and Vinjamuri 2003; Mendelhoff 2004), and other political problems (Grodsky 2009) that may cause affected publics to distrust international justice and thus sow the seeds of local failure. If public perceptions of international courts are tainted by accusations of victor's justice, Western domination, or disregard for local interests, the legitimacy of international justice will be undermined. I explore these topics by examining the meaning and importance of legitimacy in the context of international tribunals and analyzing public opinion data on views of international justice in those countries that have been the object of these international efforts, where such data are available.

## CHAPTER 6: CONCLUSION

The conclusion will summarize all of the most important findings from the preceding chapters to assess how international tribunals have performed on the set of metrics. Based on this overall performance of the tribunals I will suggest where their greatest strengths are in realizing their goals, where their greatest shortcomings are, and whether there is realistically anything that can be done to diminish the impact of the problems that prevent the tribunals from realizing their complete potential. I give the tribunals grades in each of the categories in the preceding four chapters to identify where successes have been achieved and where there is room for further improvement. I conclude this chapter by offering recommendations for the ICC and how it might better achieve justice and advance human security. Having waded through this voluminous record and considered all of the evidence, just as the judges at these courts do, the reader can pronounce his or her own verdict on whether international justice has improved human security or whether it has fallen short of these lofty aspirations.

## NOTES

1. Details about the establishment of the ICTY can be found at http://www.icty.org/sid/319.

2. From the Provisional Verbatim Record of the Three Thousand Two Hundred and Seventeenth Meeting of the United Nations Security Council on Tuesday, May 25, 1993, at 9:00 p.m.

3. This information can be found at http://www.icty.org/en/cases/key-figures-cases.

4. The reader can go to the following websites to learn about the accomplishments of the ad hoc tribunals. For the ICTY, go to http://www.icty.org/sections/AbouttheICTY; for the ICTR, go to http://www.unictr.org/en/tribunal; and for the SCSL, go to http://www.rscsl.org/index.html.

5. As found at http://www.un.org/icty/legaldoc-e/index.htm on March 30, 2007.

6. Fighting later broke out in the Yugoslav republic of Serbia in the area of Kosovo, which will be discussed later.

7. These data can be found at http://unictr.unmict.org/en/tribunal.

8. States can challenge the ICC's assertion of jurisdiction. In turn, the prosecutor can contest such state challenges on the grounds that the state with jurisdiction is genuinely unable or unwilling to carry out the investigation or prosecution. This may be demonstrated by showing that a state's proceedings were used for the purpose of shielding those responsible—there has been an unjustified delay in the initiation of proceedings or the proceedings were not conducted in an impartial or independent manner (Article 17(2) a, b, and c).

9. See the report at http://www.securitycouncilreport.org/monthly-forecast/2014-06/in_hindsight_the_council_and_the_icc.php.

10. United Nations Security Council Resolution 827 of May 25, 1993, is found at http://www.icty.org/x/file/Legal%20Library/Statute/statute_827_1993_en.pdf.

11. United Nations Security Council Resolution 955 of November 8, 1994, is found at http://www.unmict.org/ictr-remembers/docs/res955-1994_en.pdf.

12. United Nations Security Council Resolution 1315 of August 14, 2000, is found at http://www.rscsl.org/Documents/Establishment/S-Res-1315-2000.pdf.

13. The ICC treaty is found at http://www.icc-cpi.int/NR/rdonlyres/ADD16852-AEE9-4757-ABE7-9CDC7CF02886/283503/RomeStatutEng1.pdf.

14. As found at http://www.un.org/icty/legaldoc-e/index.htm and http://69.94.11.53/ENGLISH/Resolutions/955e.htm on April 2, 2007.

15. As found at http://www.un.org/press/en/1999/19991022.sc6742.doc.html.

16. As found at http://www.icc-cpi.int/NR/rdonlyres/ADD16852-AEE9-4757-ABE7-9CDC7CF02886/283503/RomeStatutEng1.pdf.

*Chapter 2*

# Human Security and International Justice

## INTRODUCTION

International tribunals are first and foremost about justice. They are supposed to deliver justice to the victims of war crimes, crimes against humanity, and genocide. They bring the accused to justice in their international courtrooms. And they are intended to provide justice for the world for it is the entire international community whose international laws have been violated. In this chapter we will delve into the issue of international tribunals and the justice they deliver. As you are no doubt aware, justice is a rather abstract concept that has multiple definitions—its meaning has been debated for centuries. Indeed, I just listed three types of justice the tribunals are supposed to provide for their different audiences. No doubt the justice the victims seek is something quite different than justice from the perspective of the defendant. Additionally, the international community is made up of states, international organizations, nongovernmental organizations, and the people of the world who all may have unique views of what kind of justice they expect to come out of an international courtroom. How are we to make sense of these different opinions about what international justice looks like and evaluate its contributions to human security?

We begin by defining justice. It is not as easy as you might think because so many of the definitions of justice use the word *just* in them, but most definitions focus on justice as a quality of being fair, reasonable, impartial, and adhering to the written rule of law. These typical definitions describe a process that possesses certain characteristics. Most of us have been socialized in an environment in which the rule of law is part of the political system and are quite familiar with the concept of justice as fairness. Those who are accused of criminal behavior will be most concerned with these qualities and ensuring they receive a fair trial. No doubt most people would have no problems with justice that is objective, unbiased, and everything else we associate with these conceptions of justice as it is personified by the blindfolded woman balancing the scales.

Generally, though, we are not content to think of justice simply as a way to describe how it is administered in a court of law—the *process* of justice. We may have an *outcome* in mind that we view as the "just" outcome. If one is a genocide survivor, it may be all well and good to have a fair trial with due process, but if the trials of those accused of genocide do not hold anyone accountable, we will probably not view such an outcome as just. For the victims and for the international community, justice is not just a means, it is also an end. Justice occurs when people are held accountable for crimes. When crimes as big as the atrocities of the former Yugoslavia, Rwanda, and Sierra Leone take place, we know that there are individuals who are responsible. Someone had to organize and order the massacres. Individuals had to execute these orders. Thus, when thousands of people die at the hands of others, in a just world the victims and the international community expect that such individuals will be called to account. International criminal justice that does not succeed in identifying, apprehending, prosecuting, and convicting those responsible becomes just a hollow exercise that is likely to leave people feeling that they have been victimized a second time.

We will explore justice using these two different perspectives. We will examine the means of justice and debate whether the justice provided in an international courtroom is fair, reasonable, and unbiased toward the accused. Have their rights, which are protected under international law, been violated? Has international justice afforded them the opportunity to contest the charges against them and to appeal against what they may perceive as shortcomings in their trials? Or are international courtrooms unfair to defendants? Are they so determined to hold people responsible for massive crimes that reasonable doubts get set aside or voices to the contrary silenced in a "rush to judgment"? We will begin by looking at the fairness of the trials from the standpoint of the defendants, starting with the decisions made about which conflicts across the world should be investigated and which parties to the conflict should be indicted and charged with violating international law. We will then explore this notion of what in international justice is called the "equality of arms." That is, does each side in a trial—the prosecution and the defense—have equal opportunity to present their case before the judges? Or is the deck stacked against the accused? Are international trials "organized to convict," as some have charged?

We will also explore justice as outcome. We will assess whether the tribunals have succeeded in their most basic responsibilities—completing trials and delivering judgments. Have the individuals who are most responsible for violating international law been apprehended and had their day in court? We will assess the track records of the four tribunals in delivering verdicts and we will analyze the punishments meted out to the guilty. Have the verdicts and sentences been fair and appropriate given the gravity of the crimes committed, and have these outcomes satisfied the desire for justice among the victims and the larger international community?

Then comes the hard part, for we must then link the quality of this international justice to human security. How has the quality of international justice affected human security, both in conflict nations and in the rest of the world? The links between justice and human security are not always so obvious because the events that occur in a courtroom in a safe and faraway land often have little bearing on societies that are rife with poverty, human rights abuses, and ineffective government. But the promise of international justice is that its provision makes nations better off than if they had let criminal perpetrators get away with murder. How well has this promise been kept? Are these nations afflicted with war crimes better off for having been the subject of international trials or has international justice made conflict resolution and the rebuilding of societies after war more difficult? We will cover this topic in the third and final portion of this chapter.

## JUSTICE AND CHOICE: THE SELECTION OF CONFLICTS TO INVESTIGATE AND INDIVIDUALS TO PROSECUTE

The very names of the first two international tribunals, "The International Tribunal for the Prosecution of Persons Responsible for Serious Violations of International Humanitarian Law Committed in the Territory of the Former Yugoslavia since 1991" and "The International Criminal Tribunal for the Prosecution of Persons Responsible for Genocide and Other Serious Violations of International Humanitarian Law Committed in the Territory of Rwanda and Rwandan Citizens Responsible for Genocide and Other Such Violations Committed in the Territory of Neighbouring States, between 1 January 1994 and 31 December 1994," are not only a mouthful, but they also seem to imply that those individuals who are being prosecuted are those who are responsible for the violations. Otherwise, why would they be on trial? The issue of the names of the tribunals may seem like quibbling over details, but there are those, especially among the defendants and their lawyers, who believe that the names are indicative of a more deep-seated need to prosecute and severely punish those who stand trial. Is there such a thing as "victor's justice" in which those who win wars or who have the support of powerful states like the United States are given leniency before international courts, while those perceived to be the villains have the full measure of the law hurled at them? To engage this debate we will first look at "who" is prosecuted before international courts and then examine "how" they are prosecuted.

Every international prosecution involves choices. Sadly, there has never been any shortage of wars and massive human rights abuses that violate international law, and violate it severely. Someone has to make a choice about which country's war to investigate, which side's generals to go after, and which among the many individuals with dirty hands in any conflict to prosecute. The choice may be a political one. Some countries have more influential allies than others, who will protect them in the United Nations Security Council or use their power to deter investigations. For example, it is extremely doubtful that the Security Council will ever refer a case involving the state of Israel to the International Criminal Court because the United States would veto any such move. The choice may be driven by the visibility of the situation. Massacres and other atrocities that are broadcast on CNN are much more likely to gain the attention of decision makers than those conflicts in faraway lands that people know almost nothing about. The choice may be practical. The ICTY and ICTR could not afford to go after every individual who violated international law in the former Yugoslavia or Rwanda, and so local institutions were left to deal with many "ordinary" perpetrators. There simply is neither the will nor the way to do so. To understand more deeply how and why these choices are made, and most importantly for us, to determine whether such choices are fair, we need to analyze the decisions that have been made about which conflicts to investigate and prosecute and which actors from which side of a conflict to investigate and potentially prosecute.

The ICTY and ICTR, created back-to-back in 1993 and 1994, illustrate nicely the dilemmas faced by international decision makers. Those nations became the subject of international investigations and prosecutions not because they finished at the top of the rankings in some sort of atrocity scale, so to speak. There were other wars occurring in the early 1990s that were also quite violent, such as the conflict between Armenia and Azerbaijan and the violence in South Africa and Colombia, to say nothing of the countries that had just thrown off communist governments that were responsible for a horrific litany of human rights violations during the Cold War. The explanations offered regarding the decision by the UN Security Council to establish the ICTY range from European horror over events taking place in their backyard, to international "guilt" over the collective failure to stop the atrocities, to the power of the news media that brought this conflict onto the international agenda (Bass 2002). Quite likely it was a combination of these and other factors. But the creation of the ICTY was not the product of some rational calculation of which nation was most in need of a war crimes tribunal. In that sense, it was a political choice to create the ICTY. The situation in the former Yugoslavia seemed to "demand" a response because of all of these compelling reasons.

The creation of the ICTR was similar. There were other ongoing bloody conflicts in Africa, such as in Liberia and Angola, albeit not nearly so enormous as the Rwandan genocide. The Rwandan genocide was exceptionally brutal in its scope and efficiency. There was a UN force there that gave it some measure of publicity and, of course, there was the example of the ICTY. The UN Security Council could hardly afford to deny such a tribunal for Rwanda when it had created the ICTY after fewer deaths. In fact, Boutros Boutros-Ghali, the UN Secretary General at the time, called the wars in the former Yugoslavia the "rich man's wars." One could imagine the charges of favoritism to the West and bias against Africa had the Security Council failed to establish the ICTR so soon after the ICTY.

If the criteria that are used in deciding when to create a tribunal are unclear or arise from the heat of the moment when people are indignant over a particular tragedy in the world, such "selections" may seem arbitrary or politically determined. And it is not a short distance to travel between believing that an institution was politically inspired to finding politics influencing many of the decisions made by the tribunal. If tribunals are born of politics, then they are political creatures, or so such thinking goes. And if they are "political," as some might argue, then they are necessarily unfair.

On one level, it is indisputable that these tribunals have political origins. In fact, let's just accept that for the sake of argument and assume all tribunals are created by politics—it is part of their DNA. They were not created as a result of review by some sort of independent panel that researched all conflicts in the world to come up with a top-ten list of best targets of prosecution. How then do we interpret their behavior? If they are political institutions, are their decisions mostly political? Is it possible, in such an environment, for judges to act fairly, neutrally, and transparently in their official conduct? Some have argued that because the ICTY and ICTR, and to a lesser extent the SCSL, were born because of the intense (political) need to punish the perpetrators of violence, they have taken steps to ensure such convictions. Mégret (2009, 76) writes,

> The hydraulic pressure of judging some of the worst crimes, often committed by individuals who will have been abundantly associated with them in public opinion, may have taken its toll on the most liberal aspects of criminal procedure, as it is sometimes conceived domestically.

Similarly, deGuzman writes (2012, 61–62),

> The concept of gravity is also invoked to justify relaxing the legal rules that protect defendants. Indeed, a Latin maxim holds that *"in delictis atrocissimus Jura transgredi liceat"* (with atrocious crimes, legal rules can be relaxed). Thus, for example, courts have invoked gravity to reject defenses based on the principle of legality—or *nullum crimen sine lege.* That principle is designed to provide notice to defendants of the types of conduct that are punishable and thus ensure the fair application of the law.

Damaska (2011) argues that because of the considerable pressure tribunals face to obtain convictions and thereby justify their existence, subtle bias may creep into the courtroom that infringes upon the defendant's rights and makes guilty verdicts more likely. But while such reasoning seems plausible on one level, finding evidence of systematic bias and unfairness toward the defendant is not easy. In fact, because such accusations of systemic bias imply that it is quite prevalent, actually finding something that is so ubiquitous is rather difficult. It is also next to impossible to disprove such arguments. The supporters of such claims need only find some evidence somewhere of bias to argue "I told you so," while the critics might have to disprove every accusation of bias. In the end, arguments that the tribunals are driven by political bias are almost impossible to disprove because almost anything can be explained as political in some fashion, especially when we do not have inside information about how and why decisions are made. The key for the truly objective researcher is to specify where evidence of bias is to be found and how such a theory would be disproven. Nonetheless, there is enough evidence of the intrusion of politics into the creation of the tribunals to monitor their actions for any indication politics is influencing their decision making. That is where we turn our attention next.

## SELECTION OF SIDES IN A CONFLICT TO PROSECUTE

All of the tribunals we examine—the ICTY, ICTR, SCSL, and ICC—investigate conflicts. They are supposed to examine allegations of violations of international law by all sides, not just one. The decisions regarding which individuals from which of the conflict actors should be prosecuted, however, are often fraught with tension. It is rare that each side is equally to blame for its fair share of crimes and hence there tend to be more defendants from one party to the conflict than another. In the case of the ICTY, we find that the Serbs in general and the Bosnian Serbs in particular have been prosecuted more frequently. In the case of the ICTR, only the Hutus have been prosecuted for the genocide against the Tutsis and other violations of international law that occurred in Rwanda in 1994. The ICC has prosecuted too few individuals for such problems to exist, although it has principally been prosecuting individuals from African states thus far, which creates its own perceptions of bias. Only in the case of the SCSL do we find a tribunal prosecuting individuals from the various key factions roughly equally in the Sierra Leone civil war. At the ICTY and ICTR, the distribution of cases across the ethnic groups has led to accusations of bias and favoritism from those groups that perceive they are being unfairly targeted.

At the ICTY, these claims of bias have come mostly from the Serbs. In general, the Serbs claim that their side has been targeted disproportionately when, as they assert, all sides are equally guilty. That point is certainly true from a purely mathematical perspective—approximately two-thirds of those indicted have been Serbs. Accusations of bias, however, rarely address whether the reason for the number of Serb defendants might be that they committed a disproportionate percentage of the crimes. Typically the accusations of bias are accompanied by claims that all sides are equally guilty or that the number or severity of the crimes with which the Serbs have been charged have been grossly exaggerated (see Clark 2014). The Serbian narrative of the wars of the former Yugoslavia is the story of Serbs trying to defend themselves and Christianity from Islam and Bosnian Muslims. When the Serbs saw that they were not treated as the saviors they perceive themselves to be, but rather as scapegoats for the violence of war, their opposition to international justice, and the West in particular, grew. Serbian nationalist leaders, who are the ones making such arguments most loudly and vociferously, view the Serb people as martyrs and thus prosecution of their "crimes" as not only unfair, but dangerous to the survival of Christianity.[1] Given the historical, religious, and political baggage of such a perspective, the frequency and vehemence with which Serb leaders make accusations of bias against the ICTY should come as no surprise (Ford 2012, 2013). In 2013, Serbian president Tomislav Nikolic stated at a United Nations conference on justice and reconciliation that,

> The proceedings against Serbs are motivated by desires to punish and retaliate; and retaliation, particularly in contemporary law, can never be justified as righteous. The Hague procedures are characterized by a total lack of justice and fairness.[2]

He later stated,

> It seems that for the greatest part, The Hague trials will not be able to lead to a real and complete truth and therefore, any reconciliation will be an imposed

> and insincere one. You cannot be fair to some and unfair to others. Also, how to explain away the fact that almost nobody, except in one case in Bosnia and in one case in Kosovo, has been convicted of crimes against Serbs.

On the other side of the coin, there have been a number of Bosnian Muslims who have been indicted by the ICTY, from prison camp guards to their military leadership. These cases have also been controversial among the Bosniak population. Some argue that their ethnic brethren were fighting a purely defensive war and that any violations of international law that might have occurred should be viewed as almost inevitable given the violence the Serbs were raining down on them. Others have argued that Bosniaks have only been prosecuted to create the impression that all sides have been prosecuted, in order to blunt Serb criticism that the ICTY is biased against them. At the same time, there have been other ICTY critics who have alleged that the trials of Bosnian Muslims have not been pursued with the same vigor as trials against Serbs, which they argue further illustrates the anti-Serb bias of the tribunal. Some defense attorneys have argued that less-than-stellar prosecution teams have been assigned to their cases so that there is a greater likelihood of acquittal (Karnavas 2011). And then there are those critics who have accused the ICTY of bias for not prosecuting leaders from the North Atlantic Treaty Organization (NATO) for alleged crimes committed during their air war over Kosovo in the spring of 1999 (see Ford 2013; Massa 2006 for discussion of such charges). There has been no shortage of accusations of unfairness by all sides.

The ICTR has also faced charges of bias and favoritism for having prosecuted no cases of Tutsi violations of international law in Rwanda during 1994, the one year over which the ICTR exercises jurisdiction. To be sure, the Rwandan genocide was perpetrated by the Hutu government and its allied militias and the victims were almost all Tutsi, although the extremist government did target moderate Hutus as well. Nonetheless, there have been allegations of Tutsi crimes and human rights abuses directed against Hutus in retaliation for the genocide as their army swept through Rwanda during the genocide and eventually overthrew the Hutu government. According to Human Rights Watch, "The International Criminal Tribunal for Rwanda's (ICTR) prosecutor's failure to date to bring cases against Rwandan Patriotic Front officers responsible for war crimes and crimes against humanity committed during the 1994 genocide risks undermining the court's legacy." Human Rights Watch refers to several credible reports by the UN Commission of Experts that initially investigated the events of 1994, as well as several other UN agencies that have looked into these events.[3] When the accused mastermind of the genocide, Theoneste Bagosora, took the stand in his own defense at the ICTR, he claimed, "The ICTR is biased against Hutus and courts Tutsi criminals who were the victors of a war they prepared."[4] Much evidence in this case, in contrast to Serb allegations of bias, comes from the UN and other nonpartisan organizations and thus carries greater weight. Thus, we must wonder why the ICTR has chosen not to pursue such cases.

There are two compelling reasons that explain this reluctance. First, one might argue that the genocide in Rwanda killed so many people with such brutal efficiency that the crimes of the perpetrators dwarf those that may have been committed by the Tutsis. Prosecuting the genocidaires not only consumed ICTR resources, it may well have overwhelmed the tribunal, making the prospect of opening up a new series of cases impractical. One might also argue that trying a small number of Tutsis for crimes that did not approach the violence of the genocide creates a false equivalency, thereby morally lessening the responsibility of the perpetrators and diminishing the severity of the genocide. Those who have accused the ICTR of bias, however, have pointed to a political reason why the tribunal has shown such reluctance to pursue cases against the Tutsis. When the ICTR gave any indication that it might pursue such charges, the response from the Tutsi-led Rwandan government was swift and severe. It threatened to deny visas to tribunal personnel who needed to travel to Rwanda to visit and escort witnesses, gather evidence, and perform other essential duties. If there was no access to Rwanda, the ICTR could not conduct its business and the tribunal would have come to a screeching halt. These were no idle threats either. When the ICTR Appeals Chamber ordered the release of one defendant, Jean-Bosco Barayagwiza, on the basis of alleged violations of his procedural rights, the Rwandan government quickly stopped cooperating with the ICTR. Shortly thereafter, the ICTR Appeals Chamber, on the basis of "new evidence" from the prosecution, reversed itself and proceedings against the defendant resumed.[5] Because of incidents like this in which the Rwandan government linked its cooperation with the actions of the ICTR, it does not stretch credulity to believe that the ICTR has declined to pursue any cases against Tutsis for political reasons.

The ICC has also been confronted with criticism for focusing its investigations on African conflicts and for prosecuting African leaders (see Du Plessis, Maluwa, and O'Reilly 2013). This, according to some critics (especially the leaders of African states), is evidence of the Western bias of the ICC located far away in Europe. While several of the conflicts the ICC is involved in were referred to it by those very states, one still cannot escape the fact that nearly all of the conflicts currently being tried are from Africa. And while there have been several other conflict situations outside of Africa that the ICC has begun preliminary investigations into, only one, at the time of this writing, outside of Africa (Georgia) has advanced any further. Some would argue that this focus on Africa, just like the decisions to create the ICTY and ICTR, demonstrates that international justice is selective. The prosecution at the ICC has picked on the African states because they are easy targets and do not have the kind of power to stop such investigations.[6] Again, while one cannot escape the fact that nearly all of its conflict situations are located in Africa, that fact, in and of itself, does not prove bias. It does raise concerns that, whether legitimate or not, can serve to undermine the legitimacy of the court over the long run.

Having reviewed the evidence of potential bias due to the prosecution of particular conflicts and groups of defendants, we can point to evidence that does suggest that such "selection effects" are not entirely free of bias. The choices made by the UN Security Council to authorize some tribunals and not others are not free of politics, especially the interests of the five permanent members. In fact, it would be quite surprising if these powerful nations acted fairly and objectively and set aside their national interests. Politics certainly intrudes into the decisions by prosecutors and judges to pursue some cases and some charges and not others. Given their finite mandate and finite resources, choices must be made and, given the realities of international criminal justice in which these tribunals must depend upon the support of the international community for their financing, political backing, and the apprehension of suspects and some amount of cooperation with local actors for access to evidence and suspects, it is not surprising that accusations of political interference arise. The ideal international justice in which tribunal personnel can conduct their affairs with justice and fairness as their only guides and not a whit of concern regarding those outside their doors is fiction. We may wish our courts to remain free of the taint of politics, but such purity has never really existed.

Does this mean that tribunals are infected with political bias in their choices and that fair trials are a chimera? Certainly not. I would urge the reader to keep in mind that there will always be tension between lofty ideals like truth, justice and fairness, and the realities of politics and running a courtroom. The very fact that these tribunals were created demonstrates their importance in international relations. And if they are important, political actors will have an interest in their actions and will seek to influence their behavior. Judges and prosecutors must struggle mightily to reduce the exercise of such influence as much as possible, but they can never remove it entirely.

Having offered a defense of the tribunals as agents of political institutions that can never entirely cut such ties, we must also recognize that the arc of history must bend toward greater justice and fairness. There were legitimate complaints raised against the Nuremberg and Tokyo Tribunals that their justice was a victor's justice. As a result, when the ICTY and ICTR were established, their founders took steps to ensure that they applied only existing international law, that there were adequate appeals processes for defendants, and that there was extensive eyewitness testimony. We should expect that future tribunals or future cases before the ICC are given the resources necessary to not depend upon the cooperation of hostile actors so as to ensure that all crimes and all parties to a conflict are investigated fairly. If the international community deems it critical to investigate, prosecute, and punish violations of its laws, it only makes sense to provide the support necessary to do the job correctly and fairly. Anything less risks undermining the legitimacy of these tribunals and thus their very existence.

## FAIRNESS OF VERDICTS AND PUNISHMENT

Judges are expected to administer justice in a manner corresponding to the highest standards of the national criminal justice systems. Antonio Cassese, former president of the ICTY, stated that "we believe that we have been able to distill as well as harmoniously amalgamate the most advanced aspects of the various legal systems, within the general framework of the principle of a 'fair trial.'"[7] To avoid the perception that they "are merely organized to convict," the tribunals have been at pains to demonstrate their impartiality. According to former chief prosecutor Richard Goldstone (2000, 123), "At all times, in the Office of the Prosecutor, the primary goal was not to achieve convictions, but rather to *ensure that those indicted would enjoy fair processes and procedure*" (emphasis added). If these institutions are to contribute to furthering peace and reconciliation in post-conflict societies, the judgment and punishment of the guilty must be fair and impartial. According to Franck (1998), fairness in international law is the most important issue now facing practitioners and scholars.

There has long been research on U.S. courts and the degree to which they are biased against defendants in criminal trials or protect the "haves" from the "have nots." Some suggest that there are significant differences in the distribution of resources between the prosecution and the defense and between well-resourced parties and those of more modest means (Black and Boyd 2012; Black and Owens 2012; Black 1996; Chambliss and Seidman 1971). The "haves" or "upperdogs" are typically characterized by access to greater resources, greater experience, and expertise in the legal process and other benefits, while underdogs are at a disadvantage in the courtroom because they are not nearly so richly supported (Box-Steffensmeier, Christenson, and Hitt 2013; Galanter 1974; Haynie and Sill 2007; Kritzer and Silbey 2003; Kuersten and Jagemann 2000; McGuire 1995; Sheehan, Mishler, and Songer 1992; Songer and Sheehan 1992).

Similar research on sentencing outcomes in U.S. courts has investigated whether the quality of the defense enjoyed by many accused is affected by their socioeconomic status, race, or ethnicity (Albonetti 1997; Brace and Hall 1997; Crow and Gertz 2008; Dixon 1995; Doerner and Demuth 2010; King, Johnson, and McGeever 2010; Mears 1998). Research tends to find that such underdog defendants are more likely to be convicted and receive harsher punishment as the quality of their legal counsel and access to the resources necessary to mount an effective case are not nearly as extensive as the prosecution (Cole 1999). Is it possible that such problems also affect defendants at the international tribunals whose lawyers do not possess many of these same advantages that the prosecution possesses?

The specific issue that has confronted judges at the international tribunals has been whether there is an "equality of arms" between the prosecution and the defense. In their classic statement regarding the meaning and importance of this term, the Tadić Appeals Chamber wrote:

> the principle of equality of arms must be given a more liberal interpretation than that normally upheld with regard to proceedings before domestic courts. This principle means that the Prosecution and the Defence must be equal before the Trial Chamber. It follows that the Chamber shall provide every practicable facility it is capable of granting under the Rules and Statute when faced with a request by a party for assistance in presenting its case.[8]

Equality of arms seems to imply, first, equality of opportunity in the courtroom, and second, that the trial chamber should provide any assistance it is required to provide and is practical. In the case cited, the defense for the accused war criminal, Duško Tadić, argued that equality of arms meant substantive as well as procedural equality. His lawyers argued that their inability to bring certain witnesses to testify in The Hague hindered their ability to present an effective defense. The Appeals Chamber held that while the Trial Chambers should provide the defense with appropriate assistance and opportunity to present its case, it was not required to grant every request made by the defense and could not be held responsible for the problems faced by the defense in bringing certain witnesses to testify.[9]

Much research has concentrated on the fairness of the rules of procedure and evidence and the degree to which they ensure an equality of arms. There are significant differences of opinion on the existence and impact of disparities in resources and expertise among the contending parties (Creta 1998; Gallant 2003; Groome 2007; Harvard Law Review 2001; Johnson 1998; Knoops 2004; Mégret 2009; Negri 2005). Few empirical analyses of such outcomes exist (see Meernik 2003), although many scholars contend that an inequality of arms does exist.

Perhaps the most consequential difference of all between the prosecution and the defense that can affect outcomes is the difference in resources and expertise between the two sides. The number of individuals in a typical defense team can be counted on one hand. The prosecution, on the other hand, may consist of dozens of attorneys, dozens of investigators, assistants, and others. You can imagine that the difference in the cost of running the Office of the Prosecutor and that of the defense probably runs in the tens of millions of dollars. Then there is the difference in expertise between the two sides. At the ad hoc tribunals, the prosecution has had years to build up a substantial level of knowledge of the conflicts, the leadership of the various sides, the signature tactics employed by the warring sides, and most other aspects of these conflicts. We would expect a less dramatic difference in expertise between the prosecution and the defense at the ICC because that court investigates and prosecutes many and more diverse conflict situations. The OTP also has substantially more familiarity with the Rules of Procedure and Evidence of their respective tribunals and institutional memory regarding the judges and the workings of the tribunals that would considerably overshadow whatever advantages the defense might have, even if some defense attorneys have defended multiple clients.

One can see that such significant differences in resources and expertise would advantage the prosecution and make it considerably easier to mount a case with the type and level of convincing evidence the judges find persuasive. Having attended many different trials myself, I can attest to the challenges faced by many defense attorneys who are unfamiliar with the hybrid legal system these tribunals have evolved. I have seen the defense attorneys struggle at times to understand and mount an effective cross-examination of a witness. I have visited their "offices," which have been just their apartments in The Hague, or perhaps a hotel room in Arusha, Tanzania. While the tribunals make a conscientious effort to enable these lawyers to mount an effective defense, one cannot escape the impression that the defense attorneys are the poor, orphan stepchildren of international justice.

Defense attorneys must also grapple with this strange hybrid system of court procedures at the international tribunals, with which few outside of the tribunals are familiar. In some ways the trials resemble the adversarial system found in common-law countries, especially the United States with lawyers battling it out to convince the judges of the plausibility of their evidence and testimony. The trials also have, and the ICC especially so, a civil law flavor in which there is an emphasis on the discovery of the truth that can be brought to light in the courtroom by the defense, the prosecution, and the judges. Indeed, the judges take an active role in questioning witnesses, directing the conduct of the attorneys in the courtroom, and even calling their own witnesses when they see a need for additional clarification or information. The prosecution can be much more nimble on its feet in the courtroom because it has dealt with this hybrid system and the particular ways in which the various presiding judges tend to run their trials, while the defense must play catch-up and learn this hybrid system on the job.

The difference in status between the prosecution and the defense at the ad hoc tribunals is perhaps best captured by the simple fact that while the Office of the Prosecutor is one of the three divisions of these tribunals, the defense has never enjoyed that kind of official recognition and status. Federova (2012, 187) writes, "Not having the status of an independent entity, an organ of the tribunal, the defence is viewed with different eyes by state authorities," especially when they are seeking evidence and witnesses. To be sure, there have been improvements in housing the defense within the ad hoc tribunals over time. I can still recall the years in the history of the ICTY when the defense attorneys were just given one office on the public ground floor to work out of during trial days. One of my most vivid memories was seeing and smelling the office when the door would occasionally open and great clouds of cigarette smoke would come billowing out (the defense attorneys were often mainly from the former Yugoslavia and smoked quite a bit). One would catch occasional glimpses into this crowded room of lawyers banging away on their computers and chain-smoking, looking more like an old-school newsroom than a law office. Otherwise the defense attorneys were expected to maintain their offices at separate locations. This situation has since been remedied at the ICC, where the defense enjoys a status somewhat like the prosecution. That, coupled with international defense lawyers associations, such as the Association of Defence Counsel Practicing before the ICTY and other organizations like the International Criminal Law Bureau, have provided greater visibility and development of training that has reduced the difference in expertise. Certainly over time and with the advent of the ICC, defense attorneys have faced fewer challenges. It may well be impossible, however, to ever eclipse the inevitable inequalities that arise when one side has the power of the international community behind it and the other seeks to defend those who have offended the laws of this community.

One critical issue that has arisen at all the tribunals and is also found in domestic jurisdictions is the disclosure of evidence, or lack thereof, by the prosecution to the defense. The prosecution is required at all the tribunals to provide such information to the defense. Indeed, at the ICC the prosecution is required to thoroughly investigate all aspects of a case in the quest for truth, not just that evidence that would implicate an individual. There have been many cases in which the defense has alleged violations of this disclosure requirement. Federova, Verhoeven, and Wouters (2009) found that in the

*Blaskic* case at the ICTY, the defendant learned of exculpatory evidence from the media.[10] More recently, during the trial of Bosnian Serb general Ratko Mladić at the ICTY, the prosecutor discovered mountains of documents that had not been shared with the defense. Here the violation was so egregious that the judges ordered an abrupt halt in the trial for several months to give the defense time to review the voluminous record.[11] The OTP claimed that computer issues were to blame. Not a few defense attorneys found such claims implausible. Federova (2012, 176) reports that such problems have also arisen at the ICC. She writes,

> Twice, the Trial Chamber has ordered a stay (in pre-trial and during trial) because it could not control the fairness of proceedings as a direct result of the prosecutor's conduct in this case. The first stay was ordered because the prosecutor could not disclose material that he had obtained under the cloak of confidentiality and that contained exculpatory elements. The second stay came when the prosecutor refused to disclose the identity of an intermediary used by the prosecution to contact witnesses, following an explicit disclosure order by the Trial Chamber.[12]

And while there are more stringent requirements in place at the ICC for prosecution disclosure of evidence, attorneys have complained that disclosure occurs so close to the beginning of courtroom proceedings that the defense's ability to mount an effective case is compromised by the difficult task of absorbing and utilizing tens of thousands of pages of documents (Khan and Shah 2014). And with so few personnel, the defense can be overwhelmed by such demands and thus present a less effective case before the judges.

Many observers have also criticized the length of time it takes to prepare for trial, conduct a trial, and reach a verdict. Defendants may find themselves in their respective tribunal's detention units for several years before they learn of their fate. And then the appellate stage begins and defendants must wait for several more years. Lengthy trials are the norm. As Zappalà has argued, "the challenge of combining expeditiousness and fairness exists in most criminal justice systems . . . international criminal courts have specific features that make them more complex and slow."[13] Even tribunal personnel admit their trials are overly long.[14] The reasons are many and often quite defensible, but they do add up to a considerable problem. First, trials are usually conducted in multiple languages, which slows down the proceedings, especially with languages for which there are few trained translators.[15] Then there are all the logistical hurdles involved in conducting trials hundreds of miles away from the scene of the crimes, which creates more delays because of the extensive amount of travel required. Because it has been so difficult to apprehend many of the suspects, there have been a number of trials of individuals that might have been combined but proceeded with only those defendants that had been captured.

In a 2008 paper with Rosa Aloisi, we found that the average length of a trial from initial defendant appearance to the announcement of the verdict was 1,056 days at the ICTY (with a minimum, at the time of writing, of 182 days and a maximum of 2,364 days). For the ICTR, the average length of a trial was 1,381 days (with a minimum and maximum of 53 and 2,561 days, respectively). Compared to the Nuremberg Tribunal, which took a little over a year from trial to sentence, and the Tokyo Tribunal, which occurred over two and a half years, the ICTY and ICTR have been somewhat slow. Is the appropriate cliché "justice delayed is justice denied" or "better late than never"?

While there certainly have been many delays in justice—the ICC only completed its first trial ten years after it was officially launched in 2002—it is difficult to sustain the argument that as a result justice has been denied. Indeed, many of the delays in some of the more prominent cases at the ad hoc tribunals have been caused by the behavior of defendants, like Slobodan Milošević, who were more interested in scoring political points back home among their supporters with their drawn-out courtroom antics and claims of illness. If anything, the delayed justice is an injustice more to the victims of these conflicts, who must wait many years before the accused are apprehended and tried. No doubt many of the victims may not survive for as long as it takes to deliver verdicts in these cases.

## CONVICTION RATE

At the time of writing, the four international tribunals have tried 193 individuals, although there was one retrial of three individuals at the ICTY. What does their conviction rate tell us of the fairness or unfairness of the tribunals? Viewed in isolation, the numbers do not necessarily mean anything. Viewed in a larger context against each other or compared to other court systems we may gain valuable insight into whether these tribunals are predisposed to convict all those who come into their courtroom. As seen in table 2.1, the overall conviction rate across the tribunals is 88 percent—170 of 193 individuals pleaded or were found guilty. I must stress that these and subsequent figures in this section are based on decisions reached at trial chambers and do not consider what may happen to cases on appeal. The numbers range from a high of 100 percent at the SCSL, where all of the nine defendants were found guilty, to the 75 percent conviction rate of the ICC, which has reached verdicts for only four individuals. At the ICTY and the ICTR, which have resolved by far the most cases, the conviction rates are 89 percent and 87 percent, respectively. That these two tribunals, sitting thousands of miles away from each other and confronting very different conflicts and trial issues (the ICTR has relied heavily on witness testimony; the ICTY has dealt with multiple, often uncooperative governments), should have such similar conviction rates is quite striking. Perhaps there is something of a "normal" rate of conviction that tribunals converge on over the course of many years and cases. It will be interesting to see if the ICC conviction rate eventually approaches this level. When we exclude the guilty plea cases and look just at the conviction rate in cases that go to trial in table 2.2 we see largely the same trends in the rank ordering of tribunals. The overall conviction rate is approximately 86 percent.

**Table 2.1 Conviction Rates at the International Tribunals at Trial**

| **Verdict** | **ICTR** | **ICTY** | **SCSL** | **ICC** | **Total** |
|---|---|---|---|---|---|
| Acquitted | 8 | 14 | 0 | 1 | 23 |
| | 11.11% | 12.96% | 0% | 25% | 11.98% |
| | | | | | |
| Guilty | 64 | 94 | 9 | 3 | 170 |
| | 88.89% | 87.04% | 100% | 75% | 88.02% |
| | | | | | |
| **Total** | **72** | **108** | **9** | **4** | **193** |
| | **100%** | **100%** | **100%** | **100%** | **100%** |

**Table 2.2 Conviction Rates at the International Tribunals at Trial without Guilty Pleas**

| **Verdict** | **ICTR** | **ICTY** | **SCSL** | **ICC** | **Total** |
|---|---|---|---|---|---|
| Acquittal | 8 | 14 | 0 | 1 | 23 |
| | 12.7% | 15.91% | 0% | 25% | 14.11% |
| | | | | | |
| Guilty | 55 | 74 | 9 | 3 | 141 |
| | 87.3% | 84.09% | 100% | 75% | 85.9% |
| | | | | | |
| **Total** | **63** | **88** | **9** | **4** | **164** |
| | **100%** | **100%** | **100%** | **100%** | **100%** |

**Table 2.3 Conviction Rates at Trial Among ICTY Defendants by Ethnicity**

| | ICTY Defendant Ethnicity | | | | | |
|---|---|---|---|---|---|---|
| **Verdict** | **Serbian** | **Croatian** | **Bosniak** | **Kosovar Albanian** | **Macedonian** | **Total** |
| Acquitted | 4 | 2 | 2 | 5 | 1 | 14 |
| | 5.88% | 8.33% | 25% | 83.33% | 50% | 12.96% |
| | | | | | | |
| Guilty | 64 | 22 | 6 | 1 | 1 | 94 |
| | 94.12% | 91.67% | 75% | 16.67% | 50% | 87.04% |
| | | | | | | |
| **Total** | **68** | **24** | **8** | **6** | **2** | **108** |
| | **100%** | **100%** | **100%** | **100%** | **100%** | **100%** |

**Table 2.4 Guilty Pleas at ICTY by Ethnicity**

| | ICTY Defendant Ethnicity | | | | | |
|---|---|---|---|---|---|---|
| **Guilty Plea** | **Serbian** | **Croatian** | **Bosniak** | **Kosovar Albanian** | **Macedonian** | **Total** |
| No | 50 | 22 | 8 | 6 | 2 | 88 |
| | 73.53% | 91.67% | 100% | 100% | 100% | 81.48% |
| | | | | | | |
| Yes | 18 | 2 | 0 | 0 | 0 | 20 |
| | 26.47% | 8.33% | 0% | 0% | 0% | 18.52% |
| | | | | | | |
| **Total** | **68** | **24** | **8** | **6** | **2** | **108** |
| | **100%** | **100%** | **100%** | **100%** | **100%** | **100%** |

**Table 2.5 Guilty Pleas at All International Tribunals**

| **Guilty Plea** | **ICTR** | **ICTY** | **SCSL** | **ICC** | **Total** |
|---|---|---|---|---|---|
| No | 63 | 88 | 9 | 4 | 164 |
| | 87.5% | 81.48% | 100% | 100% | 84.9% |
| | | | | | |
| Yes | 9 | 20 | 0 | 0 | 29 |
| | 12.5% | 18.52% | 0% | 0% | 15.1% |
| | | | | | |
| **Total** | **72** | **108** | **9** | **4** | **193** |
| | **100%** | **100%** | **100%** | **100%** | **100%** |

The reader will recall that one of the more prominent criticisms of the ICTY by the Serbs has been their charge that the tribunal is biased in favor of convicting defendants of Serb ethnicity and goes easy on Bosniak defendants. What do the results say? In fact, the numbers taken at face value would seem to suggest that Serbian defendants are convicted at a rate greater than any other ethnic group (these numbers are those from the trial outcomes again). Table 2.3 shows that Serb defendants were convicted 94.1 percent of the time (sixty-eight defendants); Croat defendants were found guilty 91.6 percent of the time (twenty-four defendants); Bosnian Muslim defendants were convicted 75 percent of the time (eight defendants); Kosovar Albanians were convicted only 16.6 percent of the time (six defendants); and of the two Macedonian defendants, one was acquitted and one was found guilty. While Serbian and Croatian defendants were convicted at roughly the same rate, defendants from the three other ethnic groups were convicted far less frequently. Perhaps part of the answer may be that some defendants were more likely to plead guilty than others and thus increase the conviction rate.

As we see in table 2.4, among defendants at the ICTY, 26.4 percent of the Serbs pleaded guilty and 8.3 percent of the Croatian defendants pleaded guilty. No member of the three other ethnic groups pleaded guilty. This may explain, at least partially, why Serbian defendants are found guilty at a higher rate than Bosniaks, Kosovar Albanians, and Macedonians. When we look at all tribunals in table 2.5, we see an interesting trend that may or may not have anything to do with perceptions of fairness. All of the guilty pleas have been entered at the ICTY and ICTR, with the ICTY in particular receiving a substantial number. Could it be the case that defendants are more likely to plead guilty if they believe they will be treated fairly when the punishments are determined? Or perhaps defendants are more likely to plead guilty because they believe they will be convicted regardless? We cannot tell at this point in time because we cannot see into the minds of the defendants, but we do know that Serbian defendant guilty pleas dwarf all others.

Each of the tribunals consists of both trial chambers that hear the cases in the typical courtroom setting with witnesses and contesting parties, but also have appeals chambers in which both the defense and the prosecution can seek reversals of the trial chamber decisions. Typical appellate procedures, from the ICTY Statute, Article 25, are as follows:

> The Appeals Chamber shall hear appeals from persons convicted by the Trial Chambers or from the Prosecutor on the following grounds:
> (a) an error on a question of law invalidating the decision; or
> (b) an error of fact which has occasioned a miscarriage of justice.

Defendants appeal everything from reliance on hearsay evidence to misapplication of command and control doctrine. The Office of the Prosecutor can appeal verdicts and sentences as well and has often argued against sentences perceived as too lenient. If the tribunals are truly fair, we would expect that there will be the occasional need to confront a miscarriage of justice (for no court is ever perfect in interpreting the evidence and the law) and reverse a conviction at trial. We see similar patterns on this issue emerging again across tribunals in table 2.6. There were no reversals at the SCSL and none at this date at the ICC. Of the seventy-two cases at the ICTR, there were only three instances in which an individual was acquitted of all charges on appeal (7.5 percent), while there were seven such cases at the ICTY (9.7 percent). Interestingly, while many of the accusations of unfairness have been leveled at the ICTY, most especially by Serbian defendants and their supporters, there are a number of cases of individuals either being acquitted at trial or on appeal, although only one of those acquittals on appeal involved a Serbian defendant.

**Table 2.6 Acquittals on Appeal at the International Tribunals**

| Acquittal on Appeal | ICTR | ICTY | SCSL | ICC | Total |
|---|---|---|---|---|---|
| No | 37 | 65 | 9 | 1 | 112 |
| | 92.5% | 90.28% | 100% | 100% | 91.8% |
| | | | | | |
| Yes | 3 | 7 | 0 | 0 | 10 |
| | 7.5% | 9.72% | 0% | 0% | 8.2% |
| | | | | | |
| **Total** | **40** | **72** | **9** | **1** | **122** |
| | **100%** | **100%** | **100%** | **100%** | **100%** |

Lastly I consider how the conviction rate at the international tribunals compares to conviction rates for federal crimes in the United States, a useful standard in comparing across institutions. One dramatic difference is that the vast majority of cases that result in conviction in U.S. federal courts are resolved through guilty pleas. According to the federal government's statistics for fiscal year 2013, "96.9 percent of all convicted defendants pleaded guilty."[16] Using the most recent data available for fiscal year 2013 and looking only at federal criminal cases that go to trial, I find that defendants were acquitted at trial 13.8 percent of the time. When we look at just those cases that go to trial at the international tribunals (table 2.2), we find that approximately 14 percent of the cases end in acquittal. There is very little difference here, which would seem to suggest that the tribunals are behaving no differently in their conviction and acquittals than U.S. federal courts.

## SENTENCING

One of the most fascinating issues in the study of war crimes tribunals, and the principal reason I began studying these institutions, is how they manage the punishment of those individuals found guilty. Nearly all of those who have been convicted have either ordered their subordinates to perpetrate human rights atrocities or are themselves the ones who engaged in horrific acts of violence. If any of these defendants had been convicted in the state of Texas (where I live), they would probably get the death penalty. How then do judges determine which individuals deserve a less severe punishment of perhaps five to fifteen years in prison, while others deserve a life sentence? (None of the tribunals allows for the death penalty.)[17] How do judges make such distinctions, and are these sentences perceived to be fair and just? The place to begin is the founding documents of the tribunals. Below I describe those factors that the judges are encouraged to consider in their deliberations and what impact they may have on sentences.

There is no doubt what the most important criterion is when sentencing the guilty. The judges universally acknowledge that "by far the most important consideration, which may be regarded as the litmus test for the appropriate sentence, is the gravity of the offence."[18] The severity of the crime, however, may be measured in any number of ways, such as by the number of people killed, the heinousness of the crimes, and the impact on the victims. Is it really possible to create some sort of "gravity scale" to measure the violence of any particular crime? Is it legally and morally defensible to create a "body count" metric in order to mete out punishment? How are the types of crimes (e.g., murder, rape, forced displacement) to be compared to the number of victims or the level of destruction? That is, what would be the equivalent level of suffering when comparing those convicted of destroying homes to those convicted of killing people? Can these things even be compared at all? We might recoil at the thought of trying to construct this sort of scale of suffering to determine how many years a war criminal should spend in prison. How exactly then do the judges determine punishment based on gravity?

In the research my colleagues and I have done over the years, we have argued that the judges will look at the broad categories of crimes when meting out punishment. We argue and find that judges punish those guilty of the crime of genocide most severely, those convicted of crimes against humanity somewhat less severely, and those found guilty of war crimes least severely (Meernik and King 2002; Meernik 2011). There is an important distinction between crimes against humanity and genocide, whose victims are *people writ large,* and war crimes committed in the course of conflict, where the violence is more indiscriminate. The crime of genocide is characterized by an attempt to deliberately target or destroy an ethnic, racial, religious, or national group, and crimes against humanity often (although not always) tend to involve the persecution of civilians (Schabas 2001; Van Schaak 1999). The element of intent in genocide and crimes against humanity is critical. In domestic law, bias crimes are also treated differently and those found guilty are often punished more severely because of the intent of their actions (see also Danner 2001). Even though war crimes may involve horrific and bloody violence done to innocent civilians, we should expect to find that those convicted of genocide especially, and crimes against humanity to a lesser extent, will be punished more severely due to the scope and intent involved in these crimes.

Another critical factor in determining punishment is the type of position held by the defendant. One of the principal purposes of the tribunals is to judge and punish individuals thought to be the most responsible for violations of international law so that blame can be properly fixed to the political and military leaders who instigated these conflicts. The hope is that if the international community can demonstrate the guilt of these leaders and appropriately punish them, victims will be less likely to blame members of other ethnic groups as collectively guilty, and thus perceive less of a need for retribution. Assuming victims and others affected by the violence can make these distinctions and attribute blame to leaders, this should help end the cycle of violence and promote reconciliation. Judges at the ad hoc tribunals have argued that, *ceteris paribus*, those who bear the most responsibility should suffer the greater punishment.[19] At the ICTY in the Blaskic decision, the judges found that

> Command position must therefore systematically increase the sentence or at least lead the Trial Chamber to give less weight to mitigating circumstances, independently of the issue of the form of participation in the crime.[20]

Therefore we should find that judges will give substantial weight to the importance of the level of responsibility exercised by the accused when determining punishment (Meernik 2003; Meernik and King 2002, 2003, 2004; Meernik, King, and Dancy 2005; Meernik 2011).

The statutes of the ICTY and ICTR also inform the judges that they should consider "the gravity of the offense and the individual circumstances of the convicted person." Rule 101(B)(i) of the Rules of Procedure and Evidence indicates that the judges shall consider "any aggravating circumstances." Judges have determined that aggravating factors must be proved by the prosecution beyond a reasonable doubt. Further, the Trial Chamber in the *Kunarac* case at the ICTY ruled that

> Only those circumstances directly related to the commission of the offense charged and to the offender himself when he committed the offense, such as the manner in which the offense was committed may be considered in aggravation.[21]

Rule 101(B)(ii) of the ICTY Rules of Procedure and Evidence provides that the judges should take into account "any mitigating circumstances including the substantial cooperation with the Prosecutor by the convicted person before or after conviction." Additionally, the judges at the ad hoc tribunals have argued that the relative weight to be accorded to any mitigating circumstance is theirs to make. In the *Kupreskic* case at the ICTY, the Appeals Chamber found that "the weight to be attached to such [mitigating] circumstances lies within the discretion of a Trial Chamber, which is under no obligation to set out in detail each and every factor relied upon."[22] Substantial cooperation with the prosecutor is the only mitigating circumstance specified by either the statutes or the rules of procedure and evidence articulated to date by the various international criminal tribunals. Further, it is also the case that the defense must demonstrate mitigating circumstances "on balance of probabilities."[23] We should expect that the more often judges cite aggravating factors in their decisions, the longer the sentence will be, while the more mitigating factors they find relevant should lead to a lighter sentence.

Perhaps the two most widely utilized mitigating circumstances at the ad hoc tribunals have been guilty pleas and cooperation with the prosecution. In our previous research on the ICTY, we found that the use of plea bargains in particular tends to result in lighter sentences (Meernik 2003, 2011; Meernik and King 2003). There are several benefits arising from the use of plea bargains, as they expedite trials, can encourage others to come forward and confess their crimes, and help establish a historical record. While plea bargains have been viewed critically by some scholars and jurists, they have been extremely useful, especially at the ICTY in expediting the tribunal's work (Scharf 2004).

To explore how the tribunals have punished the guilty, I begin by looking at the average sentences handed down by each of the four tribunals at trial. First, however, we need to separate out those who have been sentenced to life in prison because we cannot directly compare a life sentence with a sentence measured in years and months. They are qualitatively distinct things. There have been five such sentences to date at the ICTY (5.3 percent of those found guilty), while at the ICTR there have been twenty-eight such sentences (43.7 percent of those found guilty). There have been no life sentences at the ICC, and there were no life sentences at the SCSL, although some of their sentences have been so lengthy that they are basically the equivalent of a life sentence. When we remove the life sentences from the data analysis (thirty-three total cases), the average sentence at the ICTR is 261 months, with a low of 72 months and a high of 420 months. At the ICTY, the average term of incarceration thus far is 200 months, with a high of 552 and a low of 24 months. The SCSL has sentenced individuals to prison terms of 434 months, with a low of 72 months and a high of 624 months. Only two individuals have been found guilty and sentenced at the ICC thus far and their sentences were 144 and 168 months (all sentences are those imposed at the trial chamber level).

By themselves, these figures do not necessarily reveal anything about the fairness of the tribunals and their sentencing procedures, although it is clear that defendants convicted of the genocide in Rwanda by the ICTR have received the most severe sentences, as illustrated by the numerous life sentences. Next we will explore whether the factors I described above that the tribunals' founding documents indicate should be the most important sentencing determinants can help us explain the sentences. The technique I use is known as regression analysis and it allows us to evaluate the influence of many factors simultaneously on sentences. It also allows us to determine if these factors are "statistically significant" or whether their influence is more likely due to random chance.[24] I use several factors in this statistical model to predict sentence length: 1) whether the defendant was convicted of genocide; 2) whether the defendant was convicted of a crime against humanity; 3) the number of counts on which an individual was found guilty; 4) the defendant's level of responsibility;[25] 5) the number of aggravating and mitigating factors cited by the judges as important in their decision; 6) whether the defendant pleaded guilty, cooperated with the prosecution, and showed remorse; and 7) variables for the ICTY and ICTR.

**Table 2.7 Explaining Sentence Length at Trial at the International Tribunals**

| Variable | Coefficient | Standard Error | *T* Statistic | *P* Value |
|---|---|---|---|---|
| Genocide | 226.06 | 37.42 | 6.04 | 0.00 |
| Crimes against Humanity | 101.41 | 27.38 | 3.70 | 0.00 |
| Number of Guilty Counts | 7.44 | 1.96 | 3.79 | 0.00 |
| Level of Responsibility | 45.70 | 12.78 | 3.57 | 0.00 |
| Total Mitigating Factors | –25.32 | 5.29 | –4.79 | 0.00 |
| Total Aggravating Factors | 24.36 | 6.60 | 3.69 | 0.00 |
| Guilty Plea | 12.12 | 31.61 | 0.38 | 0.70 |
| ICTY | 20.51 | 36.85 | 0.56 | 0.58 |
| SCSL | 90.41 | 58.08 | 1.56 | 0.12 |
| Constant | –13.09 | 52.66 | –0.25 | 0.80 |

Number of cases = 168

As the reader can see in table 2.7, by examining the *p* value statistic, which tells us whether the impact of a variable is statistically significant and thus is a result we can have confidence in, nearly all of the factors in the model are statistically significant. The coefficients tell us the average impact of a variable on sentence length, but their effect only means something if the results are statistically significant. If the results are not statistically significant, we cannot have any faith that the results are not due to random chance. For example, the coefficient for the genocide variable is statistically significant at the 0.00001 level, which tells us there is only an infinitesimally small likelihood that the results were due to chance. The coefficient for the genocide variable is 226, which tells us that, all other things being equal, someone who is convicted of genocide can expect to receive an additional 226 months in prison from the baseline. The baseline, which we see reflected in the constant term (58.4 in this case), is basically the average sentence when all of the variables are equal to zero. Similarly, the coefficient for the variable that measures whether someone was convicted of a crime against humanity is 120.3, which means that these defendants can expect an additional 120.3 months on top of the baseline if they are convicted of such crimes.

The more charges a defendant is convicted of, the greater the sentence—9.1 months for each additional conviction. Additionally, every aggravating circumstance cited by the judges leads to 24.3 more months in prison, all other things being equal. Thus, if we consider these four factors as measures of the gravity of the crime, it would certainly appear that the judges are abiding by the sentencing guidance contained in their founding statutes and rules of procedure and evidence. The level of responsibility exercised by the accused is also important—individuals are sentenced to roughly 45.7 months, on average, for each step they take up the ladder of liability. Those who had the least power, like ordinary soldiers and concentration camp guards, are given the lightest sentences; mid-level military officers and political officials are given 45.7 months more on average in comparison to the low-level defendants; and the most high-ranking generals and political leaders are similarly given 45.7 months more, all other things being equal, than the mid-level individuals.

As stipulated in their statutes, the judges also give consideration to mitigating circumstances that tend to diminish the severity of the sentence. For every mitigating factor, such as good behavior in detention or assistance rendered to vulnerable populations during the conflict, those convicted tend to receive 25.3 fewer months on their sentence. There are also three variables whose coefficients are statistically insignificant in the estimates. First, those individuals who plead guilty, cooperate, and exhibit remorse are not statistically likely to receive a lower sentence. However, since these are all factors that are measured as mitigating circumstances as well, I dropped the variable that counts mitigating factors from the model (including both may be causing a statistical anomaly in the model) and reran it. This time the coefficient for the variable measuring guilty pleas with cooperation and remorse was statistically significant and negative like we might expect. Judges do exhibit leniency toward such individuals and so their sentences tend to be roughly 70.8 months less, on average, than other sentences. Finally, the reader can see that the coefficients for the ICTY and SCSL variables are statistically insignificant. This means that basically there are no substantial differences in the sentences handed down by the various tribunals when we take into consideration the types of crimes committed, the individual circumstances of the defendant, and other such factors. This is good news for the tribunals—none of them is a real outlier with sentences that are out of whack with the others.

The reader will recall that prominent Serbian leaders from throughout the former Yugoslavia have argued that Serbs have been unfairly targeted and punished more severely than defendants from other ethnic groups. Is there any truth to the latter claim? Do Serb defendants from Serbia, Croatia, and Bosnia receive longer prison terms than defendants from other ethnic groups? I ran another statistical model looking just at the ICTY and included a variable for Serb defendants. The coefficient for the Serb variable is statistically significant and positive—Serbian defendants who are convicted can expect to receive an additional 57.6 months in prison compared to those convicted from other ethnic groups. This does not necessarily mean that there is a bias behind these longer sentences because there may be other factors associated with the crimes for which individuals were found guilty that may be important, such as the number of victims, which I do not have data on and thus do not appear in the model. Nonetheless, these kinds of findings should certainly give us pause to consider whether there might be some sort of bias operating here. Perhaps there are biases that we cannot measure at present that might be influencing sentences.

Next I look at what happens when defendants appeal their convictions and sentences. Do they tend to receive more lenient punishment after the Appeals Chamber issues their decisions? First, I cannot find any instances where a defendant received a life sentence at trial and was then entirely acquitted on appeal, although there have been several instances at the ICTR and one case at the ICTY where an individual was given a life sentences at trial and then a lesser (although still lengthy) sentence on appeal. In general, however, I find (results not shown) that after the Appeals Chamber returns their decisions, sentences tend to decrease by approximately thirty-three months. The largest increase in sentence length after appeal occurred at the ICTR where an individual was initially sentenced to fifteen years and then received a life sentence, while the largest reduction in sentence length also occurred at the ICTR where an individual was sentenced to life at trial and then received one fifteen-year term on appeal. The reader should keep in mind that in some cases these differences are a result of individuals being completely acquitted on appeal and their sentences dropping to zero. At the ICTY, the average change on appeal is –33, which means that sentences tend to decrease by 33 months on average, while the analogous numbers are –50.1 for the ICTR and 28 months for the SCSL. In fact, no defendant at the SCSL received a more lenient sentence on appeal. There have been too few cases at the ICC to draw any reliable conclusions.

Where do all of these findings leave us in our quest to understand if the tribunals are fair in the way they adjudicate cases? There are probably some examples where the tribunals may be perceived to be unfair to a particular defendant because they were unable to gain access to witnesses or because the prosecution failed to disclose evidence or did so in a manner that had hurt the presentation of the defense case. The prosecution certainly enjoys a substantial superiority in staff, resources, and expertise that the defense can never rival. On the other hand, we also saw that the tribunals convict defendants at a rate very similar to what we find in the U.S. federal court system, which might suggest that there is something like a typical standard that such institutions tend to over time. The sentences also tend to reflect the broad guidance given to the judges in their statutes and rules of procedure and evidence. Sentences are predictable and not the result of some sort of systemic bias or random chance as some have argued (Drumbl 2007; Harmon and Gaynor 2007; Henham 2003, 2007; Olusanya 2005). That Serbs are more likely to be convicted at a higher rate than non-Serbs and receive lengthier sentences at the ICTY, however, should be of concern and should warrant further investigation to determine if there are legitimate reasons for such discrepancies. There is evidence to suggest that while international justice does not always live up to the highest standards of the law and fairness, it largely adheres to expected norms and to the very laws that established and govern the tribunals. Nonetheless, this should not detract from the need to always make things better and fairer over time. There is room for improvement.

When we evaluate the fairness of international justice against the most fair and efficient domestic systems, we can probably agree that the international justice we see does not always meet such lofty aims. The prosecution enjoys many advantages over the defense in terms of resources and expertise, for example. There are flaws in the system with witness testimony, access to evidence, and other problems unique to individual cases. When we assess international justice in terms of its progress and whether it is improving generally over time, it does not look nearly so bad. Significant strides have been made since the Nuremberg and Tokyo Tribunals in developing more of an equality of arms and providing defendants with avenues of appeal. And even since the birth of the ICTY in 1993, improvements have been made, especially at the ICC, which has been deliberately engineered to address some of the more prominent concerns with fairness that had been brought to light by the first years of the ICTY and ICTR, such as the creation of an office for the defense counsel. The arc of history would seem to be tending toward greater justice.

## IMPACT ON HUMAN SECURITY AND RECONCILIATION

So far we have been concerned with the delivery of justice as a question of fairness, which is an issue that has special relevance for the defense. Now we turn to the relationship between justice and human security. Have the tribunals' convictions and punishments provided justice to the people affected by these conflicts? Have the victims received a measure of justice that vindicates their claims and gives them some sense of closure? And most critically from our perspective, what impact has this justice had on human security? Part of the mission of international justice is to individualize guilt and lessen the felt need by some to take revenge against members of those ethnic groups they perceive as responsible for their suffering. By helping these victims understand that, for example, not all Hutus or all Serbs are guilty of crimes, these victims may be able to live more peacefully with people from these groups. We have two related questions to explore. First, how have those who live in the nations that these international tribunals have taken jurisdiction over perceived their justice? Do they believe justice has improved their security? Second, has this justice made a difference in the level of human security these people enjoy in their nations, which one would also suspect plays a significant role in their evaluations of justice? The first question is the topic of chapter 5, so we will set aside that issue for now and explore instead the answer to the second question.

The connection between the justice meted out at the international tribunals and human security is not a simple and direct one. Determining if human security in one country is a direct result of decisions made in a courtroom hundreds of miles away is no easy feat. Human security and the level of violence in any country are the result of many events and decisions that are quite far removed from international justice. It would be nice if there was a straight line we could trace from justice to security, but it is a rather complex and meandering pathway. We will explore much of the issue regarding the relationship between international justice and peace in chapter 4. For now, I want to focus more on the relationship between justice and the building blocks of peace. In particular, have international tribunals helped advance the conditions that sustain peace—reconciliation among groups that had previously been fighting each other? If international justice is functioning the way it is intended, which is to provide an unbiased truth regarding the commission of international crimes, then these truths should help individuals better understand their past and help reconcile with those whom their ethnic or religious group fought. If this truth can be accepted by all sides, however grudgingly, it *may*—the key word is *may*—create a basis for peace and human security. We will explore this issue by looking at whether the tribunals have contributed to reconciliation and the ability and willingness of opposing sides in a conflict to get along, set aside their differences, and sustain a lasting peace.

What exactly is this thing we call *reconciliation*? The term gained a great deal of attention in the 1990s, especially because of the creation of the Truth and Reconciliation Commission in South Africa. That body sought to bring out the truth of South Africa's apartheid era through the testimony of both victims of human rights abuse and those who committed such crimes. The designers of the South African TRC hoped that publicly airing the truth would give victims a sense of acceptance, legitimacy, and closure, would encourage people to confess their wrongdoings and seek forgiveness more holistically, and help everyone come to terms with apartheid and see the need to live together harmoniously. Such goals may take generations to achieve, but it did not take long before the example of the TRC was held up as a project worthy of emulation and study.

According to Staub (2006, 868), "Reconciliation may be defined as mutual acceptance by groups of each other." Others, like Gibson, have taken a more holistic view of reconciliation in the context of the South African TRC:

> Perhaps "reconciliation" is not such a difficult and complicated concept after all. When people talk about reconciliation, they often mean nothing more than people of different races getting along better with each other—that is, a diminution of racial animosities. This may mean that people come to interact with each other more (the breakdown of barriers across races), communicate more, in turn leading to greater understanding and perhaps acceptance, resulting in the appreciation and exaltation of the value of racial diversity. (2004, 13)

I believe that the fundamental notion of "acceptance" suggested by Staub and "getting along" advanced by Gibson gives us good baseline of understanding. We should like to know if the peoples whose conflicts have been adjudicated by the international tribunals are getting along with one another and are able to, at a minimum, peacefully coexist.

Research on this topic is now advancing and academics are taking the analysis of this potential linkage between international justice, reconciliation, and human security seriously. A number of scholars have argued that international justice can help establish a basis for reconciliation and human security. Wilson (2005, 909) argues that international justice can "challenge the long-held assumption in sociolegal scholarship that courts are inappropriate venues to construct wide-ranging historical explanations of past conflicts." Staub

(2013, 584–85) claims that "effective justice processes inherently acknowledge people's suffering, increase feelings of security as the world says that what was done is unacceptable, and recreate some balance in group relations after victimization diminishes a group." A number of researchers have found evidence that supports, in one form or another, that justice and reconciliation are compatible and self-reinforcing (Amstutz 2005; Biggar 2005; Digeser 2001; Noor et al. 2008; Staub 2006).

Clark (2011, 2014), however, takes a rather pessimistic view of the prospects for truth advancing reconciliation in the context of the former Yugoslavia. She argues that "the denial of truth breeds resentment, anger and frustration, and thus obstructs the reconciliation process. It does not, however, either support or undermine the notion that disclosure and acknowledgment of the truth aid the reconciliation process" (2011, 257). Her research indicates that the formerly warring communities in the former Yugoslavia tend to subscribe to their own interpretations of the events of the 1990s and deny claims advanced by the ICTY that conflict with their narratives. She writes (2009d, 372), "It is therefore imperative that the problems of denial and multiple truths, which both attest to the absence of, and fundamentally mitigate against reconciliation, are addressed. Furthermore, it is manifest that the ICTY alone cannot be expected to do this." For Clark, the critical question is not necessarily whether the ICTY can establish truths upon which reconciliation can be built, but whether the peoples of the region will accept it.

In a fascinating analysis of the use of memorials and other acts of remembrance in the Bosnian town of Prijedor, Subasić and Ćurak (2014) find that there has been an almost complete denial by the Bosnian Serb leadership and population of the many crimes committed against non-Serbs during the war. Their conclusions are worth quoting at length:

> Based on this we can assert that the absence of a public apology, avoiding participation in meetings that deal with the process of reconciliation, failure to provide full support in the ongoing search for the missing and refusing to take part in commemorations, represent examples of the denial of facts and collective and individual moral responsibility for ethnic cleansing against non-Serbs by the political elite in Bosnian Serbs in Prijedor. It also rejects the ICTY's historical record of indisputable and accurate facts and truth about the committed crimes in Prijedor, and in this way risks the resurgence of the past criminal ideologies which could endanger the process of transitional peace building, reconciliation and the future of all citizens in Prijedor. (Subasić and Ćurak 2014, 141)

This has been a topic of particular interest to me and several of my research partners. We want to know if the peoples of these nations have been building bridges among ethnic groups and creating a stable foundation for peace. Perhaps the town of Prijedor is the exception to the building of reconciliation. It is hopeful that, in the cases of those tribunals that have finished (ICTR, SCSL) or largely finished their work (ICTY), there has been lasting peace in Rwanda, Sierra Leone, and the former Yugoslavia. But how do the peoples in those nations relate to one another? Data on attitudes regarding reconciliation in Rwanda and Sierra Leone are sparse. Data on the former Yugoslavia, while not extensive, do provide us with options to assess reconciliation. That is where I and my colleagues have focused our attention in the last several years.

One of my students and I set out to test how willing people of each of the three principal ethnic groups (Bosnian Muslims or Bosniaks, Croatians, and Serbians) involved in the conflicts in the former Yugoslavia felt about members of the other ethnic groups (Meernik and Guerrero 2014). We wrote that those individuals who supported the work of the ICTY would be more likely to be willing to reconcile with their former adversaries. We defined reconciliation not so much as an opinion, but rather as an individual's willingness to interact with members of other ethnic groups. The survey questions from which we obtained these data asked individuals if they would like a person from another ethnic group living in their neighborhood, as their boss, as their political leader, a relative, or even a spouse. We believe these kinds of questions that tap into individuals' behaviors can be very revealing about what people truly believe about reconciliation and how they are prepared to act on their beliefs. To test our hypotheses we used data from the Southeast Europe Social Survey Project (SEESSP) data.[26] These data come from an extensive survey project carried out by Professor Albert Simkus from 2003 to 2004.

We found that those individuals who had positive attitudes about the ICTY and supported its work had more positive feelings toward members of other ethnic groups. We argued that because one of the missions of the ICTY has been to advance understanding of what actually happened in the former Yugoslavia during the wars of the 1990s and who has been found responsible for what crimes, those who understand this aim should be more willing to interact with members of other ethnic groups. We wrote:

> To the extent individuals support the work of the ICTY, even if they are not wholly satisfied with its effectiveness, they may also be willing to address the personal, social and political problems of the present—that is, they recognize the need for transitional justice. In effect, if individuals support the work of the ICTY as one element of this transitional justice, they should be more likely to see the importance of other elements of transitional justice, such as reconciliation. . . . In effect, we contend that support for the ICTY connotes a more open frame of mind and acceptance of the need for justice that is more likely to be reconcilable.

And that is exactly what we found. The greater the level of support expressed for the ICTY, the more likely individuals were to be more accepting of interactions with people from other ethnic groups. Additionally, we found that individuals who had a more optimistic state of mind about the present and the future were much more likely to be tolerant and reconciled. These findings tend to show that it is not just politics and justice that predict attitudes; one's underlying personal and economic situation is also critical. But clearly, support for the tribunal helps explain individual willingness to engage in behaviors that would demonstrate reconciliation.

I also conducted research with a much bigger group of faculty, graduate students, and undergraduate students on attitudes toward reconciliation among young people of the former Yugoslavia. We were given access to data that had been collected by the ICTY's Outreach Office over a number of years from presentations they made to high school and college students. The presentations were about the work of the ICTY, but after the presentations were over students were given a brief questionnaire that asked them their opinions about the ICTY and reconciliation. Students were asked whether they thought it was possible "to achieve reconciliation after the war in your country." They could answer "yes," "no," or "other." We found that opinions were very closely divided, with 42 percent of the students indicating they believed reconciliation was not possible and 49 percent indicating that it was. Students could also offer comments about the prospects for reconciliation, which were quite telling.

Many students held pessimistic but perceptive opinions about which generation was most responsible for the wars in the former Yugoslavia. One student wrote, "because from the day they're born, children are brought up in an atmosphere of inter-ethnic divisions and hatred towards other ethnic groups," while another wrote, "because the people who educate us, young people, are actually 'poisoning' our minds on religious grounds. The phenomenon of two schools under one roof explains it all." The student is referring to the schools in Bosnia-Herzegovina where two ethnic groups are taught in the same building, but where walls and rules ensure they have no contact with each other. One said, "people are far too burdened with national and religious hate, they simply do not wish to reconcile." Others expressed regret about the conflict and reconciliation, such as this remark: "because the victims of the war cannot so easily forget what happened, although I wish with all my heart that there could be reconciliation."

There were more students, however, who believed reconciliation was possible: "all this should be a lesson to us, so it never happens again, and those who are guilty should be sentenced." Another commented that reconciliation was possible: "by prosecuting criminals and bringing dignity back to all war victims regardless whether they come from BiH, Croatia or Serbia." One student saw both the problem and the solution: "I chose this answer because there is hope in me, however I think it's going to be hard because the older generations are poisoning their children with their respective theories about the war." My own favorite comment was this one that was realistic and saw to the future: "the world belongs to the young. We should not forget, but we should stop living in the past, and blame the young [for] the actions of our predecessors. We only have one life and should not spend it in hatred, but we should turn to [the] present and see how to build a brighter future."

Our findings that suggest some grounds for optimism for the prospects of reconciliation must be tempered with the research of others, like Clark (2014), who have argued that international justice cannot contribute to reconciliation and thus help advance human security unless people are receptive to the truth as communicated by the tribunal. While Clark's research focuses on the former Yugoslavia, I believe there is a strong element of truth to this observation—people must be willing to accept these legal and historical truths. I would further add that as long as people are living in conflict zones, whether subject to the scrutiny and justice of an international tribunal or not, they will be more accepting of reconciliation as their nations become more politically stable and economically prosperous. As long as the underlying conditions that helped lead to war and atrocities still exist, lack of reconciliation is much more likely. A lack of reconciliation may persist even with good governance and economics, but I would argue that these are more fundamental human needs that must be met before people can think about more deep-seated and interpersonal issues. In this respect, reconciliation and human security are not just products of justice, even though that is a necessary element. It also must be part of the national rebuilding project after war. Absent any effort to bring former adversaries together to talk through their differences, it is difficult to imagine people truly reconciling on their own.

## CONCLUSIONS

International justice has been criticized by many for its lack of fairness, and while I have discussed several of the most pressing problems, critics have pointed to what they see as numerous other flaws (Karnavas 2011). Indeed, even one of the top UN officials in international law, Ralph Zacklin, wrote in 2004, "The verdict is now largely in. The ad hoc Tribunals have been too costly, too inefficient and too ineffective. As mechanisms for dealing with justice in post-conflict societies, they exemplify an approach that is no longer politically or financially viable" (Zacklin 2004, 545). No observer of these tribunals would claim that they are perfect or that they have attained some sort of fixed gold standard of justice. Indeed, even domestic courts have their problems, as we have seen in the United States in recent years as DNA evidence continues to exonerate individuals who had been languishing in prisons for years. When the criminal justice system has the vast power of the state behind it, or in our case the international community, and the defense has only itself, such a David and Goliath contest is bound to favor the giant. Nonetheless, and despite some problems with due process, some indications that the ICTY has sentenced Serbs to lengthier sentences than other groups, as well as the issues with how these international courts were assigned some conflicts and not others to investigate, they have mostly delivered on their mission to provide justice.

I would argue that one critical basis of evaluating the fairness of the tribunals should involve assessing whether the quality of justice continues to improve. Has the justice provided by the ICTY, ICTR, and SCSL improved over Nuremberg and Tokyo? Has the justice provided by the ICC improved over the fairness of justice at the ad hoc tribunals? Viewed in that light, we can see that fairness has been improving, even if the journey sometimes involves two steps forward on some issues and one step backward on others. On one hand, problems with evidence disclosure by the prosecution and resource inequities continue to plague international justice. On the other hand, there now exists a much more robust system of appeals and an officially recognized office for the defense counsel at the ICC, as well as numerous international organizations representing the interests of defense attorneys. While most individuals who stand trial are convicted, the conviction rates are actually quite similar to what we see in the United States. We have even seen a number of high-profile defendants acquitted at the ICTY, such as the Croatian general Ante Gotovina and the Kosovar Albanian leader Ramush Haradinaj.

Our focus in this book, however, is on human security, and here the record of the tribunals is much more difficult to assess. To say that making the connection between international justice and national reconciliation is complicated is an understatement. Is it any wonder then that making international justice comprehensible and meaningful to the victims and their nations can miss the mark? Some research has shown that those who support the work of the tribunals are more inclined to support reconciliation. This is a good starting point. But for reconciliation to take hold, international justice must speak not just to those who are listening and supportive, but to those who are highly suspicious of its goals. Most importantly, it must speak to those who fall in between the supporters and the opponents—those in the middle who spend little time thinking about international justice but a great deal of time existing in nations fractured along ethnic or religious lines. Serge Brammertz, the chief prosecutor for the ICTY, put it this way:

> Reconciliation is a topic about which a lot has been said and written about. My impression is that people have normally overestimated the possibilities of international justice. I would never argue that prosecution alone can achieve reconciliation. I am certainly convinced of the fact that prosecution and accountability for crimes committed is the starting point—a condition sine qua non for reconciliation. This is something I have learned during these five years. Before the arrest of Karadžić and Mladić, I met with victims' organizations in many places. In Bosnia, I met with the mothers of Srebrenica and they always said to me: "We want to see Karadžić and Mladić arrested, otherwise we cannot start thinking about the future." I am absolutely convinced that accountability is crucial, but that it is only a starting point. Reconciliation must come from within society and cannot be achieved only by justice or imposed from the outside.[27]

I would argue that international justice is a necessary condition for human security, but not a sufficient one. As Brammertz argues in the quote above and Clark (2014) finds, the message from international tribunals must be understood on a deeply personal level. It may be the leaders of countries who are tried in these courts and who are to blame, but the mess they leave behind must be cleaned up by the people. This is easy to say for someone like me, who is also sitting in a comfortable and faraway office in a rich, democratic nation. It is quite another thing for someone who has seen their whole family executed before their eyes or for a person who was socialized in an environment in which the government tightly controlled information and conveniently blamed others for all of the ills that afflicted them. International justice does provide a building block for helping people begin to put the pieces of their lives back together and gives them a truth that can be the basis of reconciliation. With international justice, we have an imperfect system that does not always advance human security as we might hope. Without international justice, we have only the hope that political leaders who ordered severe human rights abuses and authorized widespread destruction will find it in their hearts and their interests to tell the truth and begin building a better future. Personally, I would rather take my chances with international justice than cast my lot with the war criminals. So while the evidence thus far is guardedly optimistic regarding the helpful impact tribunals have on human security and reconciliation, like the international justice system itself, it progresses slowly and fitfully, but forward.

## NOTES

1. It is also possible that some Serbs, especially in the political and military leadership, have used this narrative of a world that does not recognize their contributions to defending Christian Europe as a more cynical ploy to undermine support for Muslim communities in the former Yugoslavia.

2. As found at http://www.b92.net/eng/news/politics.php?yyyy=2013&mm=04&dd=10&nav_id=85636.

3. See "Rwanda Tribunal Should Pursue Justice for RPF Crimes," *Human Rights Watch,* December 12, 2008. As found at https://www.hrw.org/news/2008/12/12/rwanda-tribunal-should-pursue-justice-rpf-crimes.

4. As found at http://www.genocidewatch.org/images/Rwanda-24-Oct-05-Colonel_Denies_Masterminding_Rwandan_Genocide.pdf.

5. As found in the archives of the *Washington Post,* November 9, 1999, at http://www.washingtonpost.com/wp-srv/WPcap/1999-11/07/073r-110799-idx.html.

6. See the debate at http://iccforum.com/africa.

7. See the 1994 ICTY Annual Yearbook, p. 141.

8. As found at http://www.un.org/icty/tadic/appeal/judgement/index.htm, para. 52.

9. Ibid., para. 53.

10. As found in Masha Federova, Sten Verhoeven, and Jan Wouters (2009), *Safeguarding the Rights of Suspects and Accused Persons in International Criminal Proceedings,* at https://www.law.kuleuven.be/iir/nl/onderzoek/wp/wp137e.pdf.

11. See http://www.balkaninsight.com/en/article/mladic-trial-prosecution-does-not-object-to-trial-postponement.

12. As found in The Principle of Equality of Arms in International Criminal Proceedings at http://www.google.com/url?sa=t&rct=j&q=&esrc=s&source=web&cd=2&ved=0CCQQFjABahUKEwiMitCdo-rHAhXDoIAKHYdOBQM&url=http%3A%2F%2Fdspace.library.uu.nl%2Fbitstream%2Fhandle%2F1874%2F257535%2FFedorova.pdf%3Fsequence%3D1&usg=AFQjCNHRSojD0NW41c01x9tzfmxFJC-qfA&cad=rja.

13. Salvatore Zappalà (2007), "How to Ameliorate International Criminal Proceedings: Some Constructive Suggestions," *Journal of International Criminal Justice* 5: 346–47.

14. On this point see Mark Harmon and Fergal Gaynor (2004), "Prosecuting Massive Crimes with Primitive Tools: Three Difficulties Encountered by Prosecutors in International Criminal Proceedings," *Journal of International Criminal Justice* 2: 403–26 and Antonia Cassese (2004), "The ICTY: A Living and Vital Reality," *Journal of International Criminal Justice* 2: 585–97.

15. For example, it has been reported that at the ICTR until 2002, while the translation from English and French was simultaneous, the translation from Kinyarwanda into English or French was consecutive and it was tripling the amount of time witnesses would take in testifying. See Kingsley Chiedu Moghalu (2002), "Image and Reality of War Crimes Justice: External Perceptions of the International Tribunal for Rwanda," *The Fletcher Forum of World Affairs* 26/2 (Summer/Fall): 21–46.

16. Overview of Federal Criminal Cases Fiscal Year 2013, p. 5. As found at http://www.ussc.gov/sites/default/files/pdf/research-and-publications/research-publications/2014/FY13_Overview_Federal_Criminal_Cases.pdf.

17. Those convicted serve their sentences in the national prison systems of states that reach agreements with the tribunals to house those found guilty.

18. *Prosecutor vs. Zejnil Delalic et al.*, Case No. IT-96-21, Trial Chamber Judgment, November 16, 1998, para. 1225.

19. See especially *Prosecutor v. Zlatko Aleksovski*, Case No. IT-95-14/1, Trial Chamber Judgment, June 25, 1999, para. 243.

20. *Prosecutor v. Tihomir Blaskic*, Case No. IT-95-14-T, March 3, 2000, para. 789.

21. See *Prosecutor vs. Dragoljub Kunarac, Radomir Kovac and Zoran Vukovic*, IT-96-23-T&IT-96-23/1-T, para. 850.

22. *Prosecutor v. Zoran Kupreskic et al.*, Case No. IT-95-16, Appeals Chamber Judgment, October 23, 2001, para. 430.

23. *Prosecutor v. Dusko Sikirica et al.*, Case No. IT-95-8, Trial Chamber Judgment, November 13, 2001, para. 108.

24. Note that when I conduct the regression analysis of sentences, those given a life sentence are automatically measured as having been sentenced to the longest term of incarceration that is not a life sentence or in this case 624 months.

25. For this measure we use three categories of level of individual responsibility for those charged with violations of international law. Low-level war criminals, principally ordinary soldiers and prison camp guards, are coded "1"; mid-level officials, such as prison camp commanders, military officers below the rank of colonel, and political figures below cabinet level status are coded "2"; and high-level officials, including military officials at or above the rank of colonel, and political officials of cabinet-level status or higher are coded "3."

26. Extensive information on these data, the surveys, and other information about the project can be found at http://www.svt.ntnu.no/iss/ringdalweb/SEESSP%20Surveys.html.

27. As found at http://www.fletcherforum.org/2013/06/24/brammertz/.

*Chapter 3*

# Human Rights, Human Security, and International Justice

## INTRODUCTION

International criminal tribunals are supposed to provide justice when international human rights and humanitarian laws have been violated. While their reason for existence is based on this redress of specific wrongs, they are deeply rooted in a historical concern with protecting the innocent who are harmed by the ravages of war. International laws are intended to give ordinary people protection from as much of the destruction of war as possible. They are not to be *a* target or *the* target of the military fighting forces. As such, the bedrock principle of the international laws the tribunals are charged with adjudicating is the protection of the innocent. That is an all-encompassing moral principle that sets a very high bar by which to judge the impact of international tribunals on human security. Indeed, it is a core principle of international law dating back well over a century. Since the end of World War II, there has also been increasing attention and condemnation of human rights violations that occur outside the context of war, as we discussed in chapter 1, such as crimes against humanity perpetrated by governments against their own peoples.

A key principle of international humanitarian law is the Martens Clause. The clause, which was first articulated in the preamble to the 1899 Hague Convention on the laws of war, is a minimum benchmark for the protection of civilians even in the absence of any international treaty. It establishes that "until a more complete code of the laws of war is issued, the High Contracting Parties think it right to declare that in cases not included in the Regulations adopted by them, populations and belligerents remain under the protection and empire of the principles of international law, as they result from the usages established between civilized nations, from the laws of humanity and the requirements of the public conscience." It has since been repeatedly utilized by the international tribunals to extend the protections of international laws to the innocent when the laws themselves may not have criminalized every potential abuse of human rights. In effect, the Martens Clause insists that the spirit of the law is to protect the innocent even if the letter of the law does not foresee every possible way in which humans might harm each other.

Human rights and the protection of the innocent permeate the work of international justice. It is the moral imperative and the spirit guiding the creation and the business of international tribunals. This "north star" of international justice has both a backward-looking and a forward-looking face. On one hand, international justice is redress for the wrongs of the past—the abuses of human rights that have already taken place. Justice for the victims and justice for the international community whose laws have been violated certainly demands at least this much. Yet it is also forward looking in that the protection of human rights is a goal toward which justice (to say nothing of the many governments and nongovernmental organizations committed to the cause) looks beyond the reality of present-day trials in order to prevent the need for trials in the future. A perfect world in which there are no human rights abuses that would demand international justice for their redress is an ideal that is many years away. Like our own domestic criminal justice systems that seek to prevent and deter crime, we shouldn't expect the total elimination of crime. Rather, we must judge our justice systems based, in part, on how well they contribute to reducing crime. The same lesson applies to international justice and international courts. They should contribute to a reduction in violations of international law. How well have these courts fared?

At the risk of sounding like a broken record, that is a rather complex question to answer. The tribunals have all been given the mission to contribute to what we call "deterrence"—deterring future violations of the law or discouraging would-be war criminals from hurting the innocent. The preamble to the ICC treaty clearly expressed the intentions of the signatories to that agreement that they are "determined to put an end to impunity for the perpetrators of these crimes and thus to contribute to the prevention of such crimes." How exactly are the tribunals to help achieve this goal? What tools have they been given? How will we know if the tribunals have made any tangible contributions? Are they only supposed to be deterring future crimes in the conflict zones they are responsible for, such as the former Yugoslavia and Rwanda? Or is international justice supposed to help deter human rights violations the world over?

These are the questions we will be addressing in this chapter as we explore international justice and human security in the context of human rights. First,

I will discuss the concept of deterrence of human rights abuses, what it means in practice for the international tribunals, and what sorts of challenges they face in achieving this goal. I describe the relatively few tools tribunals have in their tool kits to help achieve this objective and ponder just how much influence we believe these courts have over the individuals who are in positions of power and have reason to commit human rights violations. After thinking through the obstacles and the opportunities international tribunals have for improving human rights, I examine the data. We are fortunate in that scholars have collected information on the human rights performance of governments throughout the world. In recent years, these scholars have delved into measuring many different types of human rights abuses, right down to the deaths of particular individuals. I put all these data to good use in evaluating the performance of the tribunals. After analyzing these data, we can then decide what kind of grade to give to these courts.

## DETERRENCE

Promoting human rights is not a task with which most courts would be familiar. For an international court to take on this mission would have been unthinkable one hundred years ago. It would probably have been unimaginable forty or fifty years ago. It would have been highly improbable that a series of international tribunals would have been created in the first place during the Cold War. Furthermore, because the notion that states can do as they wish within their own borders has been so sacrosanct, few could have imagined international courts created, in part, to discourage states from doing exactly that. After all, the states that do commit human rights violations do so, as they insist, to maintain internal security. Yet here we are in a world in which states are not supposed to be able to commit human rights atrocities with impunity, a world in which international tribunals are not just supposed to provide justice. They are intended to help deter such crimes from happening. All judicial systems are intended to discourage people from breaking domestic law. International courts are designed to deter powerful leaders from pursuing their own self-interest when it conflicts with international law. To understand just how well the international tribunals have fared in this mission requires delving into the concept of deterrence.

Many scholars have analyzed the (potential) deterrent impact of international tribunals (Akhavan 2001; Drumbl 2007; Minnow 2002; Sloane 2007; Snyder and Vinjamuri 2003; Stover and Weinstein 2004; Teitel 1999). As Ku and Nzelibe (2006, 779) write, "contemporary justifications for these tribunals stress their potential to deter future humanitarian atrocities." The

ICTY statute asserts that the "establishment of an international tribunal and the prosecution of persons responsible for the above-mentioned violations of international humanitarian law *will contribute to ensuring that such violations are halted* and effectively redressed" (emphasis added).[1] Deterrence of future violence is one of the most important elements of any criminal justice system, domestic or international.

There are two types of deterrence. Immediate or specific deterrence involves preventing those specific individuals who have been accused of crimes from committing such acts again. General deterrence refers to the deterrence of other would-be war criminals, wherever they may be, from carrying out their criminal enterprises for fear of international justice. It is this deterrence that we evaluate to determine what kind of impact international tribunals have on human rights and human security.

International tribunals can possibly contribute to deterrence in several ways. Most obviously their prosecution of the accused sets an example for the world and demonstrates that those who violate international law will be held accountable. The tribunals can also play an important, although indirect, role in deterring human rights abuses through the individualization of guilt (Akhavan 2001). What exactly does this mean? The conflicts in the former Yugoslavia and Rwanda, like many others, had their roots in past rivalries and bloodshed. But while historical cycles of violence and retribution are critical in understanding the present, there is no denying that political leaders often exploit these histories and tensions for their own ends. By pointing the finger of blame squarely at those who conceive, organize, and order the commission of war crimes, crimes against humanity, and genocide, international tribunals should lessen the perceived need for one ethnic group to take revenge against another (Akhavan 2001; see also Sloane 2007; Stover and Weinstein 2004).

Individualizing guilt can also shed light on the machinations such leaders employ to instill ethnic hatred and hide evidence of their atrocities. Brutal dictators typically monopolize information in their societies so their citizens remain only dimly aware of the true nature of these conflicts. They are manipulated into believing that their very survival depends on the elimination of the "other." By prosecuting these leaders, exposing their crimes, and demonstrating that there is no impunity for violating international law, tribunals can potentially advance deterrence and human rights. According to Payam Akhavan, former legal adviser at the ICTY, international tribunals can also encourage good behavior among formerly warring parties. He writes (2001, 16), "the international community's policy of using the ICTY as an instrument to remove from power indicted leaders has contributed to post conflict peace building by creating incentives for political parties to behave in a more conciliatory manner." He writes as well that the ICTR "has palpably improved the post conflict situation by impeding resurrection of the former government and enhancing the political attraction of criminal justice as an alternative to Hutu violence" (Akhavan 2001, 26).

So far we have only considered what scholars and practitioners hope or expect these tribunals to achieve in advancing human rights. Now we must consider the evidence. We will begin by considering whether the tribunals have deterred human rights violations. Have these tribunals contributed to a general deterrence of human rights violations in their target nations? Has the very existence of the tribunals, their apprehensions, prosecutions, and convictions helped to dissuade those who have the capacity to commit human rights violations?

## DETERRENCE AND HOW IT WORKS

Deterrence involves a type of human relationship in which we have to decide how best to discourage someone from doing something we do not like. Deterrence was a major topic of foreign policy during the Cold War and provides a good example from which to start. The United States and the Soviet Union deployed troops in foreign countries, stockpiled nuclear weapons, and their leaders constantly warned the other against thinking their adversary could act without consequences. The United States placed thousands of troops in Western Europe to deter the Soviets from thinking they could invade Germany, France, and the rest of its allies without a major fight. The Soviet Union in turn placed thousands of its troops in Eastern Europe, ostensibly to keep the West out (although their real purpose was to keep the populations of these countries locked in). Each side was also concerned that the other would one day believe it could get away with a surprise nuclear attack that would permanently cripple the adversary and allow the attacker to emerge dominant in the world. So each side stockpiled huge numbers of nuclear weapons that were designed to dissuade the other from thinking that it might get away with a sneak attack.

Looking back, one might well conclude that each side's deterrence policies were quite effective. There was never any invasion of Western or Eastern Europe and there was never any surprise nuclear attack. The demonstration of resolve and the horrific consequences that would result if one side was not deterred and chose to attack the other seems to have worked. But was that because the U.S. and Soviet leaders were deterred, or was it because neither side ever really intended to invade or launch a surprise attack? The odd thing about deterrence is that even when the evidence clearly shows that the desired action never took place, it is difficult to determine if those who made the decisions to not invade or not bomb ever had any intention of doing so in the first place. Or were they sufficiently impressed by the other side's threats and displays of strength to drop any plans they might have had? Short of gaining access to the secret deliberations of these leaders, it is difficult to be certain just what influenced their thinking and the lack of any military attack. Understanding deterrence of any kind requires getting inside the minds or deliberations of decision makers to figure out what really influenced their behavior. So how are scholars to confront this dilemma when it comes to international justice?

Our analysis of deterrence of human rights abuses has one key advantage over most studies of typical state-level deterrence, like U.S.-Soviet relations during the Cold War. First, think about the deterrence targets of the international tribunals—dictators, political leaders, military officials, rebel military, militia leaders, and the like. Let's focus on the dictators for a moment. We know that most dictators abuse human rights on a fairly regular basis. That's what makes them dictators! Furthermore, we know that dictators, like most politicians, want to maintain their hold on power. But where politicians in democratic countries submit themselves and their parties to regular elections, dictators try to figure out ways to stay in power using other means, which usually involve shutting down any unfavorable media coverage, tossing political opponents in jail, and convincing the people that their lack of freedom is the necessary price for security. The dictator's strategy is to abuse human rights to make people afraid to challenge him. Thus, there is little question as to whether the types of leaders international tribunals seek to deter would engage in the kind of human rights abuses on which these courts focus. They do. They do so regularly. So unlike the example of the Cold War, where neither side could ever really know the other side's intentions, we know that there are many leaders across the globe who are perfectly willing to commit human rights abuses. The only question is whether they can be deterred from carrying out these actions by international justice.

The world has tried many strategies to deter governments from abusing their citizens' human rights. The international response to the vast majority of atrocities that occurred during the Cold War was, at best, some expression of outrage and, at worst, acquiescence to the inevitability of violence. In some sense, the international community transformed the "turn the other cheek" strategy into the "look the other way" strategy. Not surprisingly, this policy convinced most dictators that they could get away with almost anything. And they did.

Is it possible to assemble a powerful coalition of states to force governments to behave? International miscreants often back down when confronted with superior force. Assembling powerful allies may well be a necessary condition for successful deterrence. Even a powerful country standing alone may tempt an aggressor who believes that the deterrence enforcer is bereft of supporters or that the international community favors the aggressor. But even large coalitions, like those that have targeted dictators such as Muamar Khadafy of Libya during the 2011 Libyan civil war or Omar Al-Bashir of Sudan during the genocide in Darfur, may fail. If these dictators believe that their grip on power is being threatened by enemies in their own society, they often become quite willing to commit horrific human rights violations to preserve their domination. If they are also confronted with an international coalition demanding that they stop such atrocities or surrender themselves to international justice, they may just as well keep fighting as long as there is some chance of winning. In their minds it is probably better to keep fighting than to give up and get carted off to a detention cell in The Hague.

What about a direct military confrontation—standing up and fighting the repressive government? This strategy can often work quite well, especially when perceptions of a bully's strength have been greatly exaggerated. Witness the rapid collapse of the Bosnian Serb military that had wrought destruction and killed thousands in Bosnia-Herzegovina before finally being confronted with a NATO air campaign. That international military response put an end to the wars in Bosnia once and for all, despite the reputation of the Bosnian Serbs as a fierce fighting force. Ultimately, there are several ways to deter a government or a rebel force from committing atrocities. Each strategy has its strength and weaknesses. The international strategy of prosecuting suspected war criminals is intended to establish the norm that human rights protection is the responsibility of all governments. But what can the law and its example do, especially when those in its sights are determined to maintain power at all costs? Can these institutions deter human rights abuses?

## WHAT WE HAVE FOUND SO FAR AND TRIBUNALS DETERRING HUMAN RIGHTS ABUSES

Trying to figure out if the tribunals have helped to deter or prevent atrocities or even just helped to make conditions better for human rights has become something of an evolving detective story. We have been searching for clues as to just what impact the tribunals have had in the conflict regions they adjudicate and the world at large. Here is some of what we have found so far.

In a fascinating piece of research, Ku and Nzelibe (2006) show that those who are most likely to commit violations of international humanitarian law (which they define and measure as leaders of coups in African nations from 1956 to 2003) are quite likely to eventually be killed or imprisoned by their political opponents. Their research suggests, on one hand, that such individuals are unlikely to be deterred by an international tribunal's threat of detention abroad if they have not already been dissuaded by the likelihood of a violent death at home. On the other hand, could it be that such individuals may surrender themselves to the ICC to fight another day in The Hague rather than die on the battlefield? In an analysis of the potential deterrent of the ICC, political scientist Michael Gilligan (2006) demonstrates that if leaders have fewer options for seeking asylum abroad (because the ICC treaty actively discourages states from accepting foreign leaders wanted by the court), they may choose to surrender. If this kind of logic does operate, then such individuals may wind up committing fewer violations of international law because they give up more easily. We have to hope that power-hungry dictators are concerned about their survival and value life (even if it means possibly being sent to prison for many years) more than playing the lottery that is the struggle for power in their country where there is a good chance they will be killed or deposed.

In contrast to studies that look for broad patterns of deterrence using data for many countries over multiple years, McAllister (2014) digs deeper to evaluate deterrence at a more fine-grained level. She analyzes the impact of the ICTY on the behavior of leaders and militaries in the conflict in Macedonia in the late 1990s and early 2000s between Albanian separatists and the Macedonian government. McAllister finds that those commanders who deliberately ordered atrocities as part of their political and military campaign were unlikely to be deterred by the threat of prosecution by the ICTY. On the other hand, when violations of human rights occur as a result of commander negligence or there is a failure to punish violators, conditions are more favorable for deterrence. Especially when leaders are seeking the assistance of governments that are strong defenders of human rights, they are more likely to ensure that their forces follow the law. The establishment of international tribunals may instill a degree of fear and caution among such leaders that encourages proactive efforts to educate and monitor their subordinates. McAllister finds that this is what happened with leaders in the Macedonian conflict. Not surprisingly, she also finds that when the international community supported the ICTY, conflict actors were more likely to restrain their forces.

David (2014) argues that only when ethnic groups see their own leaders being punished for violating human rights will their leaders stop such abuses. When one ethnic group sees only their ethnic enemies being punished, they will tend to believe that their adversaries are simply receiving their just deserts. They will not stop to examine their own behavior to consider whether they too might be prosecuted. As long as the finger of blame is being pointed at someone else, there is little likelihood that the victim group will seriously consider its own degree of culpability. It's easy to be a cheerleader for international law as long as you are not its target.

Kim and Sikkink (2010) also find that human rights prosecutions are associated with increased respect for human rights. Interestingly, they acknowledge that while there will always be some number of "spoilers" who will commit human rights abuses for their own political gain, there is evidence to suggest that human rights abuses are decreasing over the long term. They write, "we believe that the actual deterrence of future human rights violations happens through the impact of prosecutions on new generations of military and police officers, and on civilian political leaders. Future military officers may decide that prosecutions have made repression and coups too costly for use in the future" (Kim and Sikkink 2010, 958). We should not expect all leaders to instantly see the light and stop their abusive behavior, but just as the arc of history bends toward ever better and fairer justice, so too might we expect to see leaders behaving better.

Jo and Simmons (forthcoming) argue that governments that have ratified the ICC treaty should engage in less violence against civilians in general (social deterrence) and especially those with a recent history of civil war violence should experience fewer civilian deaths during wartime (prosecutorial deterrence). They suggest that states that ratify the ICC treaty will incur social costs among their own citizens should they fail to live up to its provisions. Their publics will be angry that their governments have not lived up to their commitments and might turn them out of office. Such costs should decrease the likelihood that these leaders will commit crimes that run afoul of the ICC. They also contend that rebel groups may incur similar costs, especially those with a civilian wing and high levels of civilian support, and will therefore kill fewer civilians during civil wars. They have much at stake in behaving according to international law in order to maintain an air of legitimacy and respectability among people and governments. Jo and Simmons find some support for their notions of deterrence and that the ICC can be playing a constructive role in deterring major human rights violations.

Many scholars, however, are skeptical of the notion that such tribunals can achieve a general deterrent effect (Drumbl 2007; Gordy 2003; Minnow 2002; Sloane 2007). Barria and Roper argue that "although decisions of the ICTY and the ICTR courts have referred to the deterrent effect of the tribunals, they are not a forum that can provide a general deterrent" (2005, 357). The decisions of these tribunals may not have the intended impact on politicians and generals who perceive themselves as above the law. Their effect on subordinates who know little and care less about the actions of courts in faraway lands and who place their trust in superiors with the power of life and death is likely even less. Ku and Nzelibe (2006, 780) argue that "despite the salience of these questions, hardly any academic commentary has explored in depth the merits of the deterrence justification for the ICTs." Let's begin to remedy this situation.

## THE HUMAN RIGHTS IMPACT OF THE INTERNATIONAL TRIBUNALS

The international tribunals were rightfully criticized for their early glacial pace of international justice. Nonetheless, the tribunals established a remarkable record of apprehending nearly all those they indicted. In fact, the cases of every individual indicted by the ICTY have all been addressed in some manner, mostly by trial. While some have had their cases transferred to local courts or died while in detention, the vast majority has stood trial in The Hague. The Special Court for Sierra Leone (SCSL) completed all of its trials, and the ICTR has very nearly matched the ICTY's successes in trial completion. The work of the International Criminal Court continues. Thus, while one might fault the tribunals for the cost, duration, or even the quality of justice they have provided, the achievement of their most fundamental goal of all—to provide justice—means that we have a record on which we can evaluate the deterrent effect of the tribunals. Have their trials and convictions caused would-be human rights violators to be deterred from committing atrocities?

This has been an especially important question for me personally, particularly regarding the work of the ICTY, because I studied in Yugoslavia in 1983 and fell in love with the land and the people. I was surprised and saddened by the violence and destruction of the wars of the 1990s and went back several times to see and learn for myself what had happened to this amazing place. I was especially interested in the work of the ICTY and made a point of visiting the tribunal to witness the beginning of its first trial of Duško Tadić. While Tadić was a rather unremarkable individual in the former Yugoslavia,[2] this did not diminish the sense of history in the making I experienced sitting in that crowded courtroom in the summer of 1996. It really did feel as though justice was finally being done for all of the horrible crimes I had seen on television, like the concentration camps, the siege of Sarajevo, and the destruction of the old bridge, the Stari Most, in Mostar. Because I had spent such an important part of my early life in Yugoslavia and because of my fascination with these international trials that sought to right the scales of justice, I began a personal and academic journey to understand what these international courts could do.

I began by trying to make sense of how those found guilty at these tribunals could be punished. I live in Texas, a state where if you murder someone in cold blood there is a pretty good chance you will be given the death penalty. What just punishment could possibly be meted out to someone who had the blood of hundreds or even thousands on his or her hands? I was equally as curious, however, about the impact of this work on the peoples of the former

Yugoslavia. Could these tribunals prevent such atrocities from happening again? I kept coming back to the question of what it all means. Were these trials helping to make the former Yugoslavia a more stable and peaceful land? In some of my earlier research (Meernik 2005), I found that the verdicts of the International Criminal Tribunal for the Former Yugoslavia (ICTY) have not diminished the level of interethnic group conflict in the former Yugoslavia. Later I expanded the analysis to evaluate the impact of international trials on peace and human rights in states emerging from civil war (Meernik, Nichols, and King 2010), but we still found little evidence of any impact. While I was disappointed to conclude from these analyses that the tribunals did not seem to be having a positive effect, I was still not satisfied with how we were reaching these conclusions and set about learning more.

## THE FORMER YUGOSLAVIA

If the tribunals are helping to deter human rights abuses, we might begin by looking at the human rights records of the most important nations that were under their jurisdiction—Bosnia-Herzegovina, Croatia, and Serbia (ICTY),[3] Rwanda (ICTR), and Sierra Leone (SCSL). If the tribunals are discouraging individuals from committing human rights violations because they fear prosecution or because they realize, thanks to the example set by the tribunals, that such actions are illegal and immoral, we should find that human rights conditions improve. Of course, we must never lose sight of the fact that there may be other causes at work that diminish human rights violations. Such possibilities are better left to more sophisticated analyses, which we will discuss later. The human rights scores that we will use to evaluate the impact of the tribunals come to us courtesy of the CIRI database (named for Cingranelli and Richards, the two scholars who manage the database) and measure the extent to which governments abuses their citizens' human rights.[4] Their physical integrity rights index is an additive index composed of indicators of torture, extrajudicial killing, political imprisonment, and disappearances. The index ranges from zero to eight, with zero being no respect for human rights and eight being the highest level of government respect for human rights. Established democracies like Denmark, Canada, and New Zealand attain the highest rankings, while international pariahs like North Korea anchor the bottom end of the scale. For our purposes, the reader just needs to know one thing: the higher the score, the better the human rights record. The scores of the countries in the former Yugoslavia whose citizens have been subjected to prosecution at the ICTY are shown over time in table 3.1.

**Table 3.1 Human Rights Scores in the Former Yugoslavia**

| Country | Year | Human Rights Score | Country | Year | Human Rights Score | Country | Year | Human Rights Score |
|---|---|---|---|---|---|---|---|---|
| Croatia | 1992 | 2 | Serbia | 1992 | 1 | Bosnia-Herzegovena | 1992 | n/a |
| Croatia | 1993 | 2 | Serbia | 1993 | 1 | Bosnia-Herzegovena | 1993 | n/a |
| Croatia | 1994 | 4 | Serbia | 1994 | 4 | Bosnia-Herzegovena | 1994 | n/a |
| Croatia | 1995 | 2 | Serbia | 1995 | 1 | Bosnia-Herzegovena | 1995 | n/a |
| Croatia | 1996 | 7 | Serbia | 1996 | 4 | Bosnia-Herzegovena | 1996 | n/a |
| Croatia | 1997 | 8 | Serbia | 1997 | 2 | Bosnia-Herzegovena | 1997 | n/a |
| Croatia | 1998 | 5 | Serbia | 1998 | 0 | Bosnia-Herzegovena | 1998 | n/a |
| Croatia | 1999 | 7 | Serbia | 1999 | 0 | Bosnia-Herzegovena | 1999 | n/a |
| Croatia | 2000 | 6 | Serbia | 2000 | 1 | Bosnia-Herzegovena | 2000 | n/a |
| Croatia | 2001 | 6 | Serbia | 2001 | 5 | Bosnia-Herzegovena | 2001 | 6 |
| Croatia | 2002 | 7 | Serbia | 2002 | 6 | Bosnia-Herzegovena | 2002 | 6 |
| Croatia | 2003 | 7 | Serbia | 2003 | 3 | Bosnia-Herzegovena | 2003 | 6 |
| Croatia | 2004 | 7 | Serbia | 2004 | 5 | Bosnia-Herzegovena | 2004 | 7 |
| Croatia | 2005 | 7 | Serbia | 2005 | 5 | Bosnia-Herzegovena | 2005 | 7 |
| Croatia | 2006 | 8 | Serbia | 2006 | 6 | Bosnia-Herzegovena | 2006 | 7 |
| Croatia | 2007 | 8 | Serbia | 2007 | 7 | Bosnia-Herzegovena | 2007 | 6 |
| Croatia | 2008 | 6 | Serbia | 2008 | 6 | Bosnia-Herzegovena | 2008 | 7 |
| Croatia | 2009 | 6 | Serbia | 2009 | 6 | Bosnia-Herzegovena | 2009 | 6 |
| Croatia | 2010 | 5 | Serbia | 2010 | 7 | Bosnia-Herzegovena | 2010 | 6 |
| Croatia | 2011 | 8 | Serbia | 2011 | 7 | Bosnia-Herzegovena | 2011 | 6 |

Table 3.1 shows that human rights scores are generally fairly good in Bosnia, Serbia, and Croatia.[5] Their citizens' human rights are not being systematically or substantially violated, at least since the early 2000s, which is an improvement over the repression and violence of the 1990s and is moving in the direction of the rest of European human rights practices. International justice would not appear to be associated with worsening human rights records. So far, so good.

While we have every reason to believe that these data are excellent indicators of a country's overall human rights record in a given year, it is also useful to examine other sources of information on human rights. Another record of problems countries may be experiencing with human rights comes from Amnesty International (AI), which is one of the most widely known and respected human rights organizations in the world. There are three particular pieces of information that we can glean from Amnesty International's substantial coverage of human rights issues around the world. First, there are the Urgent Actions that AI issues in response to credible reports that a particular individual or group of individuals has been subject to human rights abuses and may be in danger of further abuse. AI sends these Urgent Action notices out to its membership and asks them to write letters to government leaders asking them to release these individuals. Often these letter-writing campaigns are quite effective and shame governments into releasing these individuals. Amnesty International also produces background reports and issues news releases on significant human rights violations. These reports and press releases are also intended to call attention to egregious human rights abuses and galvanize actions to address them (see Meernik et al. 2012 for more information on these data).

We see in table 3.2 that Amnesty International Urgent Actions have not been issued with a great deal of frequency in the countries of the former Yugoslavia during this period. In fact, there are none in Croatia at all! Urgent Actions are designed to call attention to specific concerns about particular persons, and thus viewed from this perspective there would not appear to be the types of high-profile arrests or abuses that one finds in some states when prominent lawyers, journalists, or human rights activists are arrested. What of the news release and background reports, which often cover more general problems of human rights abuses?

Here we do find more evidence of concern and attention being paid by AI to the principal states of the former Yugoslavia, as we see in table 3.2. In contrast to the data on Urgent Actions, Croatia has been the target of several background reports over the years indicating some level of concern with that nation's protection of human rights, although most of these do appear during the turbulent 1990s. Bosnia-Herzegovina is also the subject of multiple reports over several years, reaching as high as fifteen in the years immediately

**Table 3.2 Amnesty International Actions in the Former Yugoslavia**

| Country | Year | Urgent Actions | Background Reports | News Releases | Country | Year | Urgent Actions | Background Reports | News Releases | Country | Year | Urgent Actions | Background Reports | News Releases |
|---|---|---|---|---|---|---|---|---|---|---|---|---|---|---|
| Bosnia-Herzegovina | 1992 | 0 | 1 | 6 | Croatia | 1992 | 0 | 1 | 0 | Serbia | 1992 | 0 | 0 | 21 |
| Bosnia-Herzegovina | 1993 | 0 | 1 | 10 | Croatia | 1993 | 0 | 7 | 0 | Serbia | 1993 | 0 | 1 | 26 |
| Bosnia-Herzegovina | 1994 | 0 | 4 | 12 | Croatia | 1994 | 0 | 3 | 0 | Serbia | 1994 | 1 | 3 | 11 |
| Bosnia-Herzegovina | 1995 | 0 | 6 | 12 | Croatia | 1995 | 0 | 4 | 3 | Serbia | 1995 | 0 | 2 | 16 |
| Bosnia-Herzegovina | 1996 | 0 | 5 | 15 | Croatia | 1996 | 0 | 5 | 1 | Serbia | 1996 | 1 | 0 | 12 |
| Bosnia-Herzegovina | 1997 | 0 | 10 | 15 | Croatia | 1997 | 0 | 8 | 1 | Serbia | 1997 | 0 | 3 | 11 |
| Bosnia-Herzegovina | 1998 | 2 | 3 | 7 | Croatia | 1998 | 0 | 6 | 5 | Serbia | 1998 | 1 | 21 | 20 |
| Bosnia-Herzegovina | 1999 | 0 | 4 | 2 | Croatia | 1999 | 0 | 5 | 1 | Serbia | 1999 | 2 | 50 | 26 |
| Bosnia-Herzegovina | 2000 | 0 | 7 | 4 | Croatia | 2000 | 0 | 3 | 0 | Serbia | 2000 | 0 | 24 | 19 |
| Bosnia-Herzegovina | 2001 | 1 | 9 | 2 | Croatia | 2001 | 0 | 1 | 0 | Serbia | 2001 | 1 | 0 | 0 |
| Bosnia-Herzegovina | 2002 | 0 | 7 | 6 | Croatia | 2002 | 0 | 1 | 0 | Serbia | 2002 | 0 | 0 | 0 |
| Bosnia-Herzegovina | 2003 | 4 | 8 | 5 | Croatia | 2003 | 0 | 0 | 0 | Serbia | 2003 | 0 | 0 | 0 |
| Bosnia-Herzegovina | 2004 | 0 | 0 | 0 | Croatia | 2004 | 0 | 3 | 3 | Serbia | 2004 | 0 | 0 | 0 |
| Bosnia-Herzegovina | 2005 | 0 | 2 | 2 | Croatia | 2005 | 0 | 0 | 4 | Serbia | 2005 | 0 | 0 | 0 |
| Bosnia-Herzegovina | 2006 | 0 | 5 | 3 | Croatia | 2006 | 0 | 0 | 1 | Serbia | 2006 | 0 | 0 | 0 |
| Bosnia-Herzegovina | 2007 | 0 | 3 | 1 | Croatia | 2007 | 0 | 0 | 1 | Serbia | 2007 | 0 | 0 | 0 |

after the war ended and refugees began to return home. In more recent years, the number of reports has declined, although there is a handful in the later years of the dataset. Serbia has been the target of the most such reports, especially when the Serbian government was significantly involved in the war in Bosnia, while the more recent increase coincides with the ethnic cleansing in the former Serbian province of Kosovo. During this period, the Serbian government of Slobodan Milošević sought to drive out the Kosovar Albanian population of the region to restore Serb domination of an area that resonates deeply in Serbian history. Shortly thereafter, Milošević, thinking he was still beloved by his people and would be reelected, called elections that resulted in his eventual loss of power, but not before there was violence and unrest in the streets.

The third measure of international concern regarding human rights are the Amnesty International news releases that seek to convey to a broad audience information about important human rights concerns. Once again we see that events in Croatia do not seem to inspire substantial attention from AI. There are some years in which there are a handful of news releases, but most of the time there are none. Bosnia-Herzegovina does attract a fair number of press releases in many years, as it experienced problems with violence against refugees returning home, with elections, and with the arrest of suspected war criminals. In Serbia, we see one rather pronounced spike in news releases in 2001 in the aftermath of the 2000 elections, in which Slobodan Milošević finally lost his grip on power. In late 2000 and the first half of 2001, there was a standoff among Serbian politicians and other powerful actors regarding what to do with Milošević, as the ICTY was demanding his surrender to The Hague. Eventually he was arrested after a tense standoff and later was spirited away to the ICTY.

Amnesty International provides another useful perspective on human rights conditions in the former Yugoslavia. While the CIRI data help us understand the overall human rights record when viewed from afar, the Amnesty International Urgent Actions, background reports, and press releases provide us with a more "real-time" frame of reference on what one prominent nongovernmental organization perceives as the most crucial issues of the day. These data indicate that there have been ongoing human rights concerns, especially in Serbia, to a significantly lesser extent in Bosnia-Herzegovina, and almost not at all in Croatia.

So we do have evidence that since the creation of the ICTY, the three nations that have been the focus of most of its work have mostly seen steady improvement in their human rights records. Naturally we must then ask how much of this is due to the influence of the ICTY and its deterrence of major human rights violations. Expecting to find evidence of scientific causation is obviously beyond the power of these data—human rights improvements did not follow the establishment of the ICTY like night follows day, but several things are clear. First, human rights did not start improving until the ICTY began apprehending suspects in large numbers toward the end of the 1990s and the beginning of the new millennium. Second, no further atrocities occurred in the region since 2001 that have resulted in more ICTY investigations. Third, the human rights records of the principal governments involved in the wars have shown steady improvement over the last fifteen years. The level of human rights protection, while not always perfect, has stabilized at a level where these countries' citizens, as well as the international community, can live in peace and security. We must, however, be mindful of where our optimistic results confront some other inconvenient truths. We know that both the Srebrenica massacre of 8,000 Bosnian Muslim men and boys (1995) and the atrocities in Kosovo war (1998 to 1999) occurred after the establishment of the ICTY. We know that there were regime changes in Croatia after its former leader Franjo Tuđman died in 1999 and in Serbia after Slobodan Milošević was arrested and sent packing to The Hague in 2001. New and more democratic leadership certainly improved human rights conditions. Hence, other factors have played a role in these human rights success stories. We cannot attribute all of this success to the ICTY.

What we can do is give the ICTY credit. First, through its indictments it caused the international community to seek the apprehension of dozens of suspected war criminals. By removing suspected war criminals from the scenes of their crimes, the tribunal not only prevented these individuals from committing further violations of international law, but also made the organization of such crimes by other regional actors far more difficult. Second, the ICTY established a necessary condition for deterrence. If there had been no international criminal justice response to the atrocities of the wars in the former Yugoslavia, the message to the international community and would-be war criminals would have been that perpetrators could expect impunity for their actions. The possibility certainly exists that the violence in the Balkans would have been far worse had there been no ICTY. Third, as our results show here, human rights did improve in the region after a time. Therefore, although we must always couch our claims with plenty of qualifiers, we can make a reasonable case that the ICTY helped the promotion of human rights in the former Yugoslavia.

## RWANDA

We next turn our attention to the ICTY's sister tribunal, the ICTR, and evaluate the human rights performance of its government. We can see in table 3.3 that Rwanda generally tends to improve over time until recently, when its scores begin a noticeable decline that ultimately place it in the ranks of some of the more repressive nations of the world, such as Saudi Arabia, Chad, and Russia. In a nation with this kind of score, there is a great deal of human rights abuse going on across the country. We know from international reports that the post-genocide government of the Rwandan Patriotic Front has been increasingly infringing upon individual rights and creating something of an authoritarian state in the name of preventing ethnic tension and conflict. While Rwanda has prospered economically and has attracted significant international investment (Dunne 2006), its government has become increasingly fearful of challenges from within and without. Security and stability have been achieved, but the cost has been a creeping authoritarianism that is stifling freedom of dissent.

**Table 3.3 Rwanda Human Rights and Amnesty International Scores and Data**

| Country | Year | Human Rights Score | Urgent Actions | Background Reports | News Releases |
|---|---|---|---|---|---|
| Rwanda | 1992 | 2 | 0 | 4 | 0 |
| Rwanda | 1993 | 1 | 0 | 3 | 0 |
| Rwanda | 1994 | 0 | 0 | 7 | 14 |
| Rwanda | 1995 | 0 | 0 | 11 | 14 |
| Rwanda | 1996 | 1 | 0 | 5 | 10 |
| Rwanda | 1997 | 0 | 0 | 10 | 10 |
| Rwanda | 1998 | 2 | 6 | 12 | 11 |
| Rwanda | 1999 | 3 | 2 | 7 | 2 |
| Rwanda | 2000 | 2 | 2 | 5 | 3 |
| Rwanda | 2001 | 3 | 1 | 0 | 1 |
| Rwanda | 2002 | 3 | 0 | 1 | 5 |
| Rwanda | 2003 | 2 | 3 | 1 | 4 |
| Rwanda | 2004 | 2 | 1 | 3 | 6 |
| Rwanda | 2005 | 4 | 0 | 0 | 1 |
| Rwanda | 2006 | 4 | 1 | 1 | 2 |
| Rwanda | 2007 | 5 | 3 | 1 | 3 |
| Rwanda | 2008 | 4 | n/a | n/a | n/a |
| Rwanda | 2009 | 3 | n/a | n/a | n/a |
| Rwanda | 2010 | 2 | n/a | n/a | n/a |
| Rwanda | 2011 | 2 | n/a | n/a | n/a |

When we turn our attention to the Amnesty International data, we see evidence of some similar trends. There are several peaks in the number of Urgent Actions in the period between the end of the genocide in 1994 and 2007, when the data conclude, as we see in table 3.3. The years right after the genocide in particular, when the Rwandan Patriotic Front government consolidated power and began to force out those in its ranks who disagreed with its policies, are particularly noteworthy. Rwanda continues to be the target of these types of "naming and shaming" activities where international groups, like Amnesty International, seek to publicize a government's human rights abuses in the hopes that the negative attention will bring about government reforms or the release of political prisoners. In the Rwandan case, it would not appear that such efforts have borne much fruit. Rwanda's human rights record in the CIRI database has only declined in recent years. So while the number of Amnesty International activities directed at Rwanda may not be as numerous as in the 1990s, Rwanda's human rights scores give us cause for concern.

The CIRI data we have been analyzing so far measure human rights violations perpetrated by governments, while the Amnesty International data usually pertain to governmental abuses. Human rights abuses, however, can be committed by governmental as well as by nongovernmental actors, such as rebel armies, militias, and others fighting for political power or perhaps control of a valuable natural resource. We will next turn our attention to some unique and very recent data that scholars have been gathering on the human rights performance of African countries. The Social Conflict in Africa Data (SCAD) measures social conflict in the period from 1998 to 2014 and is a recently developed database that relies on event coding of stories reported in major newspapers regarding various forms of non–civil war conflict in Africa.[6] These data are organized by the social conflict event—every instance of conflict is coded in each country. Hence, in order for us to use these data I organized them so that we can examine the annual count of the number of cases of social conflict each year in these states. There is also another recent and similar database that examines conflict associated with war and major political violence—the Armed Conflict Location and Event Database (ACLED).[7] These are data very similar to the SCAD data, in that researchers coded every single instance of violence associated with armed conflict. Here too I aggregate the data by year so we can look at the annual counts of such events. I do not use all of these data because both datasets cover events that do not necessarily involve human rights abuses, such as protests, strikes, and riots in the SCAD database and the various battles fought in civil wars that are recorded in the ACLED database. Instead, I focus on just those that pertain to human rights violations. In the SCAD database, I examine instances of government repression, both lethal and nonlethal, of protests. In the ACLED database, I look at instances of violence directed against civilians. Because these data are so recent and the work involved in gathering these data is so extraordinary, we only have data in SCAD and ACLED for the countries of Africa. We are not able to utilize these data for the former Yugoslavia.

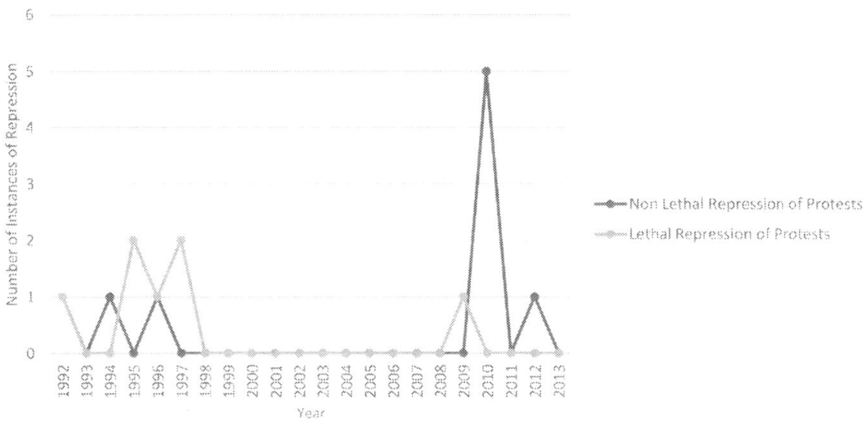


**Figure 3.1** Repression of Protests in Rwanda. *Source: Author.*

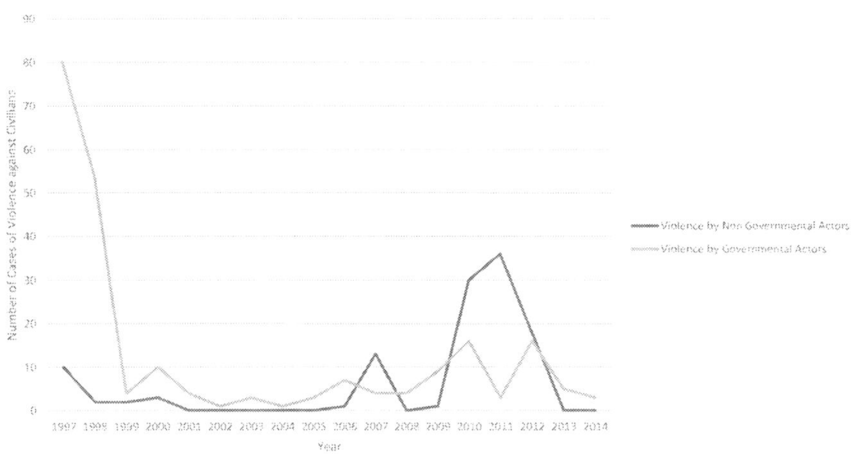


**Figure 3.2** Violence Against Civilians in Rwanda. *Source: Author.*

When we examine the number of cases of government repression of protests in Rwanda in figure 3.1, we see the same trends in evidence that the Amnesty International data revealed. There are a number of cases in the late 1990s where the Rwandan government put down protests using both nonlethal tactics, such as arresting individuals for protesting, and lethal methods, where the government takes actions that result in the deaths of some of those protesting. There are also spikes in repression in the data in more recent years. So while the government's human rights record has drawn increasing concern abroad, the government seems to be avoiding the types of massive repressive tactics that might result in actions by its supporters, such as European countries and the United States, that have applauded Rwanda's economic progress.

We next turn our attention to attacks against civilians. In figure 3.2 I have divided up the annual count of this type of human rights repression into two categories—violence against civilians committed by governmental actors (e.g., the military or the police) and by nongovernmental actors (such as the rebel movements made up of elements from the former government of Rwanda that committed the genocide and continue to carry out against in Rwanda while based in the neighboring Congo). Once again, we see a huge spike in violence in 1997 and 1998, when many of the attacks by these nongovernmental forces were at their peak. There is a steep decline in such attacks subsequently, but then another uptick in violence by both governmental and nongovernmental forces in the most recent years. Thus, despite some periods of calm, Rwandans continue to experience political violence directed against civilians despite the work of the Rwandan tribunal.

## SIERRA LEONE

Sierra Leone presents something of a human rights success story, as we see in table 3.4. While there are some years for which data are not available, in general we see an upward trajectory in Sierra Leone's protection of human rights. It had been the site of a brutal and lengthy civil war from roughly 1991 to 2002 that featured ghastly atrocities such as forced amputations, the use of child soldiers, and sexual enslavement. The war inspired the creation of the Special Court for Sierra Leone, which held several trials of the top-ranking militia and government leaders from the most prominent warring factions. All of its trials are complete and all of the individuals prosecuted, including former Liberian leader Charles Taylor, were convicted and sentenced. Perhaps this international justice has paid off.

**Table 3.4 Sierra Leone Human Rights Scores and Amnesty International Data**

| Country | Year | Human Rights Score | Urgent Actions | Background Reports | News Releases |
|---|---|---|---|---|---|
| Sierra Leone | 1992 | 0 | 0 | 3 | 1 |
| Sierra Leone | 1993 | 1 | 0 | 7 | 0 |
| Sierra Leone | 1994 | 0 | 0 | 1 | 0 |
| Sierra Leone | 1995 | 0 | 0 | 1 | 3 |
| Sierra Leone | 1996 | 3 | 0 | 1 | 3 |
| Sierra Leone | 1997 | n/a | 0 | 2 | 4 |
| Sierra Leone | 1998 | n/a | 3 | 4 | 7 |
| Sierra Leone | 1999 | n/a | 0 | 6 | 6 |
| Sierra Leone | 2000 | n/a | 0 | 12 | 24 |
| Sierra Leone | 2001 | 4 | 0 | 1 | 5 |
| Sierra Leone | 2002 | 8 | 0 | 0 | 2 |
| Sierra Leone | 2003 | 5 | 0 | 3 | 4 |
| Sierra Leone | 2004 | 6 | 0 | 2 | 3 |
| Sierra Leone | 2005 | 5 | 0 | 2 | 5 |
| Sierra Leone | 2006 | 5 | 0 | 4 | 2 |
| Sierra Leone | 2007 | 6 | 0 | 2 | 3 |
| Sierra Leone | 2008 | 6 | n/a | n/a | n/a |
| Sierra Leone | 2009 | n/a | n/a | n/a | n/a |
| Sierra Leone | 2010 | 5 | n/a | n/a | n/a |
| Sierra Leone | 2011 | 6 | n/a | n/a | n/a |

With the exception of one year, 1998, in which there were Amnesty International letter-writing campaigns, the data do not indicate that Urgent Actions were utilized at other times. It may well have been that the situation in Sierra Leone was so brutal and chaotic that the kind of information AI relies on to issue such reports was not available or it was too unsafe to report such problems. AI did issue numerous background reports about all of the violence, civil war, and international interventions during the late 1990s and early 2000s especially. While the number of background reports and new reports would still indicate that there are significant human rights problems in Sierra Leone, both sets of AI activities do decrease quite a bit and stabilize after the end of the civil war. Hence, while Sierra Leone remains one of the poorest countries in the world with numerous problems (such as the 2015 Ebola outbreak), its human rights record has begun to recover from the horrific years of its multisided civil war.

We do, however, continue to see problems with the manner in which the government of Sierra Leone handles protests associated with its political and economic problems. After the civil war ends, and perhaps because the war

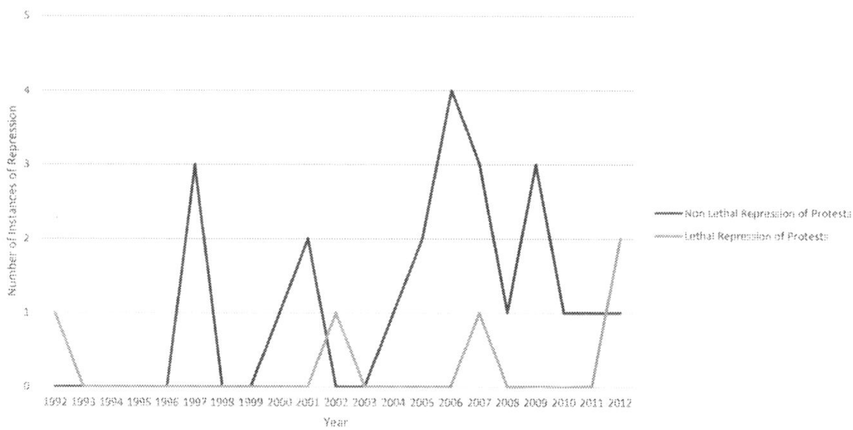


**Figure 3.3** Repression of Protests in Sierra Leone. *Source: Author.*

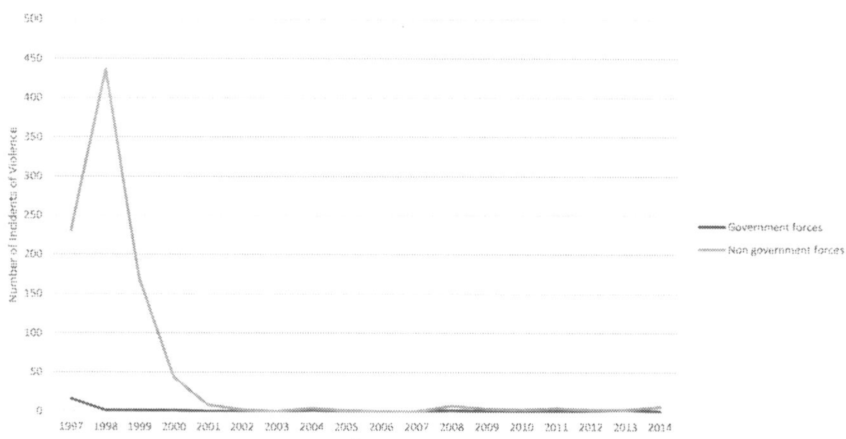


**Figure 3.4** Violence Against Civilians by Government and Nongovernment Forces in Sierra Leone. *Source: Author.*

has ended and people feel secure enough to protest, we find that the government response to protests increases. The government typically responds with nonlethal force. The outlook for Sierra Leone is much more positive when we examine the number of instances of violence against civilians. While even a small number of cases in which civilians are deliberately targeted by armies and militias is too many, there is no denying the tremendous drop in such actions.

Can we conclude that the ICTR and SCSL are at least partially responsible for the human rights successes we have seen in these nations? In the case of Rwanda, that might be a difficult claim to make. The Rwandan Patriotic Front government has been the dominant force in society and has created a semi-authoritarian government since the genocide. There is little in Rwanda that escapes its notice, especially those who raise the issue of ethnic division. Individuals who question the lack of political freedom or human rights abuses are quickly reminded of the terrible tragedy that befell the country and the rapid strides it has made since 1994. Critics are told that ethnicity no longer matters in Rwanda and that whatever infringement on human rights that does occur is a small price to pay for maintaining a society free from the threat of genocide. While certainly that explanation carried a great deal of weight in the immediate aftermath of the genocide, increasingly it would appear that Rwanda is successfully playing on the international community's "guilt" over its culpability in allowing the genocide to unfold without taking any action to stop it. Rwanda adroitly turns the finger of blame for its human rights back to the international community.

In fact, when the ICTR has taken actions in the past that might have resulted in some ICTR detainees being set free or to investigate crimes committed by the Rwandan Patriotic Army in 1994, Rwanda has swiftly and forcefully cut off cooperation with the ICTR until the tribunal reversed its positions. When the ICTR Appeals Chamber ruled that because his due process rights had been significantly harmed the tribunal would have to release Jean-Bosco Barayagwiza (suspected of taking part in the genocide), the Rwandan government wasted no time in responding. It stopped cooperating with the ICTR and refused to grant visas to any of its employees to visit Rwanda. Shortly thereafter, the ICTR Appeals Chamber reversed its decision in light of "new evidence" and the cooperation resumed. It would strain credulity to assert that the international community, through the ICTR, has played a significant role in whatever human rights protections Rwanda does currently enjoy. The Rwandan government appears to follow its strong preferences, typically regardless of the wishes of the international community or the ICTR.

There is stability, security, and prosperity in Rwanda, although international justice and the ICTR have probably not played much of a role. The

Rwandan government has conducted its own internal trials of those accused of taking part in the genocide—the gacaca initiative, in which local villages held hearings "under the tree" to hear evidence against the accused and decide upon an appropriate punishment. Indeed, thousands of such trials occurred throughout Rwanda in which accused genocidaires came back to their communities and stood accused before the whole village and were tried before elected groups of judges. At first the gacaca trials were applauded by many as a way for Rwanda to handle the immense backlog of cases from the 1994 genocide. Hundreds of thousands of individuals were imprisoned on suspicion of having taken part in the genocide. In fact, I visited one such prison in Kigali in 2001 and saw prisoners stacked three, four, and five on bunk beds in nearly every available space. But how have these community trials been perceived by the Rwandan public and have they helped prevent human rights abuses? Barbara Oomen (2005, 905) writes,

> Although early opinion surveys generally reflected the hope that the *gacaca* would indeed bring justice and reconciliation (Babola et al., 2003), public enthusiasm quickly diminished. More and more people came to see the *gacaca* as a government project, and attending them "an act of patriotism and our civil duty," as one community member put it. She saw what the international community failed to see: that this particular form of justice had been made subservient to the government's political mission.

Ultimately the price of Rwandan peace and stability has been paid with government restrictions on free speech, free press, and other democratic practices. Certainly nothing on the order of the 1994 genocide has come close to happening again. One wonders, however, whether the Rwandan government's repressive tactics may be laying their groundwork for future instability and Hutu grievances against the Tutsi-dominated government. The justice of the ICTR seems to have taken place on a parallel track to that of Rwanda's judicial remedies. The ICTR conducted its judicial affairs involving the leadership of the genocide and other important figures, while Rwanda has pursued its own strategies often heedless of the international community. It bears remembering that the one government that voted against the ICTR in the United Nations Security Council was Rwanda (it opposed the ICTR's prohibition on the death penalty and wanted to have more control over prosecution of senior leaders). International justice has soldiered on in spite of the Rwandan government and despite whatever human rights protections have emerged in the small Central African nation, not because of it.

Sierra Leone, on the other hand, has been much more of a ward of the international community. It has seen both international and British troops attempt to keep the peace. It has been the recipient of significant amounts of aid, although not nearly enough to address its crushing poverty and the destruction left in the wake of the civil war. Sierra Leone is, in a sense, the polar opposite of Rwanda. It is heavily dependent on the international community. The SCSL is located in Freetown, Sierra Leone (the ICTR is located in Arusha, Tanzania, hundreds of miles from Rwanda), which has facilitated cooperation and public awareness of the tribunal's work. Its government has been relatively open and its citizens enjoy better human rights protections than Rwanda's. We might then have some reason to believe that the SCSL is better positioned to facilitate human rights practices in Sierra Leone. As we saw in the case of the ICTR, the Sierra Leone tribunal helped remove the worst human rights violators from society. Their presence in the courtroom rather than in the countryside helped Sierra Leone transition out of the conflicts of the past. The SCSL has also been praised for its efforts at public outreach (Clark 2009). By making more of an investment telling ordinary people across the country about the work of the SCSL, it may have also helped contribute to a greater awareness and understanding of human rights. Indeed, the SCSL was a hybrid tribunal in which judges and other court personnel from Sierra Leone worked alongside their international counterparts. This too may have created a greater social and political stake in the tribunal that resonated beyond the trial chambers. Ultimately, respect for human rights requires commitment and leadership by the government and respect for these rights among those in the police, security forces, and the military who must refrain from committing abuses. The street-level implementation of human rights is, in many respects, the most critical part of all. Through its deeper integration into Sierra Leonean society, a reasonable case can be made that the SCSL has helped advance the cause of human rights, especially in light of the fairly good human rights scores we saw earlier.

## THE INTERNATIONAL CRIMINAL COURT

And what of the International Criminal Court? Have ICC investigations and prosecutions helped to improve human rights in those states in which it has been involved? The ICC is also a global tribunal. All of the states parties are subject to potential ICC investigation and prosecution if their nationals commit potential human rights violations at home or abroad. In addition, the UN Security Council has the power to refer cases to the ICC, although that, of course, requires that none of the permanent five members exercises its veto. This opens the possibility that any state could potentially find its leaders brought before the court. While countries like the United States and Russia will reflexively protect their allies from such investigations, international pariah states may well find themselves without a benefactor at the Security Council. By virtue of its power to weigh in on conflict situations and human rights atrocities on a global scale, has the ICC helped bring about an increased respect for human rights? Let's begin with the specific states the ICC has investigated.

The case of Uganda involves atrocities committed by Joseph Kony and his Lord's Resistance Army, which many readers may remember from the social media campaign of a few years ago—Kony 2012—that sought his arrest. Uganda was one of the first states to seek an ICC investigation in December 2003. Uganda utilized its right as a state party to the ICC treaty to refer the situation in the north of its territory where Kony was kidnapping children, engaging in sexual enslavement, and terrorizing the population. Since that time, the government of Uganda has run hot and cold with the ICC. When negotiations with Kony looked like a better route to peace and stability, it would keep the ICC at arm's length, but when it concluded such efforts were not likely to bear fruit, the ICC option looked more promising. Unfortunately, despite substantial international attention, the use of Ugandan and U.S. military forces in the hunt for Kony and the LRA, very little has happened in The Hague. The ICC has custody of only one suspect at the time of writing, while a second has passed away since his indictment and three others remain at large, including Kony. No trials have taken place yet. Meanwhile, Kony and whatever remains of his forces have disappeared somewhere into the jungles of the Congo, the Central African Republic, or perhaps somewhere else, and resurface occasionally to commit some barbarous act against innocent civilians. The twelve-year wait for international justice to help resolve the situation has resulted in precious little progress, although to be sure conditions in the north of Uganda have improved since Kony has mostly vacated that territory.

Of all the situations the ICC has investigated to date, the case of the Democratic Republic of the Congo (DRC, or just "the Congo") has been the most complex. Briefly, the DRC experienced years of violence following the overthrow of its government in 1996. In the eastern portion of that vast nation, which borders several other states that have experienced their own human rights atrocities and which became subject to international tribunals (Uganda, Rwanda, the Sudan, the Central African Republic), there were brutal and widespread war crimes and crimes against humanity committed by various warlords fighting for power and dominion over the region's rich natural resources, some of which continue to this day. The DRC referred the conflict in the east of the country to the ICC in early 2004. Despite the multiplicity of nations involved in the Congolese civil war, the numerous and shifting alliances among these states, the various militias, and the Congo government itself, the Congo situation has been something of a success story for the ICC, at least in comparison to its other cases. So far the International Criminal Court has completed its proceedings against four individuals, two of whom were found guilty while one other has been acquitted and released. One trial is still ongoing, while one suspect remains at large at the time of writing. But while the cause of justice has advanced, some of the most violent rebel groups (like the M23 group) have been defeated, and the human rights abuses are not as prevalent as they were at the height of the Congo wars, there are still reports of massacres of civilians in the east of the Congo. Human security has improved, but a great deal of insecurity remains for those caught in the fighting and violence in the east.

The case of the Sudan involves the genocide in the Darfur region of the country from several years ago. That situation, unlike the Congo and Uganda, which were cases referred to the ICC by the nations themselves, was handed to the ICC by the United Nations Security Council in March 2005. Unfortunately, despite the widespread attention given to the situation by many governments and international organizations, the Sudanese leaders under indictment remain free. Sudanese president Omar Bashir has even gained support in the African Union as he has railed against what he and many other leaders on the African continent see as a Western bias and neocolonialism against Africa. As of this writing, no trials have officially commenced, and it is looking increasingly like this case might be shelved for lack of defendants. The international community certainly put the human rights atrocities in Darfur on the international agenda, but otherwise proved either unwilling or incapable of doing any more. The failure in the Sudan case highlights one of the most significant challenges the ICC faces—convincing other states or organizations to apprehend those it has indicted. Despite repeated condemnations of President Bashir, especially in the West, the relative "calm" that prevails in the country, the many other crises in the Middle East, and the lack of any good options for arresting a sitting head of state have pushed Darfur off the agenda for the time being.

The Central African Republic case involves widespread violence associated with the struggle for power in 2002 and 2003, committed in part by forces from the neighboring Congo. The former president of the Movement for the Liberation of the Congo, Jean-Pierre Bemba, has since been charged with having responsibility for those forces and the crimes they committed when Bemba introduced them into the civil conflict in the CAR at the invitation of the former president of the CAR, Ange-Félix Patassé. The CAR case has been another self-referral by the government itself in December 2004. Bemba's trial recently concluded and he was found guilty of both crimes against humanity and war crimes for the actions of his forces in the Central

African Republic. Tensions remain, however, between the Christian and Muslim communities, and reports of retaliatory violence by both sides have been reported. Human Rights Watch, in its 2015 report, declared that "by the end of 2014, thousands of civilians had been killed by both sides and over 800,000 people displaced from their homes."[8] As in the Congo, despite some success in the courtroom, there has been no substantial improvement in human security in the Central African Republic. Insecurity, brought on by a different mix of forces, still prevails.

The Kenyan case was the first situation to come before the ICC as a result of the prosecutor's own decision to proceed, unlike the other cases, which have all been referred to the ICC by the states themselves or by the UN Security Council. The situation involved election-related ethnic violence in Kenya from late 2007 to early 2008. In this case, a pre-trial chamber of the ICC, whose approval must be gained before investigations are launched on the prosecution's motion, approved the prosecutor's request in March 2010 and the official investigation began. It has been subject to numerous problems, especially with witness intimidation and even the death of some witnesses. The proceedings against the current president of Kenya, Uhuru Kenyatta, have been terminated. At the time of writing, the case against the remaining two Kenyan defendants was halted because of allegations of witness intimidation. In this case, the ICC prosecution must be judged a failure (although to be fair, the ICC does not have the resources to protect witnesses in Kenya), while the level of human security, in the context of interethnic tensions, has improved.[9]

The Libyan situation, stemming from the overthrow of longtime Libyan dictator Muamar Khadafy and the ensuing civil war, was referred to the ICC by the UN Security Council in February 2011. No trials are underway because Khadafy died during the civil war and the other two suspects remain in Libya. Despite the fact that the ICC has found that the government of Libya is unable to carry out a trial for one of the three indictees, Saif Al Islam Gaddafi, it also ruled that Libyan authorities were competent to carry out a trial of Abdullah Al-Senussi. Regardless of the lack of ICC success in prosecuting any Libyan cases, the human security situation in that country is quite bad. Between the violence coming from the various militias vying for power and the horrific slaughters perpetrated by ISIS, many Libyans are living in a state of extreme insecurity.

In the case of the Ivory Coast, there are charges against former president Laurent Gbagbo, his wife Simone Gbagbo, and Charles Goude, a political leader, of crimes against humanity allegedly committed during post-election violence in between December 2010 and April 2011 as rival political groups clashed over the outcome. The government of the Ivory Coast has accepted ICC jurisdiction even though it was not an official state party to the Rome

Statute when it sought ICC assistance in 2003. The authorization from a pre-trial chamber to officially open an investigation was granted in October 2011. Former President Gbagbo and Charles Goude are in the custody of the ICC and are currently on trial. The human security situation in the Ivory Coast has improved in recent years.[10]

Because the wheels of justice have been moving ever so slowly at the ICC, it is not easy to determine just where we might expect the court to have already made a difference in these nations' human rights records. In addition, many of the cases before the court are of fairly recent origin and thus

**Table 3.5 Human Rights Scores of States Under ICC Investigation Since 2005**

| Country | Year | Human Rights Score | Country | Year | Human Rights Score | Country | Year | Human Rights Score | Country | Year | Human Rights Score |
|---|---|---|---|---|---|---|---|---|---|---|---|
| Congo | 2002 | 2 | Uganda | 2002 | 3 | Central African Republic | 2002 | 4 | Sudan | 2002 | 0 |
| Congo | 2003 | 1 | Uganda | 2003 | 2 | Central African Republic | 2003 | 4 | Sudan | 2003 | 0 |
| Congo | 2004 | 1 | Uganda | 2004 | 2 | Central African Republic | 2004 | 3 | Sudan | 2004 | 2 |
| Congo | 2005 | 2 | Uganda | 2005 | 2 | Central African Republic | 2005 | 3 | Sudan | 2005 | 1 |
| Congo | 2006 | 1 | Uganda | 2006 | 1 | Central African Republic | 2006 | 3 | Sudan | 2006 | 1 |
| Congo | 2007 | 1 | Uganda | 2007 | 3 | Central African Republic | 2007 | 3 | Sudan | 2007 | 1 |
| Congo | 2008 | 1 | Uganda | 2008 | 3 | Central African Republic | 2008 | 3 | Sudan | 2008 | 0 |
| Congo | 2009 | 1 | Uganda | 2009 | 2 | Central African Republic | 2009 | 2 | Sudan | 2009 | 1 |
| Congo | 2010 | 1 | Uganda | 2010 | 2 | Central African Republic | 2010 | 2 | Sudan | 2010 | 1 |
| Congo | 2011 | 0 | Uganda | 2011 | 2 | Central African Republic | 2011 | 3 | Sudan | 2011 | 1 |

there is little data against which to assess whether ICC investigations and prosecutions have made a difference in deterring human rights abuses. There are, however, four situations currently before the ICC that have been under adjudication for at least ten years—Uganda, the Democratic Republic of the Congo, the Central African Republic, and the Sudan. One could argue that despite the fact that only three convictions have taken place (in the DRC and CAR), these situations have been under the purview of the ICC long enough for the court to have potentially had an impact in improving human rights. What do we see in the data? I look at data from 2002 onward because that is the year in which the ICC came into being.

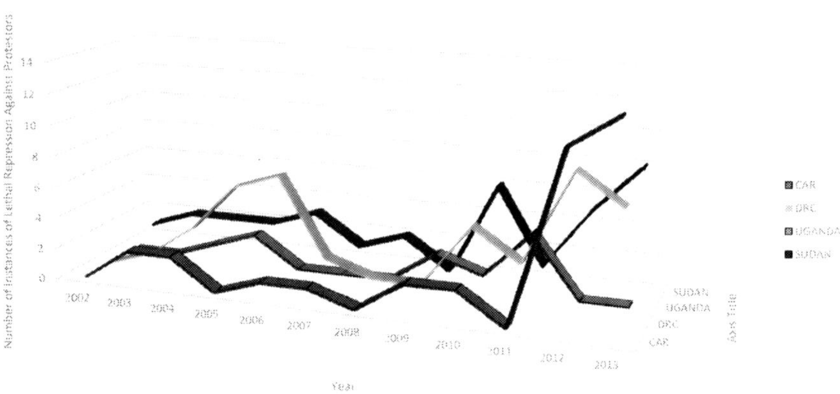


**Figure 3.5** Lethal Repression of Protestors in ICC States. *Source: Author.*

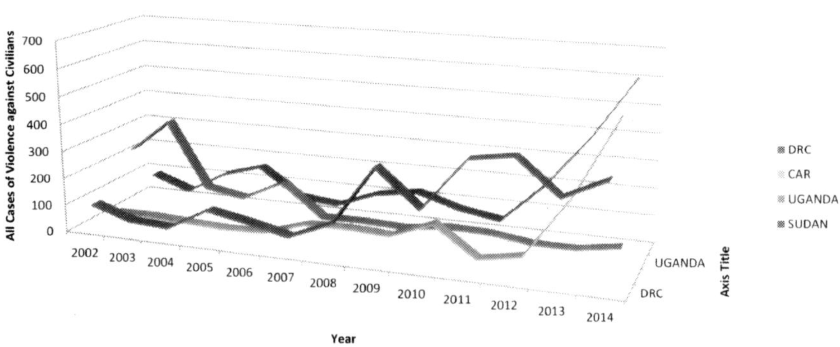


**Figure 3.6** Violence Against Civilians in ICC States. *Source: Author.*

The human rights picture in these states is not pretty—in fact, the data reveal an ugly truth, as evidenced in table 3.5. Human rights have declined in all the nations except the Sudan, which increases from "0" to "1,"—not exactly ringing the liberty bell of freedom. In the Congo, human rights scores begin at a "2," but then remain around "1" for the rest of the period. The CIRI scores begin at a "4" for the Central African Republic and drop to a "3" by 2011. And in Uganda, the scores begin at "3" and end at "2." Human rights are not improving in these states and people continue to live in societies in which governments are, at best, unwilling or unable to protect their freedoms, and at worst violently repress their rights. Whether international justice has played a role in these nations or not is a subject to which we will return shortly.

In figure 3.5 we also see that lethal repression of human rights protests have increased over time in several of the states under ICC investigation (I chose not to display the yearly instances of nonlethal repression to avoid cluttering up the chart with too much data). Especially in the Central African Republic, we find that in the most recent years the number of times when authorities have killed people in the course of clamping down on protests has increased dramatically as that nation continues to be highly unstable and riven by sectarian strife (Christian versus Muslim more recently). In fact, there have been spikes in such repression in three of the states in recent years, although there is a slight drop-off in the most recent year for the DRC (dropping from nine instances of lethal repression in 2012 to seven in 2013). Only in Uganda do we find that lethal repression has been on the decline. Even that piece of good news is tempered by the fact that in 2011 there was a high of four such instances before the decline to zero in 2012 and 2013 occurred. Conditions have improved for the Ugandan people, but there is no guarantee that the ups and downs one sees in figure 3.5 will not occur again.

And if the news so far was not depressing enough, incidents of political violence committed by all parties has been on the increase in all four states, as we see in figure 3.6. In fact, there are literally hundreds of such instances in the Central African Republic and the Sudan. Violence in the DRC continues to increase despite the presence of UN peacekeepers and the "official" end to the war. Even in Uganda violence is on the rise, although in comparison to these other nations, the number of such incidents is in the tens rather than the hundreds. Not exactly much comfort to the people of Uganda.

So what are we to conclude about the impact of international justice in these states? First, it is quite clear that human rights repression and violence against civilians has at best remained at a dangerous level and at worst has been increasing. The political and military conflicts in these states continue regardless of whatever legal proceedings may be occurring in The Hague.

While the wheels of justice turn slowly and years go by without significant or even any progress in some cases (e.g., the Sudan), the underlying ethnic tensions, battles over resources, extremist ideologies, and all the other factors that fuel this violence continue. Even in the DRC, where the ICC has been able to gain custody of all but one of its suspects, the violence goes on. Having begun its work in some of the most complex and violent conflicts in the world today, it is not surprising that the ICC appears to have, at best, no impact on these states. While the ICTY, ICTR, and SCSL had the benefit of significant international backing, especially with the apprehension of suspects and the necessity of focusing on the problems of a single state, the ICC has enjoyed neither of these advantages. Its global reach, while in theory a way of empowering the court and avoiding the need to create a series of ad hoc tribunals, has perhaps led to something of an overextension. Generating the political support and the institutional expertise necessary to deal with these complex conflicts may be a bridge too far for the ICC. Given the lack of suspects and trials and in the face of continuing violence in these societies, we must judge the ICC to have had no effect or possibly even a negative effect on human rights.

## CONCLUSIONS

The aim of this chapter has been to analyze data on human rights conditions as a key measure of human security in those countries that have been subject to the principal international criminal tribunals. These institutions are fundamentally about human rights—the laws they enforce concern the human rights of civilians and noncombatants. They are intended to advance the cause of human rights in these states by demonstrating that human rights abuses will not go unpunished when undertaken by the highest authorities. Yet these are still judicial institutions. As Alexander Hamilton once wrote about the courts in the United States, they have "neither force nor will, but judgment." Judges conduct trials in cloistered courtrooms and pronounce verdicts intended to express the condemnation of the international community. The challenge for us is to determine just how influential this message is and whether it is having the intended effect on those the tribunals are seeking to deter. The evidence we have examined would suggest the impact of international justice on human rights is positive under the right circumstances, but where it is missing support from the international community, it has accomplished little good.

To give these tribunals a thorough and fair assessment I will break down the elements of the causal process by which the tribunals are intended to advance human rights. The first step in this process is the actual administration of justice. Once the essential machinery of these tribunals has been established and there are judges, attorneys, and administration in place, the tribunals must have the evidence, the witnesses, and, most important of all, the suspects to conduct trials. As we saw, the ad hoc tribunals have all fared quite well in carrying out their judicial function. At the ICTY and SCSL, all suspects have been dealt with in some manner—the vast majority has been tried, while some others were referred to lower courts or died before their trials were completed. There are still a few ICTR suspects at large, but that tribunal too has finished its business and has now closed its doors. The ICC, on the other hand, has not been able to carry out its judicial function with the same dispatch. Several of the most prominent suspects not only remain at large, but in power, such as President Bashir of the Sudan, President Kenyatta of Kenya (whose trial was suspended after multiple witnesses refused to testify), and Joseph Kony of the Lord's Resistance Army (who remains on the loose in the wilds of Africa). After thirteen years, the ICC has completed full trials for only a handful of individuals. In a comparable period of time, the ICTY had reached verdicts in sixty-six cases, the SCSL had finished all of its cases, and the ICTR had completed forty-two trials. We can assess the performance of the ad hoc tribunal as fairly decent, although we should probably give the ICC a rather low grade. We can be generous and recognize that the ICC must look into conflict situations the world over and does not usually have the backing of the most powerful nation in the world, the United States. If the advancement of human rights through international justice requires that these tribunals first perform their most essential functions, we can check off this box for three of the four tribunals.

Now comes the tricky part. Having performed their judicial function and demonstrated that there will be no impunity for violations of international law, the message these verdicts are intended to convey to the world in general and would-be human rights violators in particular must be sent, received, and understood. The message must also ultimately cause individuals to change their behavior, but we will address that later. Certainly the leaders and the people of Bosnia-Herzegovina, Croatia, Serbia, Kosovo, Rwanda, and Sierra Leone are aware of the work of these tribunals and know that they have been convicting and sentencing individuals to incarceration. They may not always be aware of each verdict and sentence, but there is general awareness of the tribunals in each of these countries. We do not have good data on awareness of people in the states under ICC jurisdiction, so we cannot reach any conclusions about this question. The political and military leaders of these countries are the principal targets of this message, however, and it seems safe to assume that they are aware of these verdicts (leaders in government certainly are aware, as they must interact with the tribunals on a fairly regular basis as the courts seek evidence, witnesses, and suspects on their territories). We might even go out on a limb and suggest that leaders understand what these tribunals are trying to do with their verdicts—to demonstrate that those who engage in major human rights violations will be prosecuted and punished.

The real question is whether these leaders actually believe and *accept* these stated intentions or if they believe the tribunals are really trying to do something else. Some may believe that this international justice is biased against their country or their ethnic group (e.g., Bosnian Serbs). Some may believe it is just a way for the most powerful nations, especially the United States, to force compliance with its preferred international norms and rules (e.g., the Sudan). Hence, not all leaders will believe and accept this message. Is it still possible that even though the tribunals' message that justice will be done and war criminals will be punished is not accepted, leaders nonetheless adjust their behavior because they perceive a sufficiently credible threat of prosecution? I may not believe that a law is just and that the courts are fair, but I may still fear them and avoid breaking the law because I understand there is a good chance I will be caught and punished. Have leaders in these countries decided not to take actions that might land them in an international court one day? In our review of this notion of deterrence I noted that proving someone was deterred can be nearly impossible. We cannot usually know what leaders were thinking of doing unless we gain access to their thinking and planning. But we can determine if the behavior we are trying to deter still takes place. We can observe deterrence failure but not necessarily deterrence success. This is where our data on human rights violations are used.

The data we examined would suggest, but certainly not prove, that in the case of the ICTY there is some evidence to suggest that human rights have improved in the former Yugoslavia. Human rights conditions in Sierra Leone have certainly improved. In Rwanda and the countries that have been investigated thus far by the ICC, however, the evidence suggests that in some countries bad human rights conditions have not worsened, but that in other countries, human rights conditions have worsened.

Where does this leave us? First, we must acknowledge that we lack solid empirical proof that in general international justice improves human rights. I can point out the usual caveats we must make about such claims. We may be expecting too much from judicial institutions. We cannot expect that their decisions will reach deep into the political and military calculus of individuals who might be contemplating massive human rights atrocities to further their hold on power. The institutions are only as good as their stakeholders want and allow them to be. These are all potent obstacles in the path of justice. But if we were to throw up our hands and proclaim that it is nearly impossible for these tribunals to improve human rights, that would just end the conversation. The purpose of this chapter is to start, not end, the conversation.

International justice is, in many ways, like the Amnesty International Urgent Actions, reports, and news releases. It seeks to name and shame in the hope that this will cause leaders to change their behavior. Not all do, but many do. Certainly enough to keep organizations like AI going for decades with a fairly decent track record of success. AI has been successful in obtaining the release of many individuals who have been unjustly imprisoned and encouraging human rights reforms because the attention from such a high-profile international organization empowers local activists and puts pressure on governments to reform. International justice can potentially do something. It can empower local victims, nongovernmental organizations, human rights lawyers, judges, and other reform advocates to demand better human rights protections. Once justice has been done, it can also be seen to be done through outreach efforts, capacity building of local courts, and legal expertise.

Indeed, there is one school of thought in international relations, not necessarily supported by everyone, that most states would prefer to comply with international laws but often lack the capacity (Chayes and Chayes 1993). Capacity building to ensure that states better comply with international laws on human rights might well proceed on a parallel track as international justice is provided. It makes sense that if we want international justice to improve human rights that we design it and support it so that it is not just a backward-looking enterprise that settles the scores of the past. The affected states need assistance to ensure that such violations do not happen again. If we want someone to change their behavior, it is not enough to just punish them. We must also show them the right way and make sure they understand how to follow the right way. International justice should be reactive and proactive.

The tribunals do have outreach and capacity-building initiatives, but these are not always an explicit part of their mandate, nor are they given the resources to thoroughly pursue such objectives. Not all of this work need be done by employees of these tribunals. Indeed, much wonderful work is done by governments, nongovernmental organizations, and international organizations. What is needed is a plan with organization and division of responsibilities to ensure that capacity building is thorough and embedded. This may take millions of dollars and many years. But in comparison to wars, human rights atrocities, and genocidal campaigns, which can cost billions of dollars, last for years, and cost the lives of many innocents, international justice could be made to be a much better bargain. Indeed, if by embedding human rights norms and laws in such at-risk states, we reduce the likelihood of far more expensive problems.

## NOTES

1. As found at http://www.un.org/icty/legaldoc-e/index.htm on March 30, 2007.

2. Duško Tadić was convicted of war crimes and crimes against humanity for his role in the horrible conditions of detention camps set up by Bosnian Serbs in eastern Bosnia. He was, however, a fairly low-ranking individual in these camps and only came into the custody of the ICTY because he had been arrested in Germany.

3. All the nations of the former Yugoslavia fell under the jurisdiction of the ICTY, but Slovenia, Montenegro, as an independent state, and Macedonia have either not been the subject of any or just a very small number of ICTY indictments.

4. The interested reader can go to http://www.humanrightsdata.com/ to learn more about the CIRI scale of human rights abuse and the data.

5. I use "Serbia" to refer to that country and the other names it has used in recent years, such as "Serbia" and "Montenegro."

6. The Social Conflict in Africa database can be found at http://strausscenter.org/scad.html. The events coded include:

1. Organized demonstration: demonstrations organized by a formal group or organization.
2. Spontaneous demonstration: demonstrations without formal organization.
3. Organized riot: rioting organized by a formal group or organization.
4. Spontaneous riot: rioting without formal organization.
5. General strike: a labor strike affecting many industries or sectors.
6. Limited strike: a labor strike limited to a single industry or sector.
7. Pro-government violence: repression initiated by government actors or violence in support of the government.
8. Antigovernment violence: violence against government targets by permanent or semi-permanent militias.
9. Extragovernment violence: violence involving at least one permanent or semi-permanent militia group. Government forces are not included as an actor or a target (e.g., communal conflict).
10. Intragovernment violence: fighting between two armed factions within the government (e.g., mutinies or coups).

I use their data on governmental responses to these events, which are coded as no response, nonlethal response, and lethal response.

7. These data are found at http://strausscenter.org/acled.html. There are eight types of events ACLED data cover. These are the types of military battles in which 1) government forces gain an advantage; 2) rebel forces gain an advantage; and 3) neither side gains an advantage; 4) headquarters or base establishment; 5) nonviolent conflict event; 6) rioting and protesting; 7) violence against civilians; and 8) nonviolent transfer of location control. I utilize all but event types 6 and 7, as they involve events already counted in the SCAD data.

8. See the Human Rights Watch report for 2015, found at https://www.hrw.org/world-report/2015/country-chapters/central-african-republic.

9. Kenya does experience human insecurity as a result of terrorist activity by the Shahab group in Somalia, which has targeted Kenyans for their government's deployment of troops in Somalia to help bring an end to that country's violence.

10. See the Human Rights Watch report for 2015, found at https://www.hrw.org/world-report/2015/country-chapters/cote-divoire.

# *Chapter 4*

# Peace, Human Security, and International Justice

## INTRODUCTION

The international tribunals were all charged with advancing peace. Indeed, because the first two tribunals—the ICTY[1] and ICTR[2]—were established under the United Nations Security Council mandate to provide for global peace and security, this goal was a fundamental part of their institutional DNA. The Security Council found that the situation in the former Yugoslavia constituted "a threat to international peace and security" and asserted that the establishment of the tribunal was intended to "contribute to the restoration and maintenance of peace."

The SCSL and the ICC were no less designed with the aim of helping to reduce violence in the world. That the tribunals have all been given this mission there is no doubt. What has left observers of the courts puzzled and scratching their heads is how these institutions are to advance peace. Because their powers are strictly judicial, how are they supposed to influence politics in nations hundreds or thousands of miles away?

We must embark on a journey to answer this question and several related questions. First, we must determine what tools the tribunals have that might be used to advance the cause of peace. There is agreement that the tribunals have no direct tools that give them some influence in the conflicts they investigate. They have no military or police force to keep the peace. They have no direct role to play in conflict mediation or arbitration. In fact, courts are supposed to stay out of that sort of political business for fear that it may damage their reputation for impartiality and independence. They are not free to offer amnesties to the accused, even though many believe they are needed to keep suspected war criminals from refusing to negotiate and continuing the war.

Just the opposite. The tribunals often protest when it appears such deals may be in the works, as happened in the cases of Charles Taylor and the SCSL and Slobodan Milošević and the ICTY. What, then, do these tribunals have, you must be wondering?

They do have their other missions—providing justice, developing a historical record, and the deterrence of other would-be war criminals. We can trace a linkage between these objectives and the promotion of peace. It is not always straightforward or supported by the evidence, but we can evaluate the case that the international criminal tribunals can help advance peace or reduce the likelihood or occurrence of violence through the achievement of their other missions. The first part of this chapter describes these arguments in greater detail. The reader should be clear, however, that we do not always find that the tribunals have achieved these other objectives, which makes the possibility of advancing peace all the more difficult. Nor do all those scholars and lawyers who study and work in the tribunals accept the notion that the tribunals can affect peace even if they do achieve justice, create a historical record, and advance deterrence of would-be war criminals (Mendeloff 2004).

In the second part of the chapter I look at the relationship between international justice and the occurrence of conflict. We first take a largely descriptive approach to evaluating whether the ICTY, the ICTR, and the SCSL helped bring about peace in the nations over which they exercised jurisdiction. Then we take a more quantitative and statistical approach to analyzing the impact of the ICC on conflict the world over. Here there has been a growing body of research that can help us answer this question. The key, however, will be the analyses that I conduct to assess the record of the ICC. If international justice really does play an important role in advancing human security, we should have a much clearer picture of its role by the end of this chapter.

## INTERNATIONAL JUSTICE AND PEACE: HOW DO THE LINKAGES WORK?

As we discussed in chapter 2, the principal mission of international courts is to deliver justice. The provision of justice is intended to create a sense of closure and satisfaction to the victims of those prosecuted. By finding war criminals guilty beyond a reasonable doubt, the tribunals rebalance the scales of justice, thereby providing truth, retribution, and acknowledgment of the suffering of victims. But how exactly does this work? How does the truth as revealed in a courtroom in The Hague lead to peace in Bosnia or the Congo?

Justice is intended to help lead to peace because it provides an alternative to violence. The courtroom is not only a place where the truth of the matter comes out; it also comes out in a solemn and formal manner. The objectivity, formality, solemnity, and even the dress of the participants, with their judicial robes, is intended to convey just the opposite of the battlefield, where passions are high and where, in the case of the crimes before international tribunals, there have been no rules. The courtroom favors the smart and the articulate. The process of adjudication then strips the emotions and the violence out of politics (some might say too much so!) in favor of logic and evidence. It is the triumph of brains over brawn. By acting as a substitute for the violent politics of the battlefield, the courtroom creates an equivalency where the weak and those victimized by war literally have their day in court. In a very strict sense, justice is meant to provide an alternative means of dispute resolution. The problem is that justice only enters the picture after the fighting has commenced. The horse is already out of the barn by the time the accused take their place in the courtroom. Who, then, is the intended recipient of the message that justice has triumphed over violence?

The intended recipient is not just the people of the present, but is also the people of the future. In particular, the targets of this message are the leaders and the schemers huddling in their dark corners who may believe the time for violence and destruction is at hand again. They must believe that justice will be done again if more crimes are committed. But these tribunals are especially intended to demonstrate to the affected peoples that justice has been done to those who were the organizers, the instigators, and the perpetrators of violence so that they will perceive less of a need to blame all those who are members of the ethnic groups they have fought in the past. Because it is a natural human tendency to view the world in terms of those who belong to one's familial groups and ethnic, religious, or political groups and those who are "the other" and are not part of one's ties, individuals and governments alike often use these other groups as scapegoats for their society's ills. Or the narrative that develops to explain the events of the past magnifies the crimes of the other while minimizing or denying one's own group's inhumane actions. By providing justice that clearly and beyond a reasonable doubt establishes who bears responsibility for international crimes, the tribunals can undermine and potentially counteract these "us versus them" narratives that often set the stage for future conflict. The tribunals and their justice represent the insistence on the individualization of guilt, not the collectivization of blame. The tribunals must hope, however, that their more subtle and logical explanations and verdicts trump the emotional narratives offered by political and military leaders much closer to home. This is no easy task.

The tribunals must often counter very powerful and long-held beliefs. The narratives that groups of people pass down are not generally stories in which their group is the aggressor or their people are the ones to blame for the suffering of others. Rather, one finds in the version of events as told by the people like Croatians, Serbs, Bosnian Muslims, and Tutsis (to say nothing of the Turks regarding the Armenian genocide or the Japanese regarding their full responsibility for the crimes committed in East Asia during World War II) a very powerful narrative of victimization and martyrdom. Such narratives contrast the group's sacrifices and pain with a lack of acknowledgment and appreciation from an unsympathetic world, which then makes it all the more important for the group to band together to protect themselves against their adversary in the face of an indifferent world. These narratives are reinforced, sometimes to the exclusion of historical truth, by nationalist governments, xenophobic political parties, and military establishments that committed atrocities (Ford 2012).

Providing a counter-narrative for these people to demonstrate that their leaders have been exaggerating and lying about the past and that impartial judges sitting in a distant court have discovered the truth is the key. The tribunals have their outreach offices to publicize their work. They have the power of the Internet to publish their verdicts, the compelling videos of atrocities, and the powerful testimony of the witnesses and those who confess their crimes. They often have the support, or at least the voices, of human rights organizations, both local and international, that can amplify word of the verdicts and sentences of the tribunals so that more people become aware of their accomplishments. Not all groups in a society will accept these truths, but the tribunals may be able to focus on those who have not developed hardened attitudes, such as the youth, the diaspora populations returning to their homes, and others who have been themselves victimized by their own nationalist governments and political parties. Establishing justice and convincing audiences that just and fair decisions have been made is an arduous and ongoing battle, but it is perhaps the most fundamental way in which tribunals can contribute to peace.

There is a healthy debate about whether providing truth and justice can have any measureable impact in these deeply divided societies. Some scholars have found and many advocates believe that international trials can help produce a historical record and provide truth to the victims (Drumbl 2007; Neier 1999; Roht-Arriaza and Mariezcurrena 2006; Sloane 2007). Wilson (2005, 909) argues that the historical records developed by international tribunals generally "challenge the long-held assumption in sociolegal scholarship that courts are inappropriate venues to construct wide-ranging historical explanations of past conflicts." Staub (2013, 584–85) argues that "effective justice processes inherently acknowledge people's suffering, increase feelings of security as the world says that what was done is unacceptable, and recreate some balance in group relations after victimization diminishes a group." On the other hand, Clark takes a much more critical view of the prospects for truth bringing peace and reconciliation. She writes (2011, 257), "the denial of truth breeds resentment, anger and frustration, and thus obstructs the reconciliation process. It does not, however, either support or undermine the notion that disclosure and acknowledgment of the truth aid the reconciliation process."

Ultimately, these "conversions" to the truth may take time, as it did in Germany to fully come to grips with the horrors of the Nazi regime. It may only be after the tribunals conclude their trials and the contentious debates over allegations of "bias" and the fairness of verdicts end that individuals can begin to more easily hear and appreciate the "truth." We can never be certain when or how the truth will become known, and even less so understand just how the "truth" contributes to peace. But through the use of evidence and analysis, we can ourselves judge the truth of this purported connection between the truth of international justice and peace.

Lastly, the tribunals are intended to advance peace through deterrence. By demonstrating that those responsible for war crimes, crimes against humanity, and genocide will be held accountable, the tribunals are supposed to chip away at the perception that there is impunity for such crimes. The statute of the ICTY proclaims that the "establishment of an international tribunal and the prosecution of persons responsible for the above-mentioned violations of international humanitarian law *will contribute to ensuring that such violations are halted* and effectively redressed" (emphasis added).[3] Immediate or specific deterrence is achieved when those who are accused of violations of international law are brought to justice to prevent them from committing such crimes again. If the tribunals can, through the powerful and vivid evidence they accumulate, encourage the powers that be in world politics that the masterminds and ringleaders of the violence they are investigating and prosecuting are a hindrance to peace, this spur to action may also further the cause of peace.

If the tribunals can also serve as a warning to other would-be war criminals of the consequences of their actions (the general deterrence we talked about in the last chapter), they can also move the world in a more peaceful direction. Some might argue that the tribunals should be able to deter crime just like the punishments handed down in domestic courts are supposed to discourage us from breaking the law. Yet even if the tribunals were made to function more like domestic courts, their decisions may not have the intended impact on politicians and generals who perceive themselves as above the law. Their effect on subordinates who know little and care less about the actions of these international tribunals and who place their trust in superiors with the power of life and death is likely even less. It is worth emphasizing again, however, that while this message of deterrence may not be received by all because there are many hardened racist and nationalist leaders who could care less about international courts, it may be received by some. Just like there are hardened criminals who are impervious to the threat of imprisonment, the world has its share of hardcore fanatics, as well as its share of leaders dedicated to doing the right thing. The task of international justice may be to reach those who are sitting on the fence and trying to decide which of these two groups to throw in their lot with. Changing their perceptions and their decision calculus seems quite feasible. What does the evidence suggest?

## INTERNATIONAL JUSTICE AND PEACE: WHAT IS THE EVIDENCE OF IMPACT? THE ICTY

The ICTY was established as fighting raged in Bosnia-Herzegovina in May 1993. The fact of its existence did not stop the war, nor did it stop any of the atrocities that came after the tribunal began to conduct its affairs in The Hague. Quite the contrary. At about the same time as its creation, the war in Bosnia expanded as Bosnian Muslims and Bosnian Croats began fighting one another in the west around the city of Mostar. The Srebrenica genocide in July 1995 took place after the establishment of the ICTY, as did the Croatian Operation Storm that recaptured Croatian lands held by Croatian Serbs. The crimes that had begun in 1992 in Bosnia, such as the shelling and sniping in Sarajevo and the ethnic cleansing in eastern Bosnia, continued. If the United Nations Security Council believed its experiment in international justice would cause the combatants to lay down their arms, they were sadly mistaken. It is doubtful that even the most ardent supporters of the ICTY entertained such ideas. Nonetheless, it is telling that some of the worst crimes of the war came after the tribunal was established with its threat of prosecution. Strike one against international justice.

More troubling than the continuation of some crimes and the escalation of others was the beginning of another war in the former Yugoslavia in 1998 and 1999 in the Serbian province of Kosovo. Kosovo is home to a population that was 90 percent ethnic Albanian and Muslim and 10 percent Serb. Yet it is a region that had deep historical significance in Serbian history as the site of an ill-fated battle, Kosovo Polje, in which the Serbs fought against the Ottoman Turks and lost. Out of the ashes of defeat the Serbs began crafting their narrative as defenders and martyrs of the Christian faith. Slobodan Milošević had made an early assertion of his desire to foment Serb nationalism with a fiery speech on the six hundredth anniversary of that battle in 1989 and had begun consolidating power through the exploitation of nationalism and Serb fears of their Muslim countrymen. Kosovar Albanians had chafed under Milošević's increasingly authoritarian rule and a Kosovar Liberation Army was built up in the late 1990s that began to challenge Milošević and the Serb security forces. Their fighters accomplished little and were dwarfed by the Serb army. They were provocation enough, however, for Slobodan Milošević, who instigated his third (counting Croatia in 1991 and 1992 and Bosnia in 1992 through 1995) major war in the former Yugoslavia.

By 1999, the ICTY was firmly established, and while its most notorious suspects were still at large, it had held several trials and was beginning to gain support from international and national forces to arrest those individuals under indictment. One could have been forgiven for thinking the ICTY would never get off the ground from 1993 to 1995, but not so by early 1999, when the fighting began in earnest in Kosovo. The international community also understood the risks of standing idly by while the region was engulfed in another war and understood quite well the potential for human rights atrocities. Nonetheless, Milošević was not deterred from launching this war and driving hundreds of thousands of Kosovar Albanians from their homes. Not even the bombardment of his military and other targets by NATO forces led by the United States stopped him at first. It took three months of such bombing to finally bring about an end to the violence.

So what does this tell us about the ICTY's contribution to peace? Clearly, despite its existence, the violence continued and escalated in Bosnia and Croatia and new violence began in Kosovo. By this measure, international justice did not succeed. Its example did not deter any of those leaders who were motivated by nationalist designs. Politics trumped justice. While justice may have failed to deter the violence, it is important to emphasize that even the *threat* of force by the world's dominant power, the United States, and its European allies in NATO did not succeed. There had been the occasional, if insignificant, use of force in Bosnia and an increasing threat of force in the summer of 1995 by the United States and NATO. The actual use of NATO airpower in September 1995 and the renewal of violence by Croatia against Croatian Serbs in the summer of 1995 was required to stop the Bosnian war and force the parties to the negotiating table for the Dayton Peace Accords. After learning their lesson that superior force was required to deter and stop Milošević and the other Serb nationalists, the United States and NATO made it quite clear that there would be military retaliation if Milošević did not stop the ethnic cleansing and violence in Kosovo. It took three months of sustained aerial bombardment by NATO in 1999 to bring Milošević to heel. The price for ending the violence and stopping the atrocities seems to have been beyond what the ICTY was equipped to do. It took sustained and heavy aerial bombardment to do the work.

I should point out, however, that some scholars (Dijxhoorn 2014) have suggested that the ICTY indictment of Slobodan Milošević did help encourage him to finally give in to NATO demands and stop the violence. Dijxhoorn argues that the indictment was really the final and decisive nail in the coffin that not only reduced his international stature, but also seriously eroded his legitimacy at home. Milošević may have thought that his capitulation could stave off the drive to prosecute him, especially given the international community's long record of treating him as a partner for building peace rather than as a spoiler for war. If so, he was sadly mistaken. If this account is true, it does suggest that these international indictments can tip the balance in favor of peace and justice, especially for those leaders who still care about their reputation at home and abroad.

The lessons of the ICTY and the former Yugoslavia in the 1990s are very instructive. They demonstrate that international justice may be no match for strong-willed leaders with intense political preferences or ideologies who owe their positions to their implacable opposition to domestic adversaries (Clark 2014). Indeed, their unyielding stance toward the international community in general and the ICTY in particular helped to further solidify their power. International justice not only cannot bring peace until such diehard nationalist leaders have been vanquished on the battlefield or removed from positions of influence, but they also cannot accomplish their principal mission of holding such leaders accountable until that time. The greater the leaders' drive to realize their aims regardless of the amount of human suffering they cause, the lesser the likelihood any measure short of all-out war to stop them will succeed.

It is helpful to think about these effects of international justice as occurring in a two-dimensional space. Along the bottom or horizontal line is the level of domestic violence and repression leaders in a particular country would be willing to resort to in order to achieve their political objectives, no matter what those goals may be. At the left end are those leaders of states that would never entertain such ambitions, but rule peacefully and inclusively, such as in democracies like Canada and the Netherlands. At the other extreme are those leaders who would stop at nothing to realize their ambitions. Think of Adolf Hitler. For the former group of states, there is no need to deter their leaders—violent nationalism is abhorrent to them and their societies. They are peace-loving peoples. For the latter group, there is little hope that international justice, or anything else for that matter, will deter them. They are so committed to their goals and the use of whatever means seem necessary to maintain power that the abstract threat of international justice is not likely to register in their minds. It is really the group in the middle that is most susceptible to demands that they stop their violence or that they should never resort to violence. They might consider using violence and repression to achieve their goals, but they would rather remain in power without the use of violence. They are flexible enough in their tactics and desire for power that they will select the option—repression or negotiation—that would more likely keep them in power at the least cost. These leaders can be deterred under the right circumstances.

It is also clear, as we have examined the evidence of the impact of international justice on peace and human security, that international justice works best when it is paired with the threat of retaliation by the international community. The threat of prosecution may discourage them to a degree from using violence. But when justice is coupled with the threat of international military retaliation, or perhaps severe economic sanctions, they may choose negotiation over violence. The combination of both moves the dial on their decision making to convince them that peace is the preferred alternative for maintaining power.

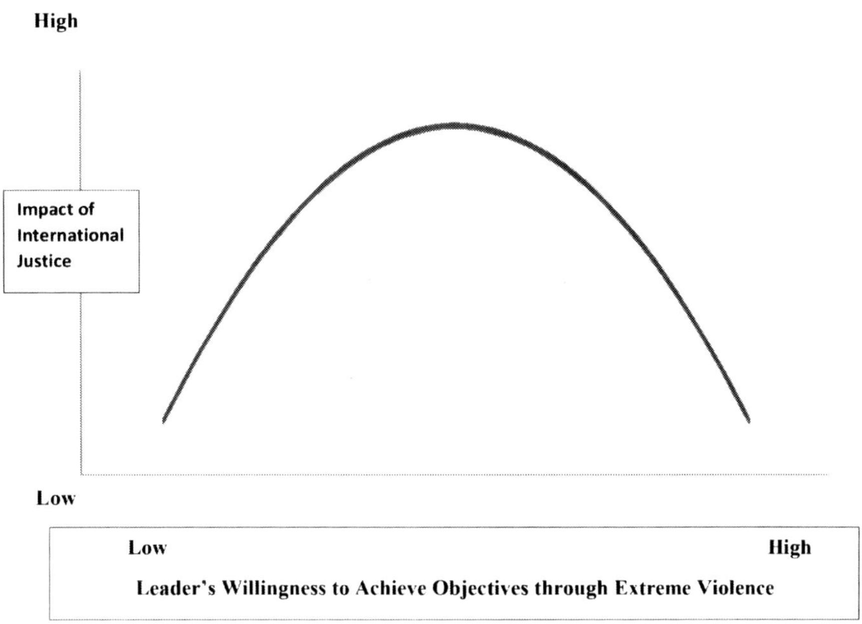


**Figure 4.1** Justice and Leaders' Willingness to Use Violence. *Source: Author.*

## THE ICTR AND THE SCSL

The impact of the ICTR and the SCSL on peace and conflict in their respective target nations is also quite clear in one sense. We know in the case of Rwanda that it was the Tutsi-led Rwandan Patriotic Army that defeated the extremist Hutu government and took power in July 1994, several months before the ICTR was created. Rwanda has, for the most part, been at peace internally ever since. Rwanda's problems with peace have been mostly related to its military actions in its neighborhood of the Great Lakes region of Central Africa, and especially its invasions of the Congo. After the RPA drove out the Hutu extremists and their militia, the Interahamwe, from Rwanda in 1994, hundreds of thousands of Hutus took refuge in neighboring states, but especially eastern Congo (Zaire as it was known then), fearing Tutsi reprisal. From their safe haven in eastern Zaire, the Hutu extremists continued to wage war against the Tutsi government and repeatedly infiltrated Rwanda. After months of such attacks and the absence of an international effort to deal with the Hutu extremists, the Rwandan government, its allies in the east of Zaire, and the government of Uganda began attacking the Hutu rebels and the Zairean army, which had been allied with the Hutu to some extent, to confront the extremists. This military campaign eventually brought about the collapse of the Zairean government, led by longtime dictator Joseph Mobutu. For years after that first invasion of Zaire in 1996, the Rwandan government has either kept forces in eastern Congo or has relied on its proxies, the various militias that have sprung up in the power vacuum in the region, to guard against a Hutu resurgence. At the same time, however, these same Rwandan and Ugandan government forces, as well as the forces of other African governments and the many local militias, continued to do battle for many years to control territory, people, and especially the rich natural resources of the region. The fighting and the destruction are not nearly so bad now, but the militias and warlords are still powerful and the UN peacekeeping force has often been unable to stop them. So while Rwanda itself has been peaceful, its neighborhood has been anything but calm (see Prunier 2011 for a thorough history of the conflicts in Central Africa).

Not surprisingly, the ICTR has not played a significant role in stopping the violence in Central Africa. Indeed, its jurisdiction is only over events that occurred in Rwanda in 1994. Despite the apprehension of the most important ringleaders of the genocide, who have stood trial at the ICTR, other Hutu extremist leaders have stepped forward to continue the fight in the Congo and occasionally inside Rwanda. These extremists have not been deterred by international justice or even by a decisive military defeat in Rwanda and a pretty severe beating in the Congo. Even the presence of a UN peacekeeping force has mostly failed to stop the violence in the eastern Congo. The ICTR provided justice for Rwanda, not Central Africa, after peace had been won. By indicting and securing the apprehension of the ringleaders of the Rwandan genocide, the ICTR has helped ensure that those individuals would not play a role in undermining the peace. The Rwandan government has ultimately been the party responsible for peace in Rwanda. Its total military victory established peace in Rwanda, just as the total victory of the allies in World War II established peace in Europe.

The same largely holds true for the Special Court for Sierra Leone. The SCSL was established just as the civil war ended, and thus its peace-facilitating mission was largely moot. Civil war violence has not started anew and, as I showed in chapter 3, human rights have been improving in Sierra Leone. Sierra Leone has been accorded a great deal of attention during and after the civil war by the United Nations, the British, and the many NGOs that have sought to help the country and its people repair their society since the atrocities of the civil war. To be sure, the SCSL has been a substantial part of this effort and its evenhanded justice that prosecuted all sides to the conflict has aided in truth telling and the construction of an accurate historical record. The SCSL also had a fairly effective outreach effort to take the story of its work and accomplishments to the people of Sierra Leone. Nonetheless, the outbreak of peace in Sierra Leone is what we call *overdetermined.* It is a child of many fathers, including local actors and international ones like the United Nations and the British. Therefore, we cannot say for certain that the SCSL has played a substantial role in sustaining the peace, only that justice has played a role in bringing peace to that troubled land along with a great deal of other efforts.

I would suspect that most diplomats and scholars would agree that the struggle for peace must be waged and won on many fronts. No one peacekeeping tool is sufficient. Peace may require military intervention to stop the fighting or to at least separate the warring sides and keep them in their corners. Peace requires reconstruction and economic development and the jobs such work brings. Peace requires responsible politics and well-intentioned leaders who place a higher value on keeping nationalism and racism out of politics than using them to exploit people's fears, and who govern for the good of the country. And peace does require justice. It requires a reckoning and confrontation with the past that only some type of justice that acknowledges the guilty and the suffering can provide. Justice does its part and may well be a necessary, although not sufficient, condition for peace in many conflicts. What this evidence has shown us is that justice standing alone cannot do the job. Its power is too soft. It must be backed by and stand along with nations that possess the hard power necessary to put an end to violence.

Peacebuilding is a holistic process in which justice contributes to a concerted effort to not only stop the fighting (what we would call "negative peace" or an absence of violence), but also address the root causes of violence to promote a "positive peace."

## THE ICC AND CONFLICT

The ad hoc tribunals, with their jurisdiction limited both in time and space, were focused on conflicts in a specific set of nations. Because of these restrictions, their ability to influence peace and human security in other parts of the globe was necessarily limited. The International Criminal Court, with its global jurisdiction, is intended to set a global example and provide justice that, in theory, should influence conflict actors among all the states that have signed on to the ICC treaty. The Rome Statute provides that the ICC has jurisdiction over situations in which 1) the state in which an alleged crime takes place is a party to the treaty; 2) the suspect(s) is a national of a state that is a party to the treaty; or 3) the case is referred to it by the United Nations Security Council. In addition to referral by the Security Council, the mechanisms by which the court may take jurisdiction over a conflict situation occur when 1) states that have ratified the Treaty of Rome refer situations meeting the first or second criteria above or 2) the prosecutor initiates an investigation on his or her own initiative (*proprio motu*) that meet the first or second criteria above.[4] Perhaps the most critical and controversial of the ICC's powers is the authority of the prosecutor to launch his or her own investigations with judicial approval.[5] This opens up the possibility that any one of the 120-plus states party to the treaty could be investigated and those most responsible for violations of the relevant international law brought before the ICC. Furthermore, the UN Security Council's power to refer cases to the ICC makes it theoretically possible that any state in the world could be investigated. Surely, if any tribunal could advance human rights it would be the powerful ICC.

Not so fast, say the critics. The ICC, like its sister international courts, is only as powerful as the world's major powers want it to be. And just like those other tribunals, the ICC must rely on international organizations and national police forces to arrest suspects. How can it accomplish anything that states, especially the most powerful ones, do not already have an interest in doing? In other words, is the ICC truly and independently powerful or must it rely on the kindness of states to do its job? Furthermore, critics argue, by meddling in ongoing, complicated, and violent conflicts, the ICC risks doing more harm than good. What rebel leader or government president, believing he or she is in the right and is going to win the struggle for power, will lay down his or her arms and let this distant court with its arcane rules and Western values dictate who is to be prosecuted and who is to be left alone? The price of justice might well be the cost of continued war. Indeed, some military commanders or militia warlords might even double down on their strategies of ethnic cleansing or indiscriminate violence if they feel backed into a corner by an international court. Leaders who are convinced they are in the right would seem to have very little incentive to surrender to the ICC. As a perceptive reader, you will no doubt realize, however, that these are all just educated guesses about what unpredictable humans might do. What does the record say? Has ICC involvement furthered the cause of justice or made things worse? We are beginning to see more research seeking to address this issue.

My colleague Mike Greig and I decided to investigate this question and looked at what happens to efforts at mediation—essentially attempts at negotiating peace—after the ICC has either launched an investigation or issued indictments regarding major human rights abuses (Greig and Meernik 2014). If supporters of international justice are correct, ICC involvement should increase the chances for peace by demonstrating that conflict resolution, rather than conflict escalation, is the better strategy. Conflict mediation should prove more attractive than continuing violence if conflict leaders are convinced that the court and its supporters are serious about ending violence. If the critics are right, we should find that when the ICC launches an investigation into a conflict, the parties may well withdraw from negotiation, perhaps for fear that by showing up to negotiate they might be arrested. At worst, one or more of the parties to the conflict may ramp up the violence, figuring they have nothing left to lose. Others may decide to increase violence to show how powerful they are in advance of negotiations, thereby hoping to get a better deal. The record actually seems to suggest a little of each. When the ICC has launched an investigation into one of the nine conflict situations that now comprise its caseload, there have been reduced chances for conflict mediation. After an investigation is initiated, parties to a conflict are less likely to enter into negotiations. However, when the ICC issues indictments as a result of such investigations, we tend to see an increase in the likelihood of mediation. How do we explain this apparent contradiction?

We can only offer an interpretation at this point and not solid evidence, but this story has an element of plausibility. It may be that when individuals first discover they are being investigated by the ICC their response is to take whatever steps are necessary to preserve their authority and throw down the gauntlet to the international community. The ICC investigation represents a threat to their continued power and freedom. They may believe that rather than seek conflict mediation, they should demonstrate their righteous indignation at being indicted by the ICC (and perhaps in their minds the Western powers that back the ICC). Refusing mediation or withdrawing from negotiation and returning to the battlefield could be a way of communicating their resolve—the high price the world will have to pay for a peace agreement. To do otherwise may, they believe, communicate weakness to their allies and their adversaries. On the other hand, if the ICC has indicted them, at that point they may believe it would be better to strike a deal in the present while negotiations are still open. Leaders may believe that the ICC and the international community are resolved to confront them and that they had better strike the best deal possible. At a minimum, such individuals may believe that they can get a better deal in the long run by demonstrating their desire for peace and by showing they are indispensable players in such mediation efforts.

There is more to the ICC story, however, than just its ability to influence events and mediation efforts in those states that have been targeted for investigation. We can also study how the ICC has influenced the behavior of all states that are parties to its treaties. Have the states that have signed and ratified the treaty engaged in less conflictual behavior? How does their record of involvement in civil wars and international wars compare to those nations that have not signed on to the Rome Statute? Some researchers have now begun to study this question and, quite interestingly, they have often found positive results!

Jo and Simmons (forthcoming) argue that governments that have ratified the ICC treaty should engage in less violence against civilians, while those states that have been involved in civil wars in their recent history should experience fewer civilian deaths during wartime. Because of the threat of prosecution and the need to live up to the provisions of the treaty, these leaders may pay a political price at home if they act contrary to international law. Such leaders may fear losing power in elections or through some other method. Jo and Simmons also argue that rebel groups should face similar costs if they engage in actions that run afoul of international law and that this will lead them to be more restrictive and careful in how they fight. Their results largely support these hypotheses and so they conclude that there is evidence to suggest that ratification of the ICC treaty has helped reduce the level of conflict among the signatory states.

Other research, however, has emphasized that many armies and rebel movements have a built-in interest in violating international law by attacking innocent civilians. Valentino, Huth, and Croco (2006, 340) argue that such violence is a "calculated military strategy designed to achieve victory by coercing the adversary or by undermining the war-related productive capacity of his civilian population." Governments and rebels may also commit such acts of violence when they are too weak to obtain victory on the battlefield, and as a means for demonstrating resolve (Hultman 2009). Cronin-Furman argues that "an analysis of empirical explanations of violence against civilians suggests that the cost-benefit calculations of commanders who affirmatively order mass atrocity are likely already to involve overriding benefits for and strong disincentives against the commission of atrocity crimes. Thus, the risk of prosecution and punishment is not likely to change their decision-making calculus." David (2014) argues that only when ethnic groups see their own leaders being punished for violating human rights will their leaders stop such abuses.

This question has fascinated me for quite some time and so I embarked on my own analysis of the ICC and conflict. While my arguments were similar to Jo and Simmons's hypotheses, I also predicted that the ICC would be most influential in improving human rights and reducing conflict in those states that had ratified the ICC treaty and were also committed to the domestic and international rule of law. Because we should maintain a healthy skepticism about why states sign treaties because many nations do so merely to look good to other countries, we must look to other evidence of commitment to the ICC beyond ratification of the treaty. I argue that if states take certain steps to implement the rule of law in their countries and support the ICC by agreeing to respect the privileges and immunities of ICC personnel in their nations (as all diplomats typically enjoy) and do not reach agreements with the United States to refuse to extradite U.S. citizens to the ICC to stand trial, this greater commitment to the ICC should reduce conflict. The hypotheses were generally supported—states that were strong supporters of the rule of law at home and supported the ICC were less likely to experience civil and ethnic violence and had better human rights records. These initial findings provide some grounds for hope and optimism that the International Criminal Court may be encouraging behavior that is more respectful of human rights and international law.

## TESTING THE ICC'S IMPACT ON PEACE

There are still many questions to explore, however, about the ICC's influence on peace in the world. To do so we will need to engage in a bit of statistical analysis ourselves. Many people who are interested in questions of international justice, like me when I began studying international relations, are not trained in the use of these statistical models. I hope my explanations of how these statistics work will be as good as those of the professor who taught me!

The first step is to give a brief introduction to the data we are using. We will be looking at whether states that have signed and ratified the ICC treaty have been more or less likely to engage in international conflict and civil war since the ICC came into force in 2002. The data we will be using come from the Major Episodes of Political Violence database. I look at both nations' involvement in civil war and conflict as well as their participation in international war. For civil war, I specifically use a ten-value measure of the "total summed magnitudes of all societal major episodes of political violence, including civil and ethnic conflict."[6] To measure state involvement in international conflict, I use information from the same dataset. The variable I use is also a cumulative (the data count the number of wars in which a state is involved) measure of all instances of state involvement in international war in a given year. We will also examine the impact of the ICC on the number of battle casualties for those states that have been involved in some type of civil war or international conflict. Lastly, we will look at whether participation in the ICC helps improve state protection of human rights. We should expect to find that states that have signed and ratified the ICC treaty will be less likely to be involved in civil or international wars, but also experience fewer battle deaths when they are involved in conflict and have better human rights records. If the ICC does not influence state behavior, then we should find that there is no statistically significant relationship between being a state party and conflict.

I use two variables to measure the impact of the ICC. First, I use a very simple measure of whether a state has signed and ratified the ICC treaty. I also use a measure of support for international law. To measure state commitment to the ICC, I developed a variable that ranges from "0" to "3," with higher values indicating a greater commitment to the ICC. States were given one point each for 1) enacting domestic legislation to implement the ICC treaty;[7] 2) ratifying the Agreement on Privileges and Immunities[8] for ICC personnel when they are in foreign countries (this ensures that ICC personnel can do their job investigating conflict situations without fear of harassment or arrest); and 3) *not* reaching a Bilateral Immunity Agreement with the United States (these agreements protect U.S. soldiers from being arrested by foreign governments and sent to the ICC for violating international law, but they are viewed as a way for the United States to use its influence in other countries to escape the consequences of any illegal activities its troops may commit).[9]

I also use several variables that are typically employed in studies of conflict to develop an accurate and thorough model of state conflict behavior. First, we will use a variable measuring how democratic states are. These data come from the Polity IV database that measures levels of democracy for all countries of the world going back many decades. The democracy variable is measured on a scale ranging from "–10" for the least democratic states to "10" for the most democratic states.[10] It is possible that democracy is driving many of these results. That is, states that are more democratic are more likely to sign the ICC treaty and to take the other steps I described above to support the court. If this is the case, then it would be that level of democracy is really responsible for encouraging good state behavior and that the ICC does not have an impact that is independent of democracy.

It is also important to take into consideration the impact of ethnicity and ethnic divisions in a society and their relationship to conflict. For this I use data from the Ethnic Power Relations dataset to measure the potential for ethnic conflict by employing a variable that is the natural log (a mathematical procedure designed to reduce the influence of outlier or extreme cases) of the share of the excluded population relative to the ethnopolitically relevant population. This is a somewhat complicated measure, but the reader only needs to know that it measures the potential for ethnically driven violence. I include a measure of a state's per capita gross national product and its urban population from the World Bank's World Development Indicators database.[11] These measures of development may also be what are really driving state commitment to peace and justice. Rich countries do so because they can afford not to fight, while poor countries may be left to struggle for themselves. I also include a variable measuring the number of states bordering each country as an indicator of the potential for conflict, and especially for civil wars to bleed over into other states. Because wealthy democratic states tend to not be involved in most wars, I include a measure for those as well and count those nations that are members of the Organization for Economic Cooperation and Development (OECD).[12]

**Table 4.1 Explaining State Involvement in Internal Wars**

| Variable | Coefficient | Standard Error | *T* Statistic | *P* Value |
|---|---|---|---|---|
| Democracy Rating | 0.047 | 0.010 | 4.840 | 0.000 |
| GDP Per Capita | 0.000 | 0.000 | 4.220 | 0.000 |
| Urban Population | –0.010 | 0.002 | –4.770 | 0.000 |
| Ethnicity | 0.122 | 0.026 | 4.690 | 0.000 |
| Number of Borders | 0.088 | 0.021 | 4.190 | 0.000 |
| ICC State | –0.384 | 0.112 | –3.420 | 0.001 |
| OECD State | –0.210 | 0.082 | –2.550 | 0.011 |
| Support for ICC | –0.314 | 0.051 | –6.120 | 0.000 |
| Constant | 0.655 | 0.156 | 4.200 | 0.000 |

Number of observations = 1,068

The first set of results we examine in table 4.1 are those for the level of violence within a country to determine if the International Criminal Court has had any noticeable effect on the frequency of such violence. The data on civil wars come from the Major Episodes of Political Violence database. This variable is coded on a ten-point scale that includes the "total summed magnitudes of all societal major episodes of political violence," including civil and ethnic conflict. It is a summative measure that ranges between 0 and 9.[13] The results strongly support this prediction. Those states that have signed onto the Rome Statute are statistically less likely than non-signatory states to experience higher levels of internal violence. In these types of analyses, to determine if a variable has a statistically significant impact we look to one indicator in particular. The lower the *p* or probability value, the less likely it is that the cause of a relationship between the independent and the dependent variable is due to chance. Here we see that the *p* value for the ICC states variable is 0.001. This means that the probability that chance was the cause of the relationship we see between ratification of the ICC treaty and internal violence is one in ten thousand. This gives us a great deal of confidence that states that have signed and ratified the ICC treaty are less likely to experience such violence than states that have not signed the treaty. Therefore, we tend to accept our hypothesis that ICC membership reduces internal violence.

The next step in interpreting the results is to examine the coefficient for the ICC states party variable to understand the size of the impact. The coefficient tells us the impact of a variable on a unit change in the dependent variable, holding all other variables constant at the mean or average. Basically, this allows us to measure the effect of a variable while making sure that the impact of the variable we are interested in is not due to the influence of other variables. In this case the coefficient for the ICC states party variable is –0.384. This means that ICC states experience 0.384 fewer units of violence than non-state parties to the treaty. What in the world does this mean, you are probably wondering right now? What it means is that because the level of violence is measured on a 0 to 9 scale, with higher levels representing greater levels of violence, the states that have signed the ICC treaty experience almost half a unit less violence than states that do not sign. States that have signed and ratified the ICC treaty are more internally peaceful, but the effect is not huge. What other factors are helping us to explain such violence?

We also find that states that are strong supporters of the ICC internationally experience lower levels of internal violence. The coefficient for this variable is –0.314, which tells us that for every one-unit increase in the level of support for the ICC, there is a corresponding decrease of 0.314 units of internal violence. You will recall that the ICC support variable is measured on a 0 to 3 scale, with higher levels indicating greater support for the ICC from states implementing the ICC treaty in their domestic law, refusing to sign non-surrender agreements with the United States, and granting ICC officials diplomatic privileges and immunities in their country. The highest score a nation can attain is "3" if they do all three. The states that score highest on the support measure experience the lowest levels of internal violence. Therefore, the results suggest that there is a benefit from signing the ICC treaty and supporting the court. There may well be a peaceful impact of international justice on the world. But before we reach any solid conclusions, we also need to examine the effects of the other variables in the model and think through any potential problems with how we are interpreting the results.

We do find a number of other factors that are related to conflict occurrence. Oddly enough, we see that more democratic and wealthier states are more likely to experience internal violence. At first, this finding would seem to be very counterintuitive and in contrast to what most of us would tend to believe—that democratic governments and nations with more wealth as measured by their per capita gross domestic product would be less likely to become embroiled in civil conflict. But there is likely something happening in these estimates that is not readily apparent, but makes sense once we think about it. The reader will notice that the sign for the coefficient for the variable for the OECD states is negative and statistically significant. The rich democratic states in Europe and elsewhere that belong to this group are not at all likely to experience civil war as we would expect. In effect, this variable captures the majority of the impact of wealth and democracy on war because it is coded "1" for these types of states. For all the other countries of the world, as they begin to increase their level of democracy and their national wealth, they become more at risk of war. The poor nations, and especially the countries presided over by dictators, which are not at all democratic, are unlikely to experience war because their dictators tolerate no opposition at all. The wealthy and democratic states also do not experience war because their peoples are largely satisfied. That leaves the countries in the middle—not dictatorships, but not democracies; not rich, but not too poor—that are most prone to violence. Those that are neither fish nor fowl, but some complex and risky combination of the two, are ripe for violence. In this case, the peaceful spot is not the middle of the continuum, but at either end of the spectrum.

We also see that countries with larger urban populations are less likely to experience war. Countries where there are more people living in rural areas are more prone to violence. As we would expect to find, the more borders with other countries a nation has, the more likely it will experience civil conflict. And countries that are more fractured along ethnic lines are more likely to experience violence. What do we find when we examine the impact of the ICC and these other factors on state involvement in international conflict?

**Table 4.2 Explaining State Involvement in International Wars**

| Variable | Coefficient | Standard Error | *T* Statistic | *P* Value |
|---|---|---|---|---|
| Democracy Rating | −0.001 | 0.003 | −0.280 | 0.779 |
| GDP Per Capita | 0.000 | 0.000 | −0.210 | 0.837 |
| Urban Population | 0.001 | 0.000 | 1.720 | 0.086 |
| Ethnicity | 0.008 | 0.005 | 1.370 | 0.170 |
| Number of Borders | 0.001 | 0.002 | 0.750 | 0.456 |
| ICC State | −0.016 | 0.010 | −1.530 | 0.126 |
| OECD State | −0.007 | 0.031 | −0.220 | 0.823 |
| Support for ICC | 0.001 | 0.010 | 0.140 | 0.886 |
| Constant | −0.034 | 0.019 | −1.720 | 0.085 |

Number of observations = 1,068

When we look at the impact of the International Criminal Court on the occurrence of international conflict in table 4.2, we do not find any evidence that either membership in the ICC or support for the ICC decreases state involvement in international war. The data on international wars also come from the Major Episodes of Political Violence database and provide us with the sum total of all episodes of international violence and war a state experiences per year.[14] The coefficients for both variables measuring ratification and support for the ICC are statistically insignificant, which means that whatever relationship we observe in the data is more likely due to chance. This is not altogether too surprising. We know that international wars are few and far between these days. Most conflicts are civil or internal wars, while wars between states do not occur with nearly the same frequency as they did before the end of the Cold War, and especially in the centuries leading up to World War II. What this means is that the event is relatively rare, so the likelihood that any particular factor will predict the occurrence of international war is pretty low. In fact, the reader will notice that none of the coefficients are statistically significant. The same set of variables that performed quite well when we analyzed levels of internal violence does not seem to be helpful in explaining the rare international wars.

Now let's turn our attention to the level of violence that results from war in table 4.3. We know that wars of all types are destructive of life and property. And we know that some wars are more violent and lead to more death than others. Is it also the case that those states that are party to the ICC treaty and those that support international justice are mindful of the destructiveness of

**Table 4.3 Explaining Battle Deaths in All War Types**

| Variable | Coefficient | Standard Error | *T* Statistic | *P* Value |
|---|---|---|---|---|
| Democracy Rating | 34.318 | 23.324 | 1.470 | 0.143 |
| GDP Per Capita | –0.030 | 0.027 | –1.100 | 0.271 |
| Urban Population | –10.895 | 9.150 | –1.190 | 0.236 |
| Ethnicity | 213.925 | 72.469 | 2.950 | 0.004 |
| Number of Borders | –26.799 | 32.929 | –0.810 | 0.417 |
| ICC State | –698.692 | 220.565 | –3.170 | 0.002 |
| OECD State | –464.387 | 127.932 | –3.630 | 0.000 |
| Support for ICC | –43.555 | 118.656 | –0.370 | 0.714 |
| Constant | 974.495 | 353.919 | 2.750 | 0.007 |

Number of observations = 167

war and so take steps to minimize the impact of the fighting? Do such states seek to reduce the occurrence of civilian casualties in order to avoid the loss of life and to avoid accusations of war crimes? In table 4.3, which looks at both military and civilian deaths resulting from battles in all types of wars,[15] we find that states that belong to the ICC tend to experience fewer casualties when they do become embroiled in any kind of war. The coefficient for the ICC membership variable is negative and statistically significant. We already saw that states that are party to the ICC treaty were less likely to be involved in internal wars. Now we know that such states, when they do experience war, tend to be involved in wars that result in fewer casualties. However, the coefficient for the variable measuring support for the ICC is not statistically significant.

Lastly, in table 4.4 we look again at human rights. For this analysis, I use the same data on human rights we examined in chapter 3. The dependent variable in this case is the CIRI index of human rights that ranges between "0" and "8," with higher values denoting better human rights records. The story here is much more positive. Once again, both membership in the International Criminal Court and support for that institution are associated with better levels of human rights protections. In these statistical analyses, we would expect a positive relationship because higher values of the human rights measure are a sign of better protection of human rights, and that is exactly what we find. The relationship between membership in the ICC and better human rights is positive and statistically significant, as is the relationship between support for the ICC and higher levels of human rights protection.

**Table 4.4 Explaining Human Rights Protections**

| Variable | Coefficient | Standard Error | *T* Statistic | *P* Value |
|---|---|---|---|---|
| Previous HR Score | 0.768 | 0.021 | 36.610 | 0.000 |
| Democracy Rating | 0.007 | 0.006 | 1.090 | 0.247 |
| GDP Per Capita | 0.000 | 0.000 | 3.000 | 0.003 |
| Urban Population | 0.002 | 0.002 | 1.270 | 0.204 |
| Ethnicity | –0.032 | 0.023 | –1.430 | 0.154 |
| Number of Borders | –0.039 | 0.013 | –3.040 | 0.002 |
| ICC State | 0.208 | 0.084 | 2.460 | 0.014 |
| OECD State | –0.191 | 0.137 | –1.400 | 0.161 |
| Support for ICC | 0.119 | 0.040 | 2.960 | 0.003 |
| Constant | 0.759 | 0.141 | 5.380 | 0.000 |

Number of observations = 1,064

What do all of these statistics tell us? It is important to emphasize that statistics do not prove anything. They can tell us whether there is a correlation between two variables holding a number of other factors constant, or "all other things being equal." A correlation demonstrates that two variables tend to move together in the same or opposite direction. We have seen that membership in and support for the ICC tend to correlate with lower levels of civil war involvement and better human rights protections in states. ICC membership is also associated with lower levels of battlefield deaths for those states that do become involved in wars. This is certainly good news and tends to show that we might be guardedly optimistic about the impact of the ICC on peace and human rights. When I finish working on a research project, if I can be "guardedly optimistic" about my findings, I'm usually pleased. The next step is to hope that others studying the impact of the ICC find similar results that bolster these analyses and help create a clearer and consistent picture of the influence of the ICC on international politics.

## CONCLUSION

One could say that in many respects the jury is still out on the strength of the relationship between international justice and peace—the evidence is incomplete. On one hand, we saw that in the cases of the Rwandan tribunal and the Sierra Leone tribunal, peace was pretty much restored in those nations before the tribunals began conducting their business. They never really had a chance to create peace, although one could make an argument that they have helped to ensure the peace in those nations in the years since their wars ended. Certainly international justice has played a role in the constellation of forces that help sustain the peace in post–civil war nations, such as international peacekeeping troops, development assistance, and support for local efforts aimed at promoting awareness of the impact of conflict, reconciliation, and other such "people to people" efforts.

In the former Yugoslavia, we saw that despite the occurrence of more violence and war crimes in Bosnia and Kosovo after the establishment of the ICTY, peace has also held since Slobodan Milošević was ousted from power in 2000. Again, international justice has worked in tandem with many national, regional, and international efforts to sustain the peace. In none of these cases do we find evidence of a direct impact of international justice on peace and conflict that would lead us to conclude the tribunals have had an independently verifiable and measurable impact on human security. The one piece of evidence that might lead us to conclude the tribunals can have direct effects on peace was the decision to indict Milošević during the 1999 air war in Kosovo. Some have suggested that his decision to accept NATO's terms was related to the ICTY indictment (Dijxhoorn 2014). Yet in looking at all the evidence of international crimes committed during the Yugoslav wars, it is clear that the perpetrators were not about to be dissuaded by the threat of an international indictment or even the threat of international military intervention. It took the act of military intervention in 1995 and 1999 to put an end to the wars. The ideals of international justice were no match for the realities of ethnonationalism in the former Yugoslavia.

The news is more optimistic when we turn our attention to the International Criminal Court. While the ICC is still in its early stages of development and struggling to find a practical, consequential, and sustainable method of identifying conflict situations, apprehending suspected war criminals, and prosecuting them in The Hague, we saw evidence to suggest that some states may be acting more peacefully in the world today as a result of the court's establishment. Those states that have signed and ratified the ICC Statute experience lower levels of internal wars, fewer casualties related to fighting when they are involved in such conflicts, and better human rights protections. Additionally, those states that take steps to support the ICC are also less likely to be involved in internal conflicts and have better human rights protections. While we cannot say for certain that these states were ever at risk for becoming involved in such violence or engaging in abusive human rights practices, it is clear that there is a difference in behavior between states that are part of the ICC and those that are not. ICC states behave in accordance with international laws. So if states join the ICC and then act appropriately, that is good. If states need to first conform their practices to what is expected under international human rights laws and then join the ICC treaty, that is good news too. Whether it is an attraction effect or a deterrent effect, the data seem to show that the ICC is making a positive contribution to peace and human security.

Peace is a critical component of human security, and perhaps the most important one because war brings with it severe and continuous threats to civilians. One only has to look at the massive migration of refugees out of Syria, Iraq, and Afghanistan toward Europe in the summer of 2015 to comprehend the lengths to which people will go to escape these horrific environments. International justice can help play a role in establishing human security in war-torn communities, but two things have to happen to make this contribution a reality. First, it is clear that the fighting must stop. It is not realistic to expect that the threat of international prosecution will cause belligerents to lay down their arms. In taking up arms, they have demonstrated the lengths to which they will go to achieve their goals, and international tribunals do not and probably never will possess the power necessary to affect that calculation. Justice cannot stop war by itself, but it can help establish the peace that brings human security.

Second, international justice can facilitate the maintenance of peace. International tribunals that fairly and effectively prosecute those most responsible and can communicate to the affected peoples just how this process works make a vital contribution to helping establish and support peace. To be sure, international justice is but one tool in the international community's tool kit for repairing nations broken by war and repression. It works alongside efforts to improve security, economic development, and political reform, each complementing and reinforcing the others when working harmoniously. Of all those needs of post-conflict nations, which include peace and security, economic growth that provides jobs, and justice for the wrongs they have endured, international justice is a critical part of two of these goals. So far the international community has recognized this important role played by the tribunals, but has not squared the circle regarding the need for international justice with the few tools they have given these institutions to advance peace and human security. International justice has often been a politically unfunded mandate. The financial means are there to support international justice, but the political will has often been lacking. The potential for international justice to bring more peace and security to the world's trouble spots is there.

It is also clear from the evidence, however, that these international courts are far more successful when the international community, and especially the major powers of the world, support them. When powerful nations determine that the pursuit of justice can also serve their ends, as was demonstrated when they became serious about apprehending the architects of the violence in the former Yugoslavia and Rwanda, much can be done. These courts do have important powers and critical moral influence in the world, but they do not possess the kind of independent power that would enable them to arrest suspects as they are indicted. That these tribunals do not have substantial independent powers should come as no surprise. Our domestic courts rely on police to do this work. The international tribunals have no such police force. Imagine if domestic courts had to cajole police forces into arresting each and every criminal suspect. That is essentially the position in which these tribunals find themselves. They are a joint endeavor among nations, and only when these nations determine they want the tribunals to succeed can we take full advantage of the power of international justice to advance peace and human security.

## NOTES

1. UN Security Council Resolution N. 808, February 22, 1993, establishing the International Criminal Tribunal for the former Yugoslavia: "The Security Council Determined to put an end to such crimes and to take effective measures to bring to justice the persons who are responsible for them, *Convinced* that in the particular circumstances of the former Yugoslavia the establishment as an ad hoc measure by the Council of an international tribunal and the prosecution of persons responsible for serious violations of international humanitarian law would enable this aim to be achieved and would contribute to the restoration and maintenance of peace, *Believing* that the establishment of an international tribunal and the prosecution of persons responsible for the above-mentioned violations of international humanitarian law will contribute to ensuring that such violations are halted and effectively redressed."

2. UN Security Council Resolution N. 955, November 8, 1994, establishing the International Criminal Tribunal for Rwanda: "The Security Council Determined to put an end to such crimes and to take effective measures to bring to justice the persons who are responsible for them, *Convinced* that in the particular circumstances of Rwanda, the prosecution of persons responsible for serious violations of international humanitarian law would enable this aim to be achieved and would contribute to the process of national reconciliation and to the restoration and maintenance of peace, *Believing* that the establishment of an international tribunal for the prosecution of persons responsible for genocide and the other above-mentioned violations of international humanitarian law will contribute to ensuring that such violations are halted and effectively redressed."

3. As found at http://www.un.org/icty/legaldoc-e/index.htm on March 30, 2007.

4. Interestingly, most of the cases currently before the ICC have been referred to it by state parties seeking investigation of alleged crimes committed on their own

territory. While the ICC is designed to be a *complement to* rather than a *replacement of* state prosecution of suspected violations of international law, many states, whether because of poor judicial infrastructure or perhaps political motivations (e.g., they seek investigation of rebel forces in their states), have asked the ICC to launch investigations on their own territory. Indeed, even nonstate parties are able to and have utilized this method (e.g., Ivory Coast).

5. States can challenge the ICC's assertion of jurisdiction. In turn, the prosecutor can contest such state challenges on the grounds that the state with jurisdiction is genuinely unable or unwilling to carry out the investigation or prosecution. This may be demonstrated by showing that a state's proceedings were used for the purpose of shielding those responsible; there has been an unjustified delay in the initiation of proceedings or the proceedings were not conducted in an impartial or independent manner (Article 17(2) a, b, & c).

6. From the Major Episodes of Political Violence Codebook as found at http://www.systemicpeace.org/inscr/MEPVcodebook2008.pdf on page 4.

7. Data on states' enactment of such legislation are found at http://www.coalitionfortheicc.org/?mod=romeimplementation. I code each state "1" for the year in which they are listed as having enacted such legislation into law, and all subsequent years.

8. Data on state ratification of the Agreement on Privileges and Immunities are found at http://treaties.un.org/Pages/ViewDetails.aspx?src=TREATY&mtdsg_no=XVIII-13&chapter=18&lang=en. I code each state "1" for the year in which they are listed as having ratified the agreement, and all subsequent years.

9. Data on BIAs are found at http://www.amicc.org/usicc/bialist. I code each state "1" for the year in which they are listed as having completed such an agreement, and all subsequent years.

10. As found at http://www.systemicpeace.org/inscr/inscr.htm.

11. As found at http://data.worldbank.org/data-catalog/world-development-indicators.

12. The independent variables are all lagged one year to allow for time to pass before their impact on the dependent variable.

13. From the Major Episodes of Political Violence Codebook, found at http://www.systemicpeace.org/inscr/MEPVcodebook2008.pdf, p. 4.

14. From the Major Episodes of Political Violence Codebook, found at http://www.systemicpeace.org/inscr/MEPVcodebook2008.pdf, p. 4.

15. These data come from the Uppsala Conflict Data Program and are described in the codebook for the battle death data found at http://www.pcr.uu.se/digitalAssets/124/124934_1codebook-ucdp-battle-related-deaths-datasets-v.5-2015.pdf.

## *Chapter 5*

# Legitimacy, Human Security, and International Justice

### INTRODUCTION

The topic of this chapter—legitimacy—goes deep into the heart of the connection between people and the political institutions that claim authority over them. It is public acceptance of a particular institution, like an international criminal tribunal, and its right to exist and carry out its affairs. It is not the popularity of the institution, although this may play a role in shaping some people's beliefs. Instead, acceptance of the right of an institution to make its decisions implies that the individual believes that the institution was properly created and entrusted with certain responsibilities and is entitled to make decisions. Generally, legitimacy also implies that even if the individual does not approve of a particular decision, he or she still accepts the right of the institution to make that decision. In the United States, as in most established democracies, people accept the legitimacy of their courts to pass judgment on the crimes and disputes of citizens. Even if these courts make mistakes or reach decisions that citizens disagree with, a court that is viewed as legitimate by the people has a reserve of belief in its legitimacy to weather such controversies. Without such legitimacy and the public willingness to entrust the handling of disputes to these courts, there would be social turmoil. Just as our domestic courts rely on their legitimacy as the proper institutions entrusted by the public with authority to provide justice, so too do international tribunals seek to establish their legitimacy.

Many different actors, such as governments, lawyers associations, individuals, and human rights groups, may have opinions about the legitimacy of international tribunals, but the acceptance of one group in particular may matter more than most others. That is the people in whose name the tribunals are providing justice. Whether you or I believe in the legitimacy of the ICTY, for example, probably matters not a whit to the tribunal. But the views of the people in the former Yugoslavia mean a great deal.

Why would this be? Why should the people who work at the ICTY or who pay its bills at the United Nations care about what the citizens of the former Yugoslavia think of the ICTY? Well, they should care a great deal. Acceptance of the legitimacy of any court, but the ICTY in this specific case, means that people accept the decisions of the court, the justice it provides, and its right to issue such rulings. Again, acceptance does not mean that people agree with 100 percent of what the court does, but it does mean that people believe in the greater good of the court. If the people of the former Yugoslavia believe in the ICTY, or the people of Rwanda believe in the ICTR, the truth as these institutions reveal it through their judgments is more likely to be more readily accepted. It implies that these people generally accept the story the tribunals produce through their judgments about who did what to whom. This is a huge step in societies in which tens if not hundreds of thousands have been killed and many of those responsible have denied any wrongdoing or even the existence of such events. It implies that individuals accept that the tribunals will dispense justice for the most powerful people in their societies—their leaders. In effect, if people accept the legitimacy of the tribunals that pass down judgments in their name, they have, in effect, taken a big step toward giving up some control over the interpretation of their past to outsiders. If tribunals have a large enough bank account of legitimacy they can draw from, they may be able to gain greater acceptance of their more unpopular decisions.

These are all big "ifs." Please keep in mind I am saying that *if* people accept the legitimacy of these tribunals, this acceptance may then lead to certain other beliefs and developments. Acceptance of the legitimacy of international justice would seem to imply that societies are coming to grips with the events of the past, which, in turn, should mean that they are working toward a better and more peaceful future. If people do not accept the legitimacy of these tribunals, such good things may not transpire. People may reject the truth. They may accept the lies, half-truths, and biased narratives of the leaders who deny their crimes. It may mean they are not willing to forgive or learn to live in peace with their neighbors. A lack of legitimacy may mean that international justice has lost out in the battle for the hearts and minds of the local people. With legitimacy, the groundwork for human security can be laid. If people do not accept the legitimacy of international justice, this may mean that there is fertile ground on which leaders may enflame ethnic hatreds and so lay the groundwork for the next war. So while the legitimacy of international justice may be a rather nebulous concept and indirectly related to human security, it is a key criterion for measuring the success of international tribunals and their hoped-for contribution to human security.

We will examine the relationship between legitimacy and human security in this manner. The first and most important objective is to delve into the meaning and implications of legitimacy for international tribunals. This means that we will spend some time on fairly abstract and theoretical issues, but ones that are nonetheless quite fascinating because the reader will come to understand just how important legitimacy is and how much we may take it for granted. We will then explore how it is that international tribunals earn legitimacy and what actions they take that have bolstered or hindered the development of their legitimacy, especially in the eyes of the publics in the affected nations. Third, we will review what is known about what people in the former Yugoslavia, Rwanda, and Sierra Leone actually think of "their" tribunals and whether they accept or reject the justice the tribunals are dispensing. We will discuss a great deal of data on public opinion polls to understand to what extent the ad hoc tribunals have earned legitimacy. Then we will examine the results of a recent worldwide poll of people's views of the International Criminal Court to better understand what early indications tell us of that court's quest for legitimacy. Throughout I will also be illustrating the connections between legitimacy, or the lack thereof, and human security. I conclude with thoughts on how best international courts may earn legitimacy and advance human security.

## LEGITIMACY AND INTERNATIONAL JUSTICE: WHAT EXACTLY IS IT?

According to Tyler (1990) and Tyler and Darley (2000), people accept judicial institutions as legitimate and accept the decisions made by these organizations if they believe that the institution is properly exercising its authority. There are three critical components to legitimacy that help explain why people grant judicial institutions such acceptance. First, legitimacy is dependent in part on the perceived fairness of court procedures and their ways of conducting business. If the rules are clear, transparent, and appropriate, people come to expect that they will be judged according to a fixed and knowable standard. If instead the methods by which courts conduct their business are opaque, arbitrary, or discriminatory, individuals will tend not to trust the outcomes of such tainted processes (Tyler 1990; Tyler and Darley 2000).

Second, individuals are more likely to accept the legitimacy of a judicial institution if they have opportunities for input into the system. When people believe that they are being listened to and that their views are being taken into consideration, even if their input is not always acted upon, they develop a greater sense of buy-in. A sense of personal efficacy—the belief that one can make a difference—about judicial institutions, even if it is slight, is critical in establishing that judicial institutions are aware of and listening to their constituents. Institutions that are too far removed from the people, appear to care very little about the views of their constituents, and claim for themselves an all-knowing infallibility have segregated their justice from the people. Justice that is arrogant and aloof is more likely to be met with contempt, if not outright hostility. People would prefer that their voices are heard and given serious consideration (Tyler 1990; Tyler and Darley 2000). When people do believe their voices have been heard and considered, they are more apt to give a court legitimacy and accept its decisions, even when they may conflict with their own opinions.

Third, and closely related, individuals are more likely to grant judicial institutions legitimacy if those who work in the criminal justice enterprise show respect toward those individuals with whom they interact. It's not always what the criminal justice system does to people, it's how it treats people that matters. Those who serve in judicial institutions and recognize that they are the custodians of a public enterprise and that they serve on behalf of the people would, we presume, act appropriately and professionally toward all those who enter the criminal justice system. If serving in such a position of public trust is a privilege, those who serve understand that the public is their boss, not the other way around. Conversely, those who see the people as objects, inputs, or as the great, unwashed masses will, we presume again, act on the basis of such beliefs and treat people accordingly. They see themselves more as entitled rather than as honored to serve and so their attitude toward the people is not one of respect, but rather of condescension. Not surprisingly, institutions that recognize the need to serve their citizens and treat them with respect will earn greater levels of legitimacy (Tyler 1990; Tyler and Darley 2000).

Institutions that possess these characteristics have established the necessary, but probably not sufficient, foundation for legitimacy. These elements are all critical determinants of legitimacy, but courts do not act in isolation from their surroundings. They are a product of, they operate in, and they must be aware of their political, social, and economic environments. These environments, or the context in which they operate, may make gaining legitimacy considerably harder. Societies in which people are inherently suspicious of politicians make it harder for courts to earn legitimacy. People who must work within a corrupt or predatory economic system may be more suspicious of authority and thereby make it more difficult for courts to earn legitimacy. Courts may even be part of the problem. Societies in which people are trained to view some of their fellow citizens as "other" or outside the dominant social group will find it difficult to accept the decisions of a court that protects the rights of these other people or takes their side in a dispute. Essentially, the international criminal justice system, like its domestic counterparts, does not exist in isolation from the rest of the world, but may be cursed or blessed with (in)fertile ground on which to develop legitimacy. For example, in the case of the former Yugoslavia, in its quest for legitimacy, the ICTY must contend with local politicians who are determined to maintain and spread their own nationalistic narratives that deny the truths delivered by the tribunal. So if acquiring legitimacy were not a difficult and lengthy process already, these international courts must earn their stripes in an often hostile environment where others seek to thwart their efforts. No one ever said gaining legitimacy was easy!

Now that we have demonstrated that legitimacy is a deep, multifaceted, and difficult to earn objective, just how exactly do these international tribunals go about this mission? I next describe some of the key methods tribunals can use to earn legitimacy in the view of the people in whose name they provide justice.

## EARNING LEGITIMACY

The tribunals are the international community's official verdicts on who bears responsibility for war crimes, crimes against humanity, and genocide. As the judges stated in the *Erdemović* decision,

> The International Tribunal, in addition to its mandate to investigate, prosecute and punish serious violations of international humanitarian law, has a duty, through its judicial functions, to contribute to the settlement of the wider issues of accountability, reconciliation and establishing the truth behind the evils perpetrated in the former Yugoslavia. Discovering the truth is a cornerstone of the rule of law and a fundamental step on the way to reconciliation: for it is the truth that cleanses the ethnic and religious hatreds and begins the healing process.[1]

But is the delivery of justice welcomed with acceptance of its legitimacy? The tribunals, like all courts, must earn legitimacy through the use of fair and proper procedures, engaging their stakeholders and responding to their concerns, and treating their constituents with respect. Let's take these criteria apart and see just how successful the tribunals have been. The third criterion is difficult to measure, as we have little way of knowing just how personnel from the various tribunals interact with stakeholders and how much respect they give them as they interact. We will briefly touch upon what the tribunals have done to demonstrate that they have delivered fair justice, and then discuss what the tribunals have done to reach out to their stakeholders and help them understand the mission of international justice.

## DELIVERING FAIR JUSTICE

For the accused, fairness is especially at stake in the notion of equality of arms—the ability of the defense to present its case on equal footing with the prosecution. Certainly there have been some noticeable lapses in the quality of justice from the perspective of the defense, as exculpatory evidence has not always been readily shared and trials have seemed to take an eternity. Nonetheless, based on what the reader will recall from chapter 2 about the quality and quantity of the justice provided by the international tribunals, we can say that, in general, the tribunals have earned decent grades for their mostly fair administration of justice. From the perspective of the prosecution representing the interests of the affected peoples, victims, and the international community, they have successfully prosecuted over 90 percent of their cases at the trial chamber level. Presumably, such a record of success, coupled with a decent if not good reputation for impartiality (despite the views of some defendants), would earn the tribunals some measure of acceptance as fair adjudicators.

In one sense, the ad hoc tribunals have realized their mission of providing justice, while the work of the ICC continues into the future. The ad hoc tribunals have dispensed with nearly all of their cases and have done so despite numerous challenges and problems. But while we might be tempted to conclude that this first determinant of legitimacy—fairness—has been mostly achieved, we must wait to discuss what the publics in the affected countries really think about international justice. Simply conducting their business in a fair and impartial manner is only half the battle. The harder half is convincing those in whose name the international courts have provided justice that they have done so fairly. For as we shall see, it may not matter that the correct verdicts were reached and the most appropriate punishment meted out if the parties to a conflict believe their own are all innocent and those from the other side are deserving of the most severe punishment.

## PROVIDING OUTREACH

As Arzt (2006, 277) argues, "if international criminal courts are to achieve their aims—one of which is to contribute to the consolidation of democracy and the triumph of the rule of law over the instinct for revenge after prolonged periods of communal violence—perception of their legitimacy by the local population is a crucial factor." One of the principal means by which the international tribunals can gain legitimacy is through their outreach work. As announced on the ICTY website,

> The Tribunal's Outreach Programme is at the heart of the institution's relationship with the region of the former Yugoslavia. . . . With the establishment of Outreach, the Tribunal recognized that it had a role to play in the process of dealing with the past in the former Yugoslavia, one of the key challenges for societies emerging from conflict. . . . Outreach not only informs, but also listens and encourages dialogue. Ultimately, the shape and success of the Tribunal's legacy in the fight against impunity and efforts to deal with the past will be determined by the local communities themselves.[2]

Outreach offices are involved in a great variety of work that is designed to both bring news and information of the tribunals to the affected populations and to bring key stakeholders from those populations to the tribunals. Outreach offices sponsor numerous visits by their personnel to the affected communities to give presentations, take part in conferences, and meet with key leaders in order to explain the work of the tribunals. One of the most noteworthy functions of outreach more generally has been in judicial capacity building. Judicial capacity building means helping local courts prosecute war crimes, crimes against humanity, and genocide on their own. While such work is generally not performed by outreach offices (it is usually the work of judges, lawyers, and others directly involved in the administration of justice), it has a strong public relations component to it that can affect public perceptions of legitimacy. The goal of judicial capacity building is twofold. First, tribunals transfer their files and evidence on international crimes to local courts so they can adjudicate their own cases. Second, judicial capacity building involves tribunal staff training local personnel in investigatory methods, case presentation, and application of international laws. By training personnel and providing evidence in cases the international courts chose not to prosecute, the tribunals are empowering local governments and demonstrating that the tribunals have been good stewards of justice (Hussain 2005). Subotic (2014, 176) writes that in the case of the ICTY capacity building efforts in Bosnia, "the Bosnian War Crimes Court has convicted 88 individuals of war crimes, crimes against humanity, genocide, and other serious violations of international humanitarian law by the end of 2011, the last year aggregate data are available (Humanitarian Law Center 2013b)." We would hope that these collaborative partnerships would create a sense of shared mission that would build legitimacy. Even more fundamentally, we would hope that as international and national teams of judges and lawyers work alongside one another, the local officials would develop a greater sense of trust in the work of the tribunals.

All the tribunals have engaged in extensive outreach efforts, but to what end? Has the quality and quantity of engagement with local populations been sufficient to earn the trust and respect of these communities? Has this engagement earned the tribunals a down payment on their legitimacy? The record of the tribunals on outreach is mixed. The ICTY now has a robust outreach effort, but such work did not start until the late 1990s and even then the ICTY did not publish its decisions in the local languages until 1999. The ICTY has been criticized for the lateness and inadequacy of its outreach efforts, as many see the court as too distant and removed to understand what happened in the former Yugoslavia (Orentlicher 2008). The ICTR's outreach efforts have also been criticized for not engaging the Rwandan people sufficiently and for also being too distant. And in both cases, there have been many opinion leaders in the former Yugoslavia and Rwanda, including in government, who have sought to push their own ethnopolitical narratives that typically blame the tribunal and the "other side" for all the ills suffered by their side (Peskin 2005). Needless to say, these nationalist politicians and agitators have much easier and almost continuous access to the media that can drown out whatever information the tribunals may be trying to share (Clark 2009). Only the SCSL has earned a good reputation for the quality of its outreach mission by making a concerted effort to visit many outlying communities in Sierra Leone and by using media strategies that were appropriate in rural and underdeveloped areas (Kelsall 2009).

Now that the reader has a basic understanding of what the tribunals have done to deliver justice and provide outreach, we can begin our investigation of what the affected peoples think of international justice. Have the tribunals succeeded in earning legitimacy by providing fair justice and outreach, despite whatever flaws there may have been in these efforts? Or have the international tribunals failed to provide fair justice and engage their stakeholders to such a degree that they have not earned legitimacy or even suffer from a deficit of such support?

## WHAT DO THE PEOPLE THINK OF INTERNATIONAL JUSTICE?

The reader knows by now that the phenomenon of international criminal tribunals is a fairly recent development in international relations, and those who reside in the states that have become the target of a particular tribunal, like the countries of the former Yugoslavia or Rwanda, or the target of a particular investigation by the ICC will know very little about what these tribunals do or what their nations are in for. What are they to think of this machinery of international justice that has grown into such a mighty edifice in The Hague? With national courts, nearly every citizen has some kind of awareness of what the courts do and what kinds of laws they adjudicate. Many individuals will have had some kind of personal experience with their local courts, even if it is just with a minor offense such as a traffic ticket. Not so with the international tribunals. How will these people evaluate the justice provided by the international community? How they will determine if the trials and verdicts are fair? What will ultimately lead them to determine that these institutions have some degree of legitimacy and that they have some right to resolve deep-seated and enduring conflicts in their nation? Most people will have little exposure to or knowledge of international law, or even understand the issues in their country that led to these tribunals taking charge of their political disputes. As it turns out, lack of knowledge of these courts and their laws is not a hindrance to opinions. Indeed, even people with little knowledge of international justice do not hesitate to express strong opinions about the job these courts are doing (Ford 2012, 425).

We will begin our exploration of public opinion, legitimacy, and the international tribunals by looking at the views of the peoples of the affected nations—principally the states of the former Yugoslavia, Rwanda, and Sierra Leone. We will later explore through some original data analysis what people around the world think about the International Criminal Court. Before we start, however, it is important to note that while there have been a number of polls taken of the people living in the former Yugoslavia about the ICTY, survey research on the opinions of Rwandans and Sierra Leoneans about the ICTR and SCSL, respectively, are rather scarce. Even the polls from the former Yugoslavia come from a variety of sources that may only administer a single poll at one point in time, which makes understanding trends in opinions over time rather difficult. Nonetheless, we shall proceed with the information we have and see just how well people evaluate the quality of international justice. We will begin with looking at public opinion in the former Yugoslavia about the ICTY.

## THE ICTY AND PUBLIC OPINION IN THE FORMER YUGOSLAVIA

Those who have studied public opinion and international justice (Clark 2009; Hagan and Ivkovic 2006; Klarin 2009; Orentlicher 2009; Subotic 2009) have found that ethnicity strongly predicts individuals' evaluations of the ICTY. Kosovar Albanians and Bosnian Muslims or Bosniaks are usually the most supportive of the ICTY. Croatians from Bosnia or from the state of Croatia tend to be less supportive, and Serbs in Bosnia and Serbia itself tend to register the lowest levels of support (Arzt 2006; Hatay 2005; Nettelfield 2010; Peskin 2005, 2008; UNDP 2005).

Serbs from Serbia and Republika Srpska have long held negative attitudes about the ICTY. Many if not most see the ICTY as biased in favor of Bosnian Muslims or Kosovar Albanians and believe that Serbs have been unfairly targeted for prosecution at much higher rates than members of other ethnic groups. They see the tribunal as unfair in many respects and even reject its very existence. They may argue that claims of genocide and other massacres have been exaggerated or even that some atrocities, such as when Bosnian Muslims have been struck and killed by artillery shells in Sarajevo, were perpetrated by the Bosnian Muslim armed forces to generate sympathy for their people in the international community. Not surprisingly, Serbs tend to believe that the ICTY is not the best venue for prosecuting war criminals. The Organization for Security and Cooperation in Europe is one of the few institutions that has regularly polled citizens in the former Yugoslavia, but they have focused principally on Serbia and the views of Serbian citizens. Surveys have been administered every four years. In their 2011 report, the OSCE found that when Serbs were asked where they thought prosecutions for war crimes and other such crimes should be located, only 11 percent thought the ICTY was the most appropriate venue. Twenty percent thought the crimes should be prosecuted where they were committed, but 45 percent thought each country should prosecute its own citizens (OSCE 2011, 10). Many people do claim to be fairly familiar with the ICTY—about 37 percent—but interestingly, awareness appears to be decreasing over time (OSCE 2011, 13). Two-thirds of the population believes the establishment of the ICTY was not necessary (OSCE 2011, 15); 40 percent believe that the ICTY was created to "put the blame for war sufferings on the Serbs" (OSCE 2011, 16), and 73 percent believe that the ICTY has different attitudes toward groups depending on their ethnicity (OSCE 2011, 22).

The more interesting questions are those that directly pertain to Serbs' overall views of the tribunal. When asked, "Do you think that trials before the ICTY contribute to finding out the truth about the events in wars on the territory of former SFRY?" in the 2011 survey, 49 percent of the population agreed with the statement "No, because real truth will never reach ordinary citizens," but 33 percent said "yes, partly," while 11 percent said "yes, completely" (OSCE 2011, 57). However, a solid 71 percent believe that the ICTY will not contribute to the reconciliation process in the region (OSCE 2011,

58) and only a combined 14 percent had a mainly or primarily positive attitude toward the ICTY, while 71 percent had a negative attitude.

While the Organization for Security and Cooperation in Europe has periodically taken polls on Serbian attitudes toward international justice and related topics, there has not been this kind of sustained attention given to citizens of Bosnia-Herzegovina by such an international organization. The UN did authorize one poll that included several questions about the ICTY. When Bosnians were asked if they had confidence in the ICTY, only 23 percent of respondents replied affirmatively. Among Bosniaks, Croats, and Serbs (all in Bosnia), the percentages were, respectively, 30 percent, 35 percent, and 7 percent. When asked whether they thought the ICTY had contributed to reconciliation, overall 53 percent said "no" or "only a little," while 38 percent said "partly," "mostly," or "yes." When breaking the population down along ethnic lines, the report finds that 38 percent of Bosniaks choose one of the three positive answers about reconciliation, close to 47 percent of the Croats chose one of three, and only 24 percent of Serbs chose a positive response (Prism Research 2013, 29).

I recently conducted research using data from the Southeast Europe Social Survey Project (SEESSP) data (Meernik 2015).[3] The data contain the responses of 21,940 people, involving almost 1,000 survey questions across 23 different independent samples in the former Yugoslavia. The survey question I analyzed asked respondents if they "support the efforts of the international court to try war criminals from the war in this country, regardless of what side they were on." Individuals were given the option to "strongly agree," "agree," "neither agree nor disagree," disagree," and "strongly disagree." I combined the "strongly agree" and "agree" categories into one variable to measure ICTY support. In the aggregate, approximately 57.2 percent of the population either agrees or strongly agrees that they support the ICTY, while 42.7 percent of the population does not agree, strongly disagrees, or expresses no opinion/doesn't know. When I looked at support among the ethnic groups of the former Yugoslavia, I found that almost 90 percent of Bosniaks supported the ICTY, 74 percent of the Kosovar Albanians supported the ICTY, 60 percent of Croatians supported the ICTY, and approximately one-third of Serbs agreed or strongly agreed that they supported the ICTY.

In a 2012 poll of residents of Kosovo, Perceptions on Transitional Justice, by the United Nations Development Program, we find results that are similar, but certainly not identical. The UNDP report provides both data on the 2012 survey and an earlier version from 2007. When asked if they were satisfied with the work of the ICTY, approximately 69 percent of Kosovar Albanians agreed that they were very or somewhat satisfied in 2007, while that number jumped to 82 percent in 2012. Among Serbs in Kosovo, however, 35 percent were very or somewhat satisfied in 2007 and 56 percent were not satisfied. In 2012, there is a huge change among the Kosovar Serbs after several Kosovar Albanian leaders on trial at the ICTY were acquitted and a number of Serbs were convicted of crimes committed in Kosovo. The percentage supporting the ICTY drops to a minuscule 2 percent and the number who indicated they were not satisfied jumps to 87 percent. These results starkly demonstrate two essential truths about public support for the ICTY in the former Yugoslavia. First, as Mirko Klarin has pointed out, public support is strongly and inversely related to the number of those from one's ethnic group on trial at the tribunal (Klarin 2009, 92). Second, the ICTY does not enjoy a foundation of support among the populace that allows it to weather the occasional verdict with which some segment of the population opposes. Rather, support for the ICTY is changing and conditional.

These views of international justice are often predicated on powerful and enduring national narratives that explain political disputes and wars within a group history that emphasizes the positive features of the group's conduct and minimizes if not denies any wrongdoing. The Serb narrative regarding their campaigns against the Bosnian and Kosovar Muslims reaches back centuries to battles against the Ottoman Empire and the Serb belief that they have been the unappreciated defenders of Christianity in Europe. These historical narratives then provide a context in which to evaluate current "threats," which must be addressed decisively if one's group is once again under "attack." As Ford (2012, 423) writes,

> people's views of themselves are intricately bound up with their social identities. Thus attacks on social or group identities can be treated as attacks on the self that will trigger the same self-defensive reasoning. As a result, group members are resistant to information that is critical of the group.

And most importantly for understanding perceptions of international courts, these narratives provide a coherent rationale for explaining why the current conflict occurred (e.g., our group was "threatened"), what actions took place (e.g., we did what we had to do to defend ourselves), and who was responsible for whatever atrocities took place (our enemies are responsible and cannot be trusted to tell the truth of their liability).

The power of these narratives means that individuals will often evaluate international justice through a potent, identity-based prism. When tribunals target individuals from the "other" groups and punish them for their crimes, support will likely be forthcoming. But when tribunals issue judgments that conflict with these narratives, the opposition is likely to be deep-seated and intense because these issues go to the very heart of what it means to be a member of the group. As Ford (2012, 433) argues, "Perceptions of the ICTY in the former Yugoslavia are driven to a large degree by whom the court indicts and whether these indictments contradict the dominant internal narratives within the various affected populations." What can we expect to find of the other ad hoc tribunals?

## THE ICTR AND PERCEPTIONS OF JUSTICE IN RWANDA

Far less research has been conducted surveying the citizens of Rwanda and Sierra Leone to inquire about their attitudes toward international justice, but there are a few surveys from which we can make some observations. One study done by Anku and Loizides (2009) found that 48.9 percent of the 227 Rwandans surveyed believed that the ICTR was doing a good job. On the other hand, 74.4 percent of the respondents believed that the gacaca courts, an older, more traditional method of providing justice, were doing a good job. The gacaca courts were set up by the Rwandan government to deal with the enormous number of people who had been arrested in connection with the genocide. People were spending years in jail with little hope of ever seeing the inside of a courtroom, given the huge backlog of cases and the horrific state of Rwanda's judicial infrastructure after the genocide. The gacaca trials were held in Rwandan villages over several years in the early 2000s and allowed Rwandans to confront those accused of the genocide and bear witness against them. Those elected by the people as judges would pronounce verdicts and determine punishment, which was often geared toward restorative rather than retributive justice. The convicted individual might have to provide something of value, such as livestock, or do work for the victim(s). Interestingly, those individuals who reported attending the gacaca court meetings in their villages more often than others were more likely to believe they were doing a good job. Perhaps this provides some indication that increased exposure to transitional justice helps create greater understanding and support for such efforts. Additionally, results reported by Pham, Weinstein, and Longman (2004) indicated that in a survey of 2,000 Rwandans only 21 percent believed that the ICTR was making a positive contribution to reconciliation.

Part of the reason for the lack of support may be a result of a lack of knowledge among Rwandans about the ICTR. According to Schulz (2014, 19),

> the empirical findings reveal that despite a development of outreach activities over the years, the general population does not seem to be significantly more aware of or more informed about the Tribunal. While in 2002, empirical findings show that a cumulated 87.2 percent of the population can be categorized

> as "not well informed" this trend certainly holds for 2006 and 2013, as well. Although technically aware about the Tribunal's existence, the overall level of knowledge and understanding—and in particular the quality and depth of information—as of 2006 and 2013 is still considered to be quite low throughout society.

Schulz (2014) also finds, however, that a majority of Rwandans do have positive attitudes in general toward the ICTR, although such attitudes did not differ between those who were exposed to ICTR outreach activities and those who were not. In fact, Schulz (2014, 23) finds that "81.5 percent of respondents of outreach participants compared to an almost identical 83.3 percent of control group respondents attest that the ICTR is either necessary for or plays an important role in promoting reconciliation in Rwanda." There would seem to be a bit of a divergence among the results of the surveys, which leads me to a couple more observations. The first is that often the survey samples do not consist of random samples, the gold standard of survey research in which every individual in the population has a theoretically equivalent chance of being selected. Such precision may be quite difficult in a country where many people lack access to phones and live in rural, underdeveloped areas. Hence, the composition of the groups surveyed may vary dramatically and may influence the results that are obtained. Second, we should also bear in mind that given the low level of knowledge about the ICTR, it is difficult to conclude that positive or negative attitudes are inherently meaningful. Perhaps the most that we can say about public opinion regarding the ICTR is that it is mixed.

## THE SCSL AND PUBLIC OPINION IN SIERRA LEONE

Evidence of the attitudes of the people of Sierra Leone toward the Special Court for Sierra Leone is even scarcer. There has been one major study of the views of citizens of both Sierra Leone and Liberia (the country of Charles Taylor, former president of Liberia and a chief instigator and organizer of the violence in Sierra Leone) by the group No Peace Without Justice and the SCSL (2012). It is not possible to determine if other private polling data about the SCSL exists. According to the No Peace Without Justice survey, 91 percent of those surveyed in Sierra Leone indicated that they believed that the SCSL had contributed toward bringing peace to their country, while 78 percent of the people of Liberia believed the same (No Peace Without Justice 2012, 21). Additionally, 64 percent of those surveyed in Sierra Leone and 75 percent of those surveyed in Liberia believe that the SCSL had contributed toward ending the culture of impunity for committing such crimes, while more generally 82 percent overall in both countries believe that the court has helped bring justice (No Peace Without Justice 2012, 29). A similar percentage in both countries indicated that they believed the court has contributed to greater respect for human rights and the rule of law (2012, 30). The report also found that the outreach section of the SCSL had been very well received in Sierra Leone and has reached a substantial number of people (Kerr and Lincoln 2008).

Popular views of international justice in the nations that have been subjected to this modern invention of global politics and human rights have been quite diverse. As we saw with the ICTY, individuals' evaluations of the tribunal vary significantly by ethnicity. Those who believe that leaders from their ethnic group have been singled out for prosecution and that members of the other groups have largely escaped such justice see the ICTY as an ethnically biased institution. In particular, the Serbs in Bosnia, Kosovo, and Serbia proper have fairly negative views of the tribunal, which are informed considerably by the narratives of ethnonationalist politicians and rather spotty media coverage. Bosnian Muslims and Kosovar Albanians, the principal victims of Serb aggression, have much more positive views of the ICTY. Survey research regarding the ICTR has found fairly divergent results. Some research finds quite high levels of support, while others find startlingly low opinions of the tribunal. The little research that has focused on the SCSL has found that institution enjoys fairly wide support.

Does this mean that international tribunals have earned legitimacy in the eyes of the affected population? The verdict must be that in the case of the ICTY, it depends on whom one is asking. For the ICTR it is rather difficult to tell, but some indications are that the tribunal has gained support, while the SCSL appears to have earned a significant degree of respect, especially in comparison to other efforts at transitional justice in Sierra Leone.

One of the key determinants of popular support for these tribunals is the extent to which these institutions have done an effective job communicating the nature and purposes of their work and their accomplishments. Outreach efforts are critical in earning legitimacy, especially for these new and rather alien forms of international justice. The ICTY was rather late to the game of outreach, and this tardiness, coupled with a very difficult political and media environment in the former Yugoslavia where the tribunal has had to compete against powerful counter-narratives, has made understanding and acceptance of the tribunal's mission quite difficult. Since those inauspicious beginnings, the ICTY has undertaken numerous outreach activities that may have helped create more of a positive impression of the tribunal's work, but it must struggle to convey its message among some publics who deny that some crimes ever took place. In situations like this, it is not clear that anything short of enlightened local leadership that clearly and consistently acknowledges the crimes committed by many leaders would not be effective in countering these ethnonationalist beliefs.

At the other end of the spectrum in Sierra Leone, where the SCSL tried just the principal leaders of the main armies and political movements contesting for power during the civil war and where the court had an early and extensive outreach mission, the reception of the court has been better. Additionally, the SCSL was located in Freetown, the capital of Sierra Leone, which generated more of a sense of local ownership of international justice. Courts located in distant lands face considerable hurdles in communication and local understanding that dramatically increase the difficulties of earning legitimacy. As we discussed at the beginning of this chapter, one of the key criteria in determining the legitimacy of any court is the extent to which people believe the court is engaging them and listening to them. While there are good reasons why international tribunals, and especially the ICC, are located outside of these conflict zones, this comes at a price. International justice becomes more important and relevant to the international community concerned with specific deterrence (convicting and punishing war criminals to prevent them from further fomenting violence) and general deterrence (dissuading other would-be war criminals from engaging in such behavior) than local communities.

As two of the ad hoc tribunals (ICTR and SCSL) have basically ceased operations and the ICTY is about to, earning legitimacy now and into the future largely moves from actions of these courts to the journalists, historians, educators, and others in the affected nations who will write about and comment on them. The development and publication of their legacy projects will provide some input into popular perceptions, but much of the influence over their legitimacy will no longer be in the hands of the tribunals. This is not the case with the ICC, which can certainly learn lessons from these tribunals. There is especially the need to earn legitimacy through consistent and effective outreach programs. We will next turn to looking at popular perceptions of the International Criminal Court.

## POPULAR VIEWS OF THE INTERNATIONAL CRIMINAL COURT

There has been little research to date on popular views of the International Criminal Court. There is, however, one recent survey on the attitudes of people around the world toward the court that can help us shed light on what people think about it, how factors such as age, education, and gender affect opinions, and especially whether where one lives is an important determinant of such attitudes. At this stage, we will depart from describing what other researchers have found and explore the data from the 2012 survey "The Voice of the People End of the Year Survey" ourselves. These data were collected by Gallup International and the Worldwide Independent Network of Market Research. Much of the survey was concerned with issues other than the ICC, but there was one question that is of great interest to us. The pollsters asked citizens of fifty-six different countries, "Currently, world leaders accused of severe violations of human rights are tried by an international court. Do you support or oppose the existence of such an international court which is not under the authority of your own state?" This is the question that we will use to gauge popular support for the ICC and begin to understand whether the court has begun to earn international legitimacy.

Individuals were given three options when answering this question. These were: "support," "oppose," or "neither support, nor oppose." Additionally, for some respondents there were missing data or individuals did not express an opinion, but because much of this category was missing data we cannot include it in the analysis. The basic breakdown of responses to this question can be seen in figure 5.1. Approximately 60 percent of those surveyed support the ICC, 19 percent oppose the existence of the ICC, and 20 percent neither support nor oppose the existence of the court.

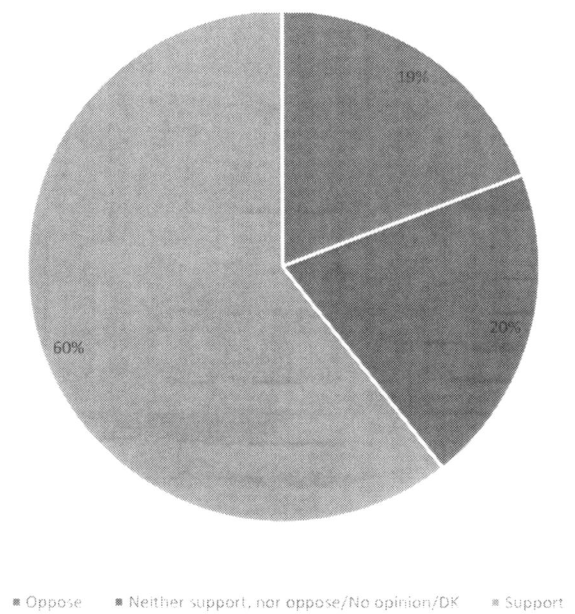


**Figure 5.1** Support of the International Criminal Court. *Source: Author.*

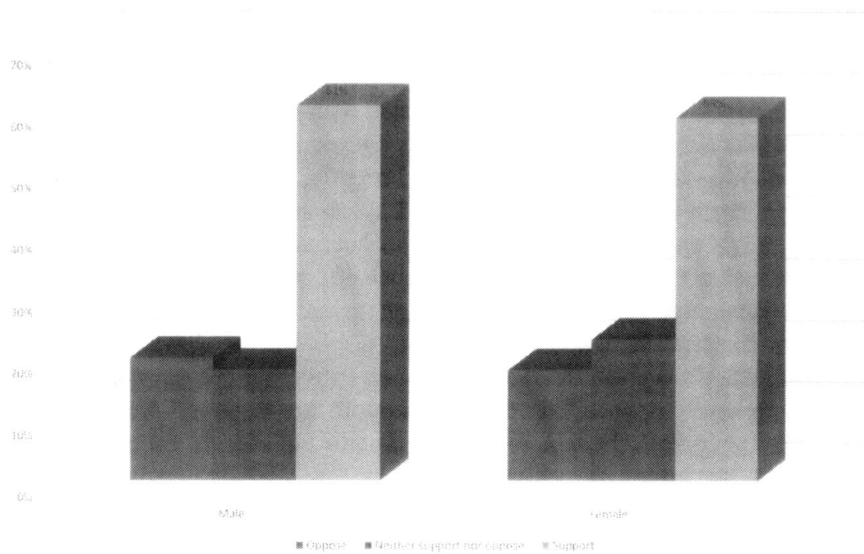


**Figure 5.2** Gender and Support for the ICC. *Source: Author.*

We begin by looking at whether men and women differ in their attitudes toward international justice, as it has become increasingly clear that there is a distinct gender dimension to the violence of war (Hudson et al. 2012). When we examine support along gender lines, as shown in figure 5.2, we find that men are just slightly more likely to support the existence of the ICC than women. Approximately 61 percent of men support the ICC, while 59 percent of the women surveyed do. As I was exploring these data, however, I saw that women were more likely than men to not respond to the ICC question or to express no opinion (12 percent of the women surveyed did not respond and 8 percent of the men did not respond). Additionally, women (23 percent) were more likely than men (18 percent) to neither support nor oppose the existence of the ICC. This may mean that greater awareness of the ICC among women could help bolster support for the court.

As we see in figure 5.3, there is a clear trend in the data that shows that greater levels of education lead to greater levels of support, as well as decreasing levels of opposition and indifference. Those who have the greatest level of education—measured in the survey as completion of a graduate degree (a master's degree, professional degree, or a PhD)—are most likely to support the ICC at 69 percent. Among those who complete a higher education degree, support for the ICC stands at 65 percent, while of those who complete just secondary education, 59 percent support the court. Lastly, among those who have no education or who have completed just a primary school education or less, only 53 percent support the ICC. Even though the trends in this relationship clearly demonstrate that education increases support, it is still striking that there is always majority support for the ICC.

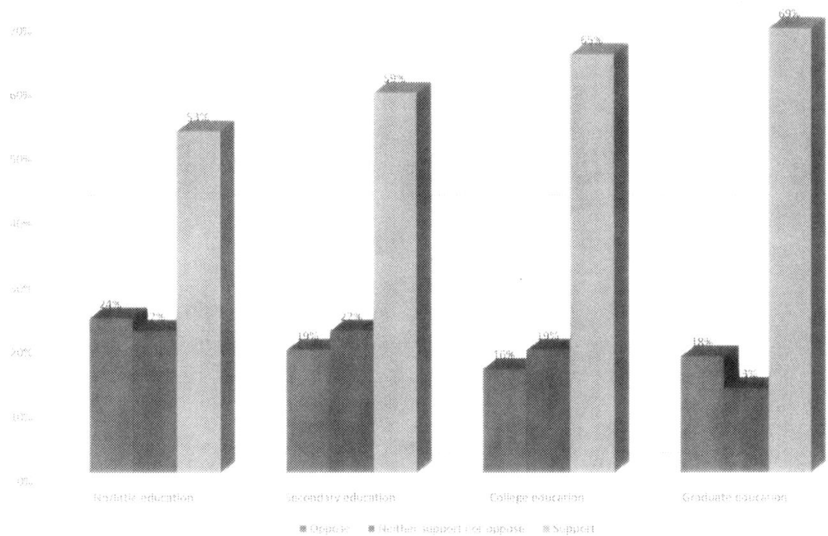


**Figure 5.3** Education Level and Support for the ICC. *Source: Author.*

Perhaps even more striking than the positive relationship between education and support for the ICC is the even stronger trend between age and support in figure 5.4. The older the respondents, the more likely they are to support the court. The youngest group—those under eighteen—only support the ICC at 54 percent, although one might expect that given the pronounced relationship between education and support for the ICC that support may well rise for many young people as they move through the educational system. Among the oldest group, those sixty-five and older, we see that two-thirds support the existence of the ICC. Interestingly, however, there is little movement in the percentages of those who indicate they neither support nor oppose the existence of the ICC across the age groups.

Of all these categories, we see the most striking differences in support for the ICC across regions in figure 5.5. Interestingly, some of these regional

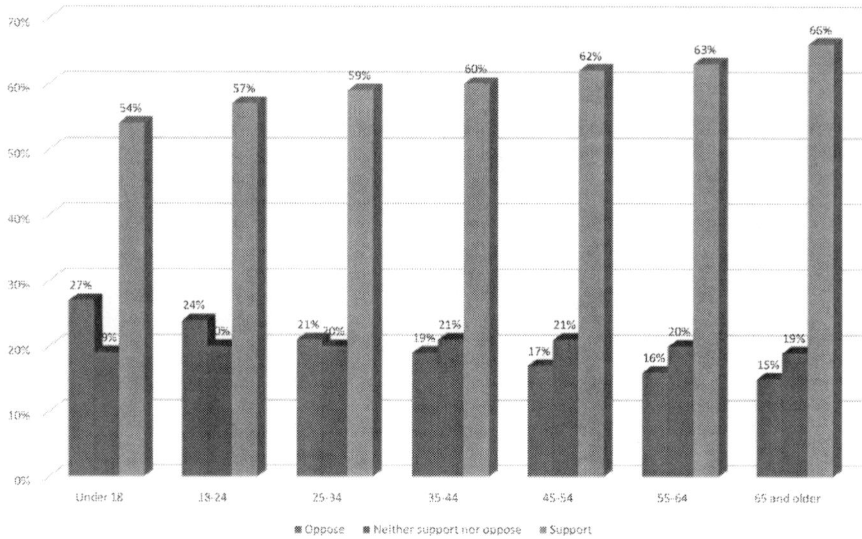


**Figure 5.4** Age and Support for the ICC. *Source: Author.*

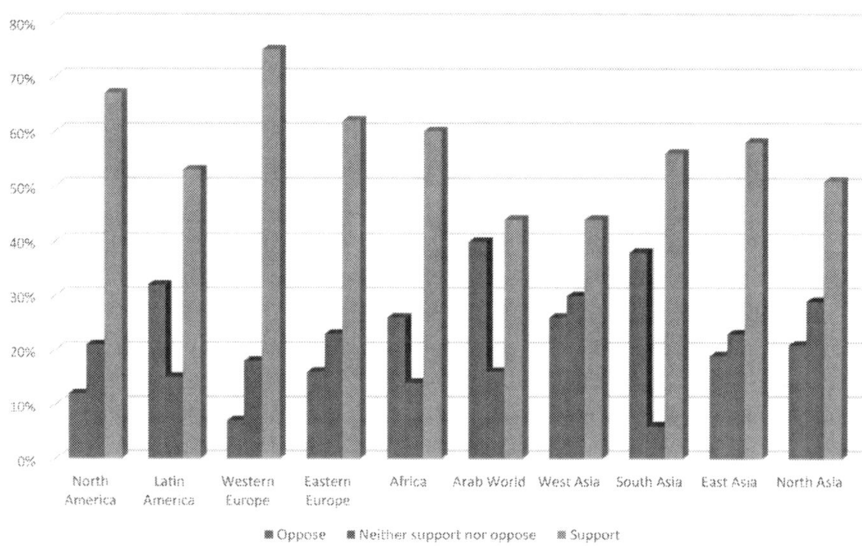


**Figure 5.5** Regions and Support for the ICC. *Source: Author.*

trends are not at all what we might expect, given popular accounts in the media. For example, support for the ICC is fairly low in Latin America at only 53 percent, while opposition is relatively high at 32 percent—the third highest of any of the regions. The Latin American states were among the earliest and strongest of the ICC proponents, and it was an Argentinean, Luis Moreno-Ocampo, who was the first chief prosecutor of the ICC. Yet support for the ICC is lower in this region than in North America, which includes the country that has been one of the loudest and most persistent critics of the ICC—the United States. In North America, we see that 67 percent of the respondents surveyed support the existence of the ICC, while only 22 percent are opposed to it. Perhaps the respondents from Latin America agree that the court has focused too much on the conflicts of the underdeveloped parts of the globe. Contrarily, it is also possible that those surveyed in this region would like the ICC to investigate human rights abuses that have been occurring in Latin America since the establishment of the ICC. Unfortunately, we cannot say for sure because we do not have data on the reasons why respondents support or oppose the court.

In order to delve more deeply into how people's views of the court may differ depending on where they live, I break down support by country. Table 5.1 lists support for the ICC according to country of residence and is ranked from highest support to lowest support. As we might have suspected, people from Western European nations are giving the ICC the highest levels of support. The top four supportive nations are, in order, Sweden, Iceland, Belgium, and Switzerland, with support ranging from 82 percent to 83 percent. European nations have been among the chief backers of the ICC and have even made support for the ICC a condition of EU membership.

Quite interestingly, however, we see that the East African nation of Kenya is ranked number five on the list, at 80 percent support. The reader may recall that not only is Kenya one of the nations whose troubles have resulted in an ICC investigation, it is also the first, and so far the only, nation at the time of writing whose investigation was brought under the independent authority of the chief prosecutor (all other nations either self-referred their case to the ICC or the case was referred by the United Nations Security Council). We would expect that awareness in Kenya would be fairly high because of this, but at the same time the ICC investigation has been quite controversial and has met with vociferous government opposition. In fact, and again at the time of writing, the ICC case has basically been suspended because of witness intimidation and other problems with local cooperation. Kenya is also notable in that the percentage of individuals who neither support nor oppose the ICC is quite low (4 percent), while opposition is the second highest among the top twenty court supporters at 16 percent (Hong Kong is highest at 18 percent

**Table 5.1 Support for the ICC Across States**

| Rank | Country | Support | Oppose | Neither Support Nor Oppose |
|---|---|---|---|---|
| 1 | Sweden | 85% | 3% | 12% |
| 2 | Iceland | 82% | 4% | 13% |
| 3 | Belgium | 80% | 5% | 15% |
| 4 | Switzerland | 80% | 6% | 14% |
| 5 | Kenya | 80% | 16% | 4% |
| 6 | Finland | 79% | 6% | 15% |
| 7 | Portugal | 79% | 7% | 14% |
| 8 | Germany | 79% | 5% | 16% |
| 9 | Ireland | 78% | 6% | 16% |
| 10 | Georgia | 76% | 9% | 15% |
| 11 | Armenia | 76% | 7% | 18% |
| 12 | Bulgaria | 75% | 6% | 19% |
| 13 | Vietnam | 75% | 10% | 15% |
| 14 | Spain | 74% | 8% | 18% |
| 15 | Canada | 74% | 8% | 18% |
| 16 | Australia | 72% | 8% | 20% |
| 17 | Ukraine | 72% | 11% | 17% |
| 18 | France | 70% | 10% | 21% |
| 19 | Romania | 69% | 6% | 25% |
| 20 | Hong Kong | 68% | 28% | 4% |
| 21 | Austria | 67% | 8% | 25% |
| 22 | Poland | 66% | 6% | 27% |
| 23 | Russian Federation | 64% | 13% | 24% |
| 24 | Singapore | 63% | 15% | 22% |
| 25 | Italy | 62% | 12% | 26% |
| 26 | Czech Republic | 62% | 12% | 26% |
| 27 | United Kingdom | 62% | 12% | 26% |
| 28 | United States | 60% | 16% | 23% |
| 29 | Iraq | 59% | 28% | 13% |
| 30 | Peru | 58% | 24% | 18% |
| 31 | Lithuania | 58% | 13% | 29% |

| Rank | Country | Support | Oppose | Neither Support Nor Oppose |
|---|---|---|---|---|
| 32 | Argentina | 57% | 28% | 15% |
| 33 | Korea, Rep (South) | 57% | 15% | 28% |
| 34 | India | 56% | 38% | 6% |
| 35 | Afghanistan | 54% | 28% | 19% |
| 36 | South Africa | 53% | 33% | 13% |
| 37 | Brazil | 53% | 36% | 11% |
| 38 | Malaysia | 53% | 24% | 24% |
| 39 | Mozambique | 52% | 24% | 24% |
| 40 | Bosnia-Herzegovina | 52% | 31% | 17% |
| 41 | Japan | 52% | 17% | 31% |
| 42 | Tunisia | 51% | 33% | 15% |
| 43 | Cameroon | 49% | 36% | 15% |
| 44 | Philippines | 46% | 27% | 27% |
| 45 | Colombia | 45% | 26% | 29% |
| 46 | Turkey | 45% | 45% | 11% |
| 47 | Macedonia | 44% | 30% | 27% |
| 48 | Ecuador | 42% | 48% | 11% |
| 49 | Morocco | 41% | 36% | 23% |
| 50 | Pakistan | 41% | 20% | 39% |
| 51 | Palestinian Territories | 39% | 33% | 27% |
| 52 | Azerbaijan | 31% | 10% | 59% |
| 53 | Serbia | 28% | 44% | 28% |
| 54 | Lebanon | 27% | 64% | 9% |
| 55 | China | 18% | 34% | 48% |
| | **Total** | **60%** | **19%** | **20%** |

opposition among the most supportive states). It would certainly appear that when we have reason to believe that awareness of the ICC is likely to be quite high, that opinions will more readily form.

In fact, Kenya is the only nation surveyed that has become subject to the International Criminal Court's jurisdiction, so its support for the court is quite significant as we look to see just what kind of legitimacy the ICC has earned.

While this is only one poll using one specific question to gauge individuals' support for the court, this finding would suggest that perhaps the ICC is not quite as unpopular among ordinary people in one critical African nation as it would seem to be among their political elite. Perhaps Kenyans are quite aware of what their leaders have been doing to gain political power, as was seen during the violent elections of 2007, and appreciate the role of the ICC in adjudicating these human rights abuses.

Another interesting trend is the support we see among nations that have been targets of violence by other powerful states. While I must caution that these are just impressions, it is interesting to see that support ranks quite high in Vietnam at 75 percent (which has been involved in wars with both China and the United States) and Georgia (which has been the target of Russian aggression and where the ICC has had a long-running, but seemingly inconclusive, preliminary investigation) at 76 percent.

There are three states in the sample of nations that were the subject of the ICTY—Bosnia-Hercegovina, Macedonia, and Serbia. While there is majority support in Bosnia, it is a rather low 52 percent. Indeed, even the United States, whose government has been a harsh critic of the ICC at times, ranks higher in support. In Serbia, whose citizens have never been big fans of international justice, support is among the lowest of any nation at 28 percent. Indeed, only two nations are less enamored of the ICC. Support in Macedonia, which saw only two of its citizens brought before the ICTY, is a rather paltry 44 percent. In contrast to Kenya, exposure among these states to international justice has resulted in only tepid support at best.

Among the states whose peoples are not supporters of the ICC, there are a variety of nations from throughout the globe. There are several on the African continent including Cameroon (49 percent), Morocco (41 percent), and two in the Middle East—the Palestinian territories (39 percent) and Lebanon (second lowest at 27 percent). Lebanon is another interesting case because not only does it have the highest level of opposition by far of any nation in the survey sample at 64 percent, it has also been the subject of an ongoing, but quite inconclusive, investigation of an international tribunal—the Special Tribunal for Lebanon. That tribunal has yet to bring to justice a single suspect in the death of former prime minister Rafik Hariri, whose assassination is the sole crime under the jurisdiction of the court. It would not stretch credulity to believe that their lack of support for the ICC reflects their own unsatisfying experience with international justice.

The reader will also recall the surprising lack of support among Latin American nations given their leadership on transitional justice issues. There are two nations in South America where there is not majority support—Colombia and Ecuador. Colombia is another case, like Georgia, where there has been an ongoing but inconclusive preliminary investigation of human rights abuses committed during long-running civil wars and other types of violence. In Colombia, there is only 45 percent support for the ICC and also a great deal of indifference—29 percent neither support nor oppose the court. In Ecuador, there is 42 percent support for the ICC. Finally, the nation whose people provide the lowest level of support for the ICC is China, which is not a member state and has long criticized many international justice efforts as violations of state sovereignty rights. Chinese citizens also exhibit a high level of opposition to the ICC at 34 percent.

What can we conclude about support for the ICC and its legitimacy given such widely varying opinions across the globe? First, judging by the comparatively low levels of support given the ICC by countries that have had prior experience with international tribunals—namely Bosnia-Herzegovina, Serbia, Macedonia, and Lebanon—it may be tempting to conclude that familiarity breeds contempt. In only one of these cases did support rise above the 50 percent benchmark, which was in Bosnia, a country whose people certainly have diverse views of their own about international tribunals, but which has been the most supportive of the ICTY among the former Yugoslav republics. Do international courts create high expectations among the people in whose name they provide justice, which then leads to an inevitable deterioration in support when international justice cannot deliver on such expectations? While many people's expectations for international justice may well be unreasonable (which can be forgiven in part given many of the grandiose promises made about what these institutions could deliver), we must square the lack of support among these four nations with the remarkably high levels of confidence exhibited by the people of Kenya.

Not only do Kenyans provide the ICC with some of the highest levels of support the world over, they do so in spite of the failures of the ICC to deliver justice for Kenyan leaders who have been indicted by the ICC. How do we explain this? A full explanation probably requires considerably more data on the attitudes of Kenyans about the ICC, their leaders, and the problems with their own justice system. There are, however, a couple of intriguing potential explanations. While the ICC could be faulted for many shortcomings in Kenya and elsewhere, it did indict Kenyan leaders across the political spectrum and may be perceived by Kenyans as evenhanded in its selection of targets for indictment. You will recall that among the criticisms of the ICTY and ICTR one charge has been that they have singled out some groups for prosecution and not others. In fact, this *possible* perception of the evenhandedness of international justice is something we also saw in the case of the Sierra Leone tribunal, which enjoyed the greatest support among the three ad hoc tribunals. Further data on Kenyan attitudes, as well as data from other nations that have become subjects of the ICC, would help us answer this question.

The other possibility is that individuals in both Kenya and Sierra Leone compare international justice to their own local justice and have concluded that the latter works better. This will also be important for us to consider in the future. International justice is not evaluated in a vacuum. It occurs in local political contexts, and it is also evaluated alongside other efforts at transitional justice, such a domestic prosecutions, truth commissions, reparations, and so on. To the extent that those institutions do not measure up to people's hopes, international justice may look like a pretty good deal.

## LEGITIMACY AND HUMAN SECURITY

Legitimacy is not an easy thing to come by for any institution that must make difficult and unpopular decisions. It is doubly more complicated when that institution applies international laws about subjects that arouse great passions and does so far removed from the people for whom it is supposed to be delivering justice. But earning legitimacy is not impossible and it is quite important in laying the political and social foundation upon which human security must rest. The evidence we have examined, gathered, and analyzed in this chapter can help us understand just how legitimacy can be earned and what it can do to help advance human security.

When legitimacy is earned, it helps advance peace. Real and true legitimacy connotes acceptance of the right of an institution to make decisions—it means the people have accepted the need for the institution and recognize that the decisions it makes are made on behalf of society. For an international tribunal, this means that there is an acceptance of the need for objective truth to be conveyed regarding who was responsible for wrongdoing and what the proper outcome is for those who are found to be liable. If people cannot agree that there has been wrongdoing and that individuals from their ethnic group, religious affiliation, or political party had something to do with it, they can hardly be expected to see the need for international justice. They have not yet dealt with the more underlying divisions in society that brought about violence and so are facing deeper problems that will hinder, if not prevent, any acceptance of the right of an international court to weigh into their disputes.

This would seem to be the case with many if not all of the former Yugoslav republics. The support provided by each of them is conditional. It depends on whether the Yugoslav tribunal upholds or upends their version of the events of the 1990s. There would seem to be little general unconditional support of the ICTY in the region; instead, support is lost or gained each time a verdict is announced. Some part of this is no doubt due to shortcomings of the ICTY and its ability to effectively communicate its mandate, its processes, and its outcomes. Nonetheless, we should recognize that the ethnic divisions of those countries have remained essentially frozen in time. International aid and international military intervention have bought and maintained a great deal of human security to which international justice has contributed, but such peace has endured despite the national, religious, and political divisions among peoples that have been enshrined in law (as in Bosnia) or have been exploited by nationalist politicians. It may well be a necessary condition of human security, especially in the absence of meaningful local alternative models of transitional justice. Yet those stubborn underlying ethnic and religious fault lines continue to rumble, as evidenced in the levels of support accorded the ICTY, and create an unstable foundation upon which human security rests. The international community can provide justice for the citizens of the former Yugoslavia, but it cannot want justice more than the people do if it is going to work. The former Yugoslavia remains a work in progress. International justice has done mostly all it has been capable of doing. The rest is up to the people and their leaders with support from the international community.

If the former Yugoslavia presents us with something of a cautionary tale of the limits of international tribunals in earning legitimacy and contributing to human security because of the weakness or inability of international and local actors, Rwanda presents a study in contrast. Ethnic divisions remain in that society to be sure and, like the former Yugoslavia, it may take years to heal the rifts that course through society. The Rwandan government, however, has moved forward with determination to deal with the genocide through local justice, such as gacaca, and other political moves such as banning the use of ethnic identity cards. While the human rights record of the Tutsi-dominated government has deteriorated in recent years and many of its efforts to promote harmony have been rather heavy handed, it has confronted the past more directly and forcefully than have the governments of the former Yugoslavia. This, coupled with a fairly good record of economic growth, might just create a self-sustaining peace that may outweigh whatever shortcomings we see in local and international efforts.

The role of the ICTR in advancing human security in Rwanda through acceptance of its legitimacy is difficult to assess, as we saw that opinion polls have produced varying results. There is evidence in the polls that does suggest the Rwandan people support the justice of the ICTR, but that they also have greater confidence in their own judicial enterprise. This, coupled with the domineering role played by the government in Rwandan society, probably means that human security in Rwanda is largely internally driven. International justice may have played an important role in confronting and punishing the ringleaders of the genocide and calling the genocide by its rightful name. What we cannot know is the degree to which social and political problems may have arisen in Rwanda had there been no international justice and condemnation. But we cannot say if the ICTR's legitimacy or lack thereof among the people of Rwanda has contributed to advancing human security in that country. We see a powerful government that has been determined to establish security and stability in Rwanda at whatever cost and an international tribunal that awkwardly accompanied the Rwandan people in the journey toward truth and justice.

The reader may be forgiven at this point for thinking that we have very little in the way of good news or optimism about the legitimacy of international justice and its contribution to human security. But while the former Yugoslavia and Rwanda may show us the limits of international justice in the face of local opposition and the interests of local government, Sierra Leone and even the case of Kenya give us some solid ground for optimism. The Special Court for Sierra Leone enjoys widespread and strong support among the people of that nation. It certainly earned a great deal of legitimacy during its existence and was helped in large part by three crucial factors. First, it was located in Freetown, the capitol of Sierra Leone, which made the job of outreach and communication considerably easier and also created more of a sense of local ownership. Its many and extensive efforts at going into the community to educate the people no doubt helped foster greater awareness and recognition that the bad actors who had plagued their society were being prosecuted and punished (Clark 2009).

Second, the Special Court for Sierra Leone pursued a nonpartisan strategy of targeting the leadership of those groups that were responsible for the most brutal and widespread atrocities. While the court certainly had to contend with the same sorts of divisions in society that prompted some people to wonder why the court was going after some political and military leaders and not others, the SCSL does not seem to have attracted nearly the same charges of bias that have been leveled against the ICTY and to a lesser extent the ICTR. Its justice has not been perfect, but what people probably desire most is some form of reckoning and retribution that demonstrates their problems have been recognized and their voices heard.

Third, the SCSL completed its business in relatively short order. Unlike the ICTY, ICTR, and ICC, where trials have been dragging on for years, the Special Court for Sierra Leone wrapped up its business in about ten years. To be sure, that court had only four trials to conduct, but perhaps that is part of their success. Having identified a select number of individuals to prosecute (including one safely ensconced in another country, Charles Taylor) instead of casting a wide net, the court ensured that its business would be dealt with quickly, that a large number of trials would not confuse the issue, and that attention would be focused on the trials instead of the long delays and complications. This is the strategy being pursued by the ICC, but it has not enjoyed nearly the same level of success as the SCSL, for many reasons, but perhaps it too has become too thinly spread.

But has the support the SCSL has earned in Sierra Leone advanced human security there? As we saw in the data on human rights in Sierra Leone, it is one of the few success stories among the states targeted by international tribunals. It has also been largely spared any further violence from internal war or external interventions. There is every reason to believe that the SCSL played an important role in helping solidify these gains in Sierra Leone, along with the international military intervention, international aid, and other forms of assistance. International justice done right is a critical component of sustaining the peace and protecting human security. Without justice, the likelihood that the truth will be undermined by emboldened ethnonational politicians increases. Without international justice, these bad actors can continue to wreak havoc in their countries and spoil the peace. And without international justice, people are likely to fear that these bad actors will continue to plague their societies and so will take whatever measures they feel are necessary to protect themselves. The key is that the justice has to be done expeditiously, fairly, and, if not locally, then accessibly to the population. The SCSL seems to have met these basic criteria.

Perhaps most surprisingly of all, the ICC does seem to have earned a strong degree of support in Kenya, the one nation in the survey data we examined that has been an ICC target. That the ICC has gained the support of the Kenyan people despite its many setbacks (several of which occurred after the survey was administered) speaks well for the potential for the court to earn the trust of other peoples whose conflicts it adjudicates. Further evidence regarding attitudes toward the ICC in other states is essential. Kenya is a relatively stable and prosperous nation compared to many of the other nations whose wars it is investigating, many of whom are still in the grip of violence and fear.

From these several cases of international justice we have explored, I would advance several recommendations. First, international justice should be brought in only after the violence has ended and there is widespread agreement on the need to prosecute a select number of perpetrators from all sides. It should also only be utilized when the nation itself is incapable of using or unwilling to use its own domestic criminal justice system. An exact balance of individuals from the various sides is not necessary, but each should believe its concerns have been addressed. This will not be perfect and perfectly fair justice in that these post-conflict situations must bow to politics to an extent.

There is a risk that such "moral parity" (Akhavan 2013, 533) will offend more than it will help. Nonetheless, the perfect cannot become the enemy of the good. We will return to this subject in the concluding chapter. Second, the appropriate degree of local engagement and control should be negotiated up front. The ICC will need to seriously consider holding trials where the victims live. It must ensure that its justice resonates locally or its truth may not be heard.

Third, international justice should be swift and short and focus on the primary leaders. The ICC will have to function this way and it is unlikely that any other tribunals will ever go after as many targets as the ICTY and ICTR did in their formative years. The longer trials drag on, the greater the chance that spoilers will exploit such problems for their own ends and undermine justice and peace. The longer the trials drag on, the greater the likelihood that the people will lose confidence and listen to the spoilers. This may well mean that the ICC should eschew investigating some conflicts where the chances of gaining custody of suspects are fairly low. At least until the court has earned some degree of legitimacy, discretion may be the better part of valor.

## NOTES

1. *Prosecutor v. Dražen Erdemović*, IT-96-22-Tbis, para. 21
2. As found on the ICTY website, http://www.icty.org/sections/Outreach/Outreach Programme, on April 12, 2013.
3. Extensive information on these data, the surveys, and other information about the project can be found at http://www.svt.ntnu.no/iss/ringdalweb/SEESSP%20Surveys .html. There were 2,500 residents of Croatia surveyed, 6,830 residents of Bosnia-Herzegovina, 3,639 residents of Serbia, 1,850 respondents from Montenegro, 2,504 residents of Kosovo, 2,593 from Macedonia, and 2,024 citizens of Albania (the Albanians were not included in this analysis). In Bosnia, 6,830 respondents were surveyed and of those, 2,100 were from Croat municipalities, 2,530 from Bosniak municipalities, and 2,100 from Republika Srpska. Another 3,639 respondents were surveyed in Serbia. The remainder comes from the other regions of the former Yugoslavia.

# *Chapter 6*

# Conclusion

## INTRODUCTION

The purpose of this book has been to evaluate the contribution of international justice to human security. Toward that end, we have analyzed the mechanics of how international tribunals are supposed to contribute to human security. How is it exactly that international tribunals are able to advance human security by providing justice, promoting human rights and peace, and earning legitimacy? The ad hoc international tribunals—the International Criminal Tribunal for the Former Yugoslavia, the International Criminal Tribunal for Rwanda, and the Special Court for Sierra Leone—and the permanent International Criminal Court were all expected to do a lot more for the world than simply deliver verdicts and pronounce punishment for the guilty. The promise of international justice is that it would go beyond what our domestic criminal justice systems do and help rid the world of international crimes and massive human rights atrocities. These are noble ambitions and even just the creation of these courts represents a victory for human rights. International justice has come a long way from the Armenian genocide to the Holocaust to the horrific human rights abuses of the Cold War communist dictatorships. But has its performance lived up to its promise? And how has the potential—the capacity of international justice—to promote peace, human rights, and all manner of other good and just causes affected its accomplishments? We will make our closing arguments here.

There are many ways by which we might evaluate the performance of these tribunals in advancing justice, human rights, peace, and earning legitimacy. As I suspect that many of the readers of this book are students, teachers, professors, and others who work in the business of international justice, I will use an assessment method we are all familiar with—letter grades. I will rate the overall performance of all the tribunals in realizing each of these four goals, while at the same time commenting on the performance of the individual courts. International justice is something like a group project, with each tribunal contributing to the overall mission. Where the performance in aggregate has been excellent, we will give the courts the gold standard, the "A" grade. When their performance has been mostly satisfactory with a combination of problems and accomplishments, they will earn the "average" grade of a "C." Where overall performance has been lacking and perhaps doing more harm than good, we must give international justice a failing grade of "F." I will, however, create a bit of a grading curve for the tribunals in recognition that they were not always given the tools or resources to be successful in achieving their goals. Just as it would be unfair to evaluate student performance over material that was not covered in class, so too is it inappropriate to fault the international courts for their failures when they were not equipped by their creators to be successful. Let's begin!

## JUSTICE AND HUMAN SECURITY

The ICTY and ICTR have mostly finished conducting their trials and the Special Court for Sierra Leone has dispensed with all of its trials and their appeals. The ICTR has a few more cases to finish at the appellate level, but the doors to its headquarters in Arusha, Tanzania, have all but closed. The ICTY still has two trials of first instance to be finished, but barring any unforeseen circumstances it should finish its last two trials sometime in 2017–2018. Hence, in all three cases, the ad hoc tribunals will have accomplished their principal mission of providing justice by holding trials, handing down verdicts, and meting out punishment. There have been no cases in which prominent accused persons have escaped justice, although there are still a handful of suspects wanted by the ICTR (indeed, one was just captured recently and transferred to Rwanda to stand trial).[1] The ICTY and SCSL were able to hold trials for all of those individuals they indicted and sought to prosecute (some ICTY cases were dropped or referred to national courts in the former Yugoslavia).[2] There have been no cases in which trials had to be halted because of circumstances within or beyond the control of the tribunals, as has happened with trials at the ICC involving Kenya and the Sudan (there have been delays and some died before completion of their trial, but nothing of the magnitude of the ICC problems). We can conclude that for the ICTY, ICTR, and SCSL, justice has been served and their principal missions accomplished. And while reasonable (as well as unreasonable) people may hold different opinions on just how fair these courts have been, the quality of their justice represents a substantial improvement over the Nuremberg and Tokyo Tribunals and has also improved as they have further developed.

We will need to give the tribunals a two-part grade in this initial portion of our grading exercise, first for the quality of their justice and second for the impact of this justice on human security. In terms of their delivery of justice, we must give the three ad hoc tribunals a fairly high grade for their completion of their trials. Because there have legitimate complaints regarding some critical issues such as excessively long trials (in the case of the ICTY and ICTR) and concerns about the sharing of exculpatory and other evidence with the defense, we cannot give the tribunals a straight "A" grade. I would judge their performance as an "A–" in delivering justice through completion of their trials and the delivery of verdicts and sentences. And lest the reader think that we may have set the bar too low and been too easy on the tribunals for simply having held trials, we should again bear in mind the comparison with the ICC. Delivering justice is not as easy as it might seem.

The jury is still out on the International Criminal Court, but the early indicators would suggest we have an "at-risk" institution on our hands. The court has tried only a handful of suspects from a few cases all arising out of conflicts in Central Africa. Other cases have been undermined by local politics (Kenya and Libya) and by the international community's unwillingness to exert pressure on the perpetrators (the Sudan). Prosecutions involving the situations in Uganda and Libya have been hampered by a lack of suspects in custody. The ICC has launched only one case on its own initiative—Kenya, again.

The ICC has been accused in the media, in academia, and among political leaders of bias against Africa. Although those governments and other groups that criticize the ICC for focusing on Africa conveniently overlook that a majority of those cases were self-referred by African states, the opaque methods by which the ICC has chosen to proceed with full-scale investigations has given such charges traction. It is not clear just how and why the ICC has decided that some conflict situations are worthy of investigation and prosecution and others not. In its history to date, we must regrettably conclude that the ICC does not have much to show for its efforts. Certainly the broad mandate of the court to investigate conflicts the world over, coupled with a lack of support from the international community to apprehend suspects, has made its work significantly more difficult than was the case with the ad hoc tribunals. Nonetheless, we cannot give the ICC a good grade. It has not failed entirely, but I would assign a "C–" grade to the ICC. That may be a bit generous, but we must keep in mind that the world has not always provided the kind of political and economic pressure on target states that seems to be necessary for the apprehension of suspects in some cases. If international justice was a group project, we would find that one member of the group has hurt the rest of the members and would bring the group grade down to a "B."

The difficult part of this portion of the evaluation is linking the provision of justice to the achievement of human security. Has the quality of the justice provided advanced the level of human security in each of the target nations? I have argued throughout this book that justice should be viewed as a necessary condition for human security in the aftermath of war and other forms of violence in which civilians have been targeted for atrocities. Absent any kind of reckoning with the past, any peace that is achieved is built on very thin ice and may well break in the future and lead to further acts of violence. The difficulty for us is that we will never know what would have happened in these target nations without international justice. We can speculate about how their politics would have evolved without these tribunals, but these counter-factual thought experiments are a poor substitute for real evidence. We can see that in one case, that of Rwanda, its government was going to pursue its own vision of peace building and reconciliation regardless of whatever the ICTR did. The international community has never had the kind of presence in Rwanda that would give it leverage over human security there, so the impact of international justice in Rwanda would have been limited no matter what. Yet as Akhavan (2013, 530) points out, "Holding ICTR trials in Arusha while the spillover violence of the genocide wipes out millions in eastern DRC, is an abominable contradiction." The ICTR was not equipped to stop the violence, but the force of its example was meaningless in the face of this new violence.

In the case of the former Yugoslavia and Sierra Leone, however, the international community, including the tribunals, has had a strong and lengthy presence. Those nations needed international intervention to bring peace and to sustain it. The international community ended the wars there, just as the Rwandan Patriotic Army ended the war in Rwanda. The international tribunals have always been a key component of the international community's peace-building strategy. Therefore, one might reasonably ask what would have happened to those nations had there been no international justice, but local justice or no justice at all instead. It is difficult to imagine how the political and military situations in those countries would have been helped by an absence of justice. Had the perpetrators been allowed to go free and presumably become part of the political process in these nations, it strains credulity to expect that those groups targeted by these leaders in Sierra Leone, and especially Bosnia-Herzegovina, would have acquiesced and made nice. Just the opposite would probably have occurred. The visible and ongoing presence of people like the leaders of the rebel armies in Sierra Leone and figures like Radovan Karadžić and Ratko Mladić in Bosnia would have undermined the peace and destabilized those nations had there not been international tribunals demanding their apprehension.[3]

In effect, a lack of international justice in the face of widespread, severe, and chronic human rights atrocities sends a strong signal that local parties are free to address such problems as they see fit. In some cases where the conflict actors, whether in countries like Sierra Leone and Bosnia-Herzegovina, may have goals that are open to negotiation with their adversaries, it may be possible for these local forces to reach a peace without the support of the international community or international justice. But all too often the goals of the conflict actors are not open to negotiation. If the conflict goals reflect a deep-rooted sense of national identity in which one group does not feel secure in the presence of the other or the conflict goals are driven by other ideological agendas that are not open to negotiation (think of ISIS), then international intervention, including international justice, is probably necessary to halt the fighting and establish conditions in which peace can be created and sustained. One could certainly argue that this was the case in an "identity" war such as in Bosnia.

To be sure, international justice can sometimes enflame passions where national, ethnic, and religious affiliations are at the core of the conflicts, but without international justice that removes those whose goals are to fan the flames of such violence, it is difficult to see how long-term human security can be achieved. International justice has helped to provide the foundation for a secure and stable society. No foundation built with justice, no peace. But the rest of the house must be built too in order to provide the shelter needed to weather the political storms that still swirl around places like Bosnia-Herzegovina.

It is not as clear that the ICTY has played such a central role in other conflicts under its jurisdiction in contributing to peace, such as in Croatia and Kosovo. The ICTY prosecuted far fewer cases involving the Kosovo war and the violence in Croatia in 1991 and the summer of 1995 and has tended to acquit those whom it did prosecute in several prominent cases. Both countries are now at peace and both have been served to an extent by international justice, but the impact of the ICTY in creating a stable foundation for human security in those states has been much more limited. Rather, the international community through the KFOR force in Kosovo has played a substantial role in that country's development and relationship with the country from which it seceded, Serbia. Croatia resolved its disputes with Serbia and its Serbian population either through military force or negotiation.

The overall grade for the ad hoc international tribunals in advancing human security through the provision of justice must be a mixed grade of "C." In some instances, we can argue with a degree of confidence that justice has played an important and perhaps even necessary role, such as in Sierra Leone and Bosnia-Herzegovina. In other conflict situations, such as in Rwanda, Croatia, and Kosovo, its effect has been much more limited and we should be hesitant to conclude, especially based on the kind of counter-factual reasoning I have been using, that the ICTR and the ICTY have made a necessary contribution.[4]

With the ICC it is still far too early to tell just how much of an impact its prosecutorial efforts have had on helping to advance human security, but based on the limited information we have thus far, there are many indications that its efforts have not played much, if any, role in helping to establish human security. Indeed, the violence in places like the Congo, the Central African Republic, and Uganda continued on despite ICC involvement, although human security has improved somewhat in the Congo and Uganda. The UN intervention in the Congo and U.S. efforts to train Ugandan forces and assist in the capture of Joseph Kony and other leaders of the Lord's Resistance Army have helped improve the situations in those countries. But the ICC contribution, by serving as a vehicle for justice and the attribution of responsibility for atrocities, has contributed in some ways. The lengthy trials involving the Congo and the lack of trials for indictees from Uganda have made the ICC seem rather ineffective. In other situations, political conflicts evolved independently of the ICC, such as in Kenya, the Sudan, and Libya. While the ICC has not been entirely irrelevant in these situations, we would be hard pressed to find evidence that its international justice has proven necessary or even important in helping establish human security in conflict situations. Its midterm grade would probably again have to be a "D."

## HUMAN RIGHTS

The ad hoc tribunals (not so much the ICC) have been reasonably effective in delivering justice, which has generally helped provide a solid foundation for human security. Now we must take a step further and evaluate whether the tribunals have made any contributions to advancement in the area of human rights. The reader will recall that the evidence was mixed in chapter 3.

## THE FORMER YUGOSLAVIA AND THE ICTY

There was limited evidence to suggest that the ICTY may have contributed to advancements in human rights. We know that human rights improvements took some number of years to occur in the region after the ICTY was created, but that they did occur and have mostly improved in the following years. We also know that large-scale human rights abuses have not occurred at all since the end of the wars in Croatia and Bosnia-Herzegovina. No further atrocities have occurred anywhere in the region since 2001 (after the war in Kosovo in 1999 and the brief period of fighting in Macedonia in 2001) that have resulted in more ICTY investigations. The difficult part lies in assigning some degree of responsibility for these improvements to the ICTY. From chapter 3 we know that regime changes in Croatia and Serbia played a major role in removing repressive leaders from power. To the extent that the ICTY can be given partial credit for playing a role in facilitating the removal from power of individuals like Slobodan Milošević, and in making public life impossible for many other wartime leaders, such as Radovan Karadžić and Ratko Mladić, which lessened the ability of these spoilers to sabotage the peace, it can be given partial credit for helping to improve human rights. Our data on human rights scores in the region show that these indicators did eventually improve as well. To be sure, these observations are made alongside the knowledge that even after the ICTY was created, there were horrific massacres at Srebrenica and in Kosovo. The ICTY alone was not sufficient to deter ethnonationalist politicians. Rather, once international support made the apprehension of increasing numbers of key political and military figures possible in the former Yugoslavia, human rights improvements became a reality.

Therefore, because human rights conditions in general have improved, because there have been no significant human rights atrocities since 2001, and because ICTY pressure was important in removing repressive leaders from power, we can assign a grade of "B" to the ICTY. It was not a decisive player in bringing about human rights improvements in the region. That likely depended to a considerable extent on European and American pressure (Kerr 2007). Nonetheless, ICTY pressure also forced the hand of those organizations to take international justice seriously and provide the necessary support to the ICTY.

## RWANDA AND THE ICTR

Human rights conditions in Rwanda are certainly not as bad as they were during the period leading up to and into the 1994 genocide, but human rights repression is an ever-present reality in that nation and Central Africa more generally. There is stability, security, and prosperity in Rwanda, but the Rwandan government has achieved these goals through economic strategies of growth and liberalization and the development of an attractive market for private and public sector investment (Dunne 2006). On the political side, the repressive tactics of the Rwandan Patriotic Front government, which has evinced little reluctance to go after and silence critics at home and abroad, have ensured security and stability, but have hurt human rights. The Rwandan government has also employed its own local, restorative justice vehicle in the gacaca initiative, in which local villages conducted their own trials.

The ICTR grade for advancing human security through promotion of human rights must be judged a "C." The tribunal did encourage and play some role in facilitating the removal of a large number of individuals from power who might have been spoilers of the peace or provided real leadership to the Hutu extremists who fled over the Rwandan border into Zaire (so called at the time) in 1994. Hence, it made a valuable contribution in helping to remove potential threats to human rights from Hutu extremists. The ICTR has not, however, been in any position to encourage the Rwandan government to improve its human rights practices. That government has assertively forged its own type of political development and has become an obstacle in the path to the improvement of human rights. Therefore, we must conclude that the ICTR, while contributing to the removal of many individuals who would have posed an ongoing threat to human rights in Rwanda, has not had significant influence over events in that nation.

## SIERRA LEONE AND THE SCSL

Sierra Leone has experienced the most improvement in human rights of any of the nations that we have examined. While its human rights scores are not the highest, it has improved substantially from the dark days of the civil war of the 1990s. There has been little violent or nonviolent repression of protests, and violence against civilians has dropped to quite low levels. How much of this success story can be attributed to the SCSL? To be sure, Sierra Leone was targeted with a sizeable military intervention, foreign assistance, and NGO help after the war ended. As I argued in chapter 3, Sierra Leone is really the polar opposite of Rwanda. Rwanda has certainly received considerable amounts of international support, but it has largely charted its own path with regard to internal peace and security. The international community, including and especially the SCSL, has played a major role in advancing human rights on the ground in Sierra Leone. From the location of the SCSL in the capital of Freetown, to the SCSL's extensive outreach efforts, the court functioned within Sierra Leonean society. Hence, its ability to advance internal change was significantly greater than the tribunals that were not so advantaged.

In addition, the Sierra Leone tribunal, like the ICTY and ICTR, has helped remove the worst human rights violators from politics, where they had done considerable damage to society. The SCSL was reached by an agreement between the United Nations and the Sierra Leone government and borrowed from some of the best features of the ICTY and ICTR, such as their Rules of Procedure and Evidence, while avoiding many of the difficulties those tribunals have encountered in how their work is perceived among their stakeholders. Local outreach and greater levels of engagement with the local population have resulted in significant local support and have been part of a comprehensive engagement in Sierra Leone that has contributed to a sharp decline in human rights violations (Kerr and Lincoln 2008). For these reasons, we shall award the SCSL a grade of "A–." It is not the best possible grade because we cannot overlook the vital role played by the international community in establishing the peaceful and secure conditions that made the court a success. At the same time, there is much to learn from the successes of the SCSL that can be used as we look to the future of the ICC.

## THE WORLD AND THE INTERNATIONAL CRIMINAL COURT

The evidence in chapter 3 indicated that among the states that have been subject to ICC investigations, human rights are not improving. Human rights repression and violence against civilians remain at exceptionally high levels, and in some places under ICC jurisdiction it has been getting worse. In places like the Congo, Libya, the Sudan, and the Central African Republic, human rights conditions are quite precarious and life as a civilian remains dangerous in the face of militias, terrorist organizations, other groups, and even their governments, which continue to prey on civilians. While these problems are mostly due to complex international and local political interests beyond the ICC's control, ICC involvement has not made an appreciable positive difference in any of these cases.

In contrast to the ad hoc tribunals that dealt with conflicts that had either ended before they were established (ICTR and SCSL) or had mostly ended before the tribunal was fully functioning (ICTY), the ICC is dealing with many violent and unstable nations or very difficult political environments, such as the Sudan, Libya, the Congo, Uganda, and Kenya, that have hindered the ICC's effectiveness. The ICC's problems are numerous. Its inability to gain custody of those individuals whom it has indicted does not help in deterring other would-be war criminals, who see a toothless organization and an indifferent international community. Its diverse caseload, along with its inability to enter many of the countries whose situations it is investigating, means that its outreach activities will not be as substantial as will be needed in these politically fraught nations. Indeed, given the ICC's diverse caseload and the location of its target states in some of the most challenging regions on the planet, it is doubtful that the court is equipped at all to help advance human rights. While the example of its justice may deter some would-be war criminals and its apprehension of a small number of suspects will limit their ability to make mischief back home, the ICC has more pressing issues to attend to than human rights. The lack of prosecutions and the near end of cases in Kenya, the Sudan, and Libya seem to indicate that the ICC may be accumulating more problems than answers over time. We would have to give the ICC a "D" grade. Because the ICC does not have control over its entire jurisdiction and must take cases on referral, its impact will be limited. Yet despite those caveats, it is clear that the ICC is foundering.

Overall, the international criminal tribunals are probably deserving of a "C+" grade in human rights. The SCSL is a success story and the ICTY is a partial success story, while the ICTR and ICC have not played a significant role in human rights improvements. Improvements in human rights can be facilitated by the tribunals, as they remove bad actors from societies and contribute to more general deterrence. Human rights improvements, however, also require local reforms of internal security laws, policing, and the practices of local courts. These internal changes are not under the purview of the tribunals, but as the tribunals assist local courts in prosecuting lower-ranking individuals and building capacity, they can help set the stage for future improvements. If the ICC is able to become a more effective force for international justice, that is where it may wish to expend its limited resources in outreach activities.

## PEACE AND HUMAN SECURITY

The record of the tribunals regarding the advancement of peace is not unlike their human rights record. Peace, like human rights, is overdetermined. That is, there are multiple factors accounting for peace in the countries targeted for investigation, each one of which has likely played an important role. Isolating which factors were responsible for how much of the peace is a rather speculative exercise. Attributing responsibility to the tribunals is equally, if not even more, speculative in nature. Let's see what we know for sure.

We know that one war and one minor civil war broke out in the former Yugoslavia after the establishment of the ICTY. We know that no wars have occurred inside Rwanda (Central Africa is another matter entirely) and no wars have occurred within Sierra Leone. The states that have been targeted by the ICC were often still at war when investigations began, and if the wars are over, there has been dangerous instability left in their wake. Violence has not flared up again in Kenya or the Ivory Coast and it has diminished in the Congo and Uganda, although atrocities still occur in the areas that have been the principal focus of the ICC investigations. Conflict continues in the Sudan and the Central African Republic, while instability and violence still plague Mali and Libya. We must also remember the findings that those states that were members of the ICC and were more supportive of the court were less likely to experience civil wars and enjoyed greater human rights protections. The creation of the ICC does not seem to have contributed to greater human security more generally in Africa.

Based on the data we saw in chapter 4, our assessment of the record of the ad hoc tribunals would be mostly good. The SCSL would receive another excellent grade, as all forms of violence in that nation have declined and that tribunal played the most active role of the three in Sierra Leonean society. The grade of the ICTR would not be nearly so high due to the overwhelming role played by the Rwandan Patriotic Front government in dominating the internal and external security needs of Rwanda. We should give the ICTR a "C" grade again for its limited role in Rwandan society, while at the same time we must recognize that the arrest of nearly all the major culprits in the Rwandan genocide has eliminated their ability to foment unrest and violence within Rwanda. The ICTY would also receive a "C" grade on the basis of the wars that occurred after the tribunal was established. As I argued in chapter 4, however, given that the threat of NATO airpower was not sufficient to dissuade the Serbian leadership from launching yet another war, it is highly doubtful that any tribunal could have done more. And the jury is still out on the ICC, although the early indicators do not look good. For now, let's leave the past behind us and think about whether today's peace will hold into the future for the countries of the former Yugoslavia, Rwanda, and Sierra Leone.

As we have discussed earlier, those who would spoil the peace have been removed from power and the threat of ICC prosecution will hang over the heads of all those leaders in Africa whose strategies entail human rights abuses. The coming years will tell if the peace that has been purchased for the price of many lives and much destruction and buttressed by international justice will last. UN and NATO forces have been out of Bosnia for well over a decade, and thus the long-standing international military presence in the region has ended for the most part (the EU still provides assistance with some military tasks in the region). International forces are no longer in Rwanda or Sierra Leone. Whether any of these nations will relapse into civil war is an open question, as there is a fairly high likelihood that once a state has experienced civil war, it will fight another (Mason and Meernik 2008).

The international community has invested a considerable amount of resources into these nations and, despite the high recidivism rate of civil war states, peace seems likely to hold in the countries of the former Yugoslavia, Rwanda, and Sierra Leone for the foreseeable future. The bigger issue is likely to be whether some level of reconciliation has been achieved that can reinforce the peace and be drawn upon in times of distress. If ethnic tensions continue to simmer, they may tear society up again in the event that a future economic or political crisis arises. Just like an old wound that never heals and breaks open under exertion, ethnic tensions can undermine years of peace building if not treated properly. And to continue with the medical analogy, that treatment is reconciliation. Reconciliation is an ongoing process, not a onetime event, and societies that do not address the divisions and lack of trust that led to war may well find the same problems arising again.

The former Yugoslavia and Rwanda have ethnic tensions that predate their wars of the 1990s, while there is less of a history of extensive state-organized violence and systemic repression in Sierra Leone. The Rwandan government has engineered a somewhat heavy-handed effort at reconciliation with its gacaca trials, elimination of ethnic identity cards, and its emphasis on one Rwanda for all. The most important tool it has in tamping down tensions is probably economic growth. Ethnic tensions between the Hutus and Tutsis may well remain, but prosperity will probably make these problems less salient. That is not the case with the former Yugoslavia, and especially Bosnia-Herzegovina, where former adversaries must still live alongside one another. While there have been national and international efforts at reconciliation, the Bosnian government and its basic functions are still divided along ethnic lines. The conflict has become frozen. Politicians continue to exploit divisions and one group's fear of the "other" to gain and maintain power, while unemployment and economic problems abound. If Rwanda were the patient, yearly checkups to evaluate its health and ability to fight off the infection of another conflict would seem reasonable. If Bosnia-Herzegovina were the patient, quarterly assessments might be the more risk-averse strategy. While there is no immediate threat of war in any of the nations that were subjects of the ad hoc tribunals, peace and reconciliation must be constantly attended to and warning signs must be taken seriously. It was the world's refusal or inability to heed the warning signs that helped lead to their earlier wars. One would hope that we have learned a lesson.

## THE LEGITIMACY OF INTERNATIONAL JUSTICE AND HUMAN SECURITY

The legitimacy of the international criminal tribunals—the acceptance of the right of these institutions to make decisions and the justice they provide—helps establish a foundation for human security. In particular, the acceptance of the peoples of the states subject to international justice of the truth as discovered during trial is essentially the beginning of acceptance or acknowledgment of who did what to whom during their nation's conflicts. Legitimacy, however, must be earned, especially in the case of international courts that intrude upon a state's sovereign right to provide justice to its own people. The people will want to see results; they will likely have some very definitive ideas about who should and should not go on trial and be punished. This creates something of a conundrum for these courts. Without acceptance of their right to deliver justice and a basic acceptance of the truth and justice they do provide, it is unlikely that the tribunals can create this foundation upon which human security can be built. But if legitimacy is premised on the tribunals providing a truth that is in accord with one's narrative about what happened during a conflict, the acceptance and legitimacy of the tribunals are conditional. If legitimacy is viewed through the lens of one's ethnic group and hinges on the outcome of each and every verdict, the tribunals may be reinforcing the very ethnic divisions their truths were intended to overcome.

This is the risk of international justice every time a tribunal adjudicates political and military conflicts. Earning legitimacy is inherently an uphill struggle against entrenched interests and popular passions. It demands very effective prosecutorial efforts, clear, compelling, and credible judicial decision making, and an engaging and ongoing communications strategy. Nonetheless, earning legitimacy is not impossible, as the reader learned in chapter 5. Let's review what we have learned about how each of the tribunals fared in this quest and how their efforts to earn legitimacy have helped or hindered human security.

The ICTY has faced significant challenges earning legitimacy, as each of the major ethnic groups involved in the wars of the former Yugoslavia have largely held fast to their own ethnonationalist narratives (Ford 2012). Support for the ICTY is contingent on ethnicity—the greater the number of one's ethnic group on trial, the lower the support. In effect, the ICTY has not earned robust legitimacy because this type of conditional support is not genuine. Conditional legitimacy does not create a foundation upon which the responsibility of each group for wartime crimes is accepted. Just the opposite. Conditional legitimacy can perpetuate the divisions and biased truths that helped contribute to the outbreak of conflict. We discussed at length in chapter 5 the reasons why the ICTY has faced many challenges in developing an enduring legitimacy, from the lateness of its outreach programs to the ineffectiveness of its communications strategies in a region where government-controlled media provides counter-narratives that resonate more deeply with the people. Whether the problems with the ICTY's inability to earn real legitimacy were mostly in or out of its control, in one sense, does not matter because the result is still the same—divided societies that, in many cases, have not accepted international truth. They have not, for the most part, used the truth provided by international justice to establish a foundation for peace and reconciliation. Legitimacy has been weak and has hindered the advancement of human security in the region. We would have to give the ICTY a fairly low grade of "C" in recognition of its efforts that have not risen to the challenges of earning legitimacy in the war-torn Balkans.

The legitimacy of the ICTR in the eyes of the Rwandan public was difficult to determine, as the few opinion polls that have been conducted provide diverse results. Even if we accept that in general Rwandan attitudes have been supportive of the ICTR, and certainly more acceptant of its legitimacy than many people from the former Yugoslavia have been of the ICTY, the ICTR almost seems to operate in a parallel universe from Rwanda. The Rwandan government provides its justice independently of the ICTR's and has a much more dominant role in establishing its truth in the eyes of the Rwandan public. Indeed, lest we forget, the Rwandan government was the only vote in opposition in the UN Security Council to the creation of the ICTR. The decisions of the ICTR have not, albeit with some exceptions, provoked hostility or fanned the flames of ethnic tension, but it is not clear if these verdicts have contributed to helping to provide a truth that establishes a foundation for human security, as the Rwandan government has taken ownership of that task. The ICTR earns a grade of "C+/B–," as its efforts have met with some support and it has largely avoided reaching decisions that have been divisive (although some would say this is only because the ICTR has only ever tried Hutu leaders for their crimes and not the Tutsi-led Rwandan Patriotic Front army for its alleged crimes in 1994).

The Special Court for Sierra Leone is the one true success of the three ad hoc tribunals. It has earned support from the people of Sierra Leone; it developed an effective outreach program and it prosecuted individuals from all the major factions of the civil war without perpetuating underlying ethnic tensions (Wu 2013). Its international-national partnership model can give us some important lessons on how international justice works best, as we will discuss later. The SCSL appears to have earned legitimacy and its success in this regard has helped establish a good foundation for the peace that has held in Sierra Leone for almost fifteen years. The SCSL gets an "A" and the star pupil award.

The International Criminal Court presents something of a mixed bag. On one hand, the court enjoys solid support among the peoples of the world of approximately 60 percent and even from those in one nation—Kenya—that has been subject to ICC jurisdiction. On the other hand, its selection of cases for prosecution has aroused controversy. It has lost support among many African leaders, even in South Africa, whose dominant party, the African National Congress, adopted a resolution calling on African leaders to withdraw from the ICC. The challenges it will face in the future as it navigates the treacherous political waters of the nations it investigates, to say nothing of the larger international community whose support will be critical in gaining access to evidence, testimony, and suspects, are substantial. So while early indicators of the ICC's legitimacy in the opinion poll data we examined are promising, the court's ability to convert this support into legitimacy in its target states is difficult to assess. The linkage between whatever legitimacy the court does enjoy in the eight nations that it has investigated and human security is even more difficult to measure. Therefore, we must give the ICC a grade of "I" or incomplete on the question of its legitimacy and contribution to human security.

Our overall grade for the four tribunals is a "C." There have been notable successes like the SCSL, but there are also the problems with the ICTY and the conditional support it enjoys among the people of the former Yugoslavia. The evidence of ICTR and ICC legitimacy is mixed, but also insufficient with which to judge its impact on human security. To the extent that any of these tribunals is able to provide truth in a form and a way that resonates with the affected peoples, they can provide a basis for acceptance of responsibility and perhaps some level of reconciliation. Providing such a truth is not trivial. In nations whose leaders are the most unyielding in their ethno-nationalist narratives, whose conflicts are the most complex, or whose communications infrastructure is poor, it may well take an army of public relations experts to set about earning legitimacy. That is not what the international community is prepared to offer, however. So what can be done? That is the last subject of this chapter and the book.

## CONCLUSION

It is a simple truism that the benefits of international justice are quite difficult to quantify and measure, while the costs have been significant. The UN budgets for the ad hoc tribunals have run in the hundreds of millions of dollars annually. Our analyses reveal that their records have been mixed. National trials or truth commissions would cost considerably less, assuming that governments would vigorously strive to prosecute and tell the truth. The international community has, however, through its international conventions on war crimes and genocide, its establishment of war crimes tribunals through the United Nations, and the creation of an International Criminal Court, made it abundantly clear that some crimes are so heinous as to demand an international response. International justice is a project conceived and executed through the international community. The world must take ownership of it or come up with a better way going forward. If international tribunals are to work and advance human security, then I would suggest doing the following.

First, international justice should be more locally anchored and locally accessible. If international justice is going to work for people who live hundreds or thousands of miles away from its headquarters, then something needs to be done to provide more effective and consistent connections and communications to the people whose conflicts are the target of international prosecutions. Our analysis of the legitimacy of the tribunals revealed that the establishment of the SCSL in Freetown, Sierra Leone, made communication with local audiences much more feasible and gave them a much greater sense of ownership of justice. Local buy-in then made the justice delivered by the SCSL more understandable, which in turn gave the SCSL greater levels of support. The acceptance of the SCSL and the justice it delivered facilitated the long-term maintenance of human security. Our measures of human rights improvements and peace showed the greatest progress in Sierra Leone. For the ICC, this will probably require a substantial revision of its treaty. While it may not be possible for the entire court to go traipsing around the world from conflict zone to conflict zone, it can bring its operations closer to the people by better explaining the process by which it determines to launch investigations and holding significant numbers of trials in the countries that are being investigated. If these nations are too dangerous to conduct such activities, they are probably not ready for justice.

Second, the ICC should continue to indict just those leaders who are most responsible for substantial violations of human rights. More controversially, however, the ICC should strive to provide political balance in its selection of individuals to prosecute. It is quite clear that given the powerful ethnonationalist narratives that people have been taught and even indoctrinated in, that prosecutorial strategies that focus on one group while not targeting others will lead to opposition and resistance to the truth. Justice may not resonate locally under such circumstances and may even create greater tensions. If nothing else, justice should do no harm. The prevention of harm may well mean that it is not possible to prosecute only on the basis of who committed the most human rights violations. Prosecution may have to incorporate considerations of politics, group identity, and other factors to ensure that it is viewed as evenhanded. This does not mean that there is a "moral parity" among the sides in a civil war or that tribunals should indict individuals when evidence is lacking in order to achieve balance. Rather, it is recognition that in order for international justice to work, it must be cognizant of national politics—it cannot pretend that these divisions do not matter. Consideration of such "extrajudicial" factors may be anathema to those of us brought up with the idealized view of justice as blind, but it is probably the lesser of two evils. To do otherwise may mean that justice does not "work" for the affected populations at best or that it leads to greater violence at worst.

Implicit in these two recommendations is the third and final one. Creating greater local ownership of international justice and determining how to appropriately balance the targets of prosecution suggests that justice will need to be consciously tailored to fit local situations. It cannot be a "one-size-fits-all" model. Instead, the ICC, as the only permanent tribunal after the ad hoc tribunals have all closed down, should negotiate the terms of its relationship with the governments whose people it will be prosecuting. Without such agreement up front on who the ICC is likely to target and where and how it will hold its trials, the local acceptance of the ICC will probably be insufficient to develop the legitimacy it needs to deliver justice and ultimately advance human security. This does require a significant revision of the ICC treaty, but the precedent already exists because many of the court's current cases were the result of self-referral. This process of self-referral should involve a binding agreement by all relevant parties regarding the location and nature of the ICC investigation. This will substantially increase, although it can never guarantee, acceptance of the ICC's legitimacy in the local population. A freely given acceptance of the right of the ICC to conduct its business means a much greater chance that the people will accept its legal and historical truths and establish a foundation upon which human security can be built.

This may not be the model that most governments envisioned when they created the ICC, but it is based on two fundamental principles. First, international justice should strive to do no harm. If its provision creates or risks greater violence and suffering among the people in whose name justice is being provided, we must reconsider the ethical and moral dimensions of international justice. If the international community's goal of justice privileges the prosecution of its laws over the interests of the people whose conflicts have led to this justice, human rights will once again be made subservient to politics. Where before it was national governments and their desire for power and security that trumped human rights, the current model of justice could lead to the international community's interest in upholding its precedents and its laws trumping human rights. The irony in this is disturbing. The cost for human security would be substantial.

Second, we cannot want something more than the people or country we are trying to assist. If justice is going to work, it needs local buy-in. The international community, through the ICC, cannot expect that its insistence on its right to investigate and prosecute will ensure that local people will accept this right and accord the ICC the legitimacy it requires. To be sure, the ICC has the rightful power to investigate conflicts on its own initiative because the states that signed the ICC statute give it that very right. They surrendered some degree of their sovereignty in the process. It is clear, however, that while the "right" to seize jurisdiction is a necessary condition for initiating a case, it is not a sufficient condition for establishing legitimacy. There is no power that any court has that can force people to accept its legitimacy. That must be earned. For it to be earned, there must be some degree of popular acceptance or democratic legitimacy according to the ICC. The people should speak, in whatever manner they choose, to signal their acceptance of the ICC and most especially their readiness to accept, even reluctantly, its judgments. This international justice may not always be popular and no one will likely be happy with everything the court does. But popular acceptance of the ICC's legitimacy means that there is a much greater likelihood that it can provide the kind of justice that leaves people more, not less, secure. And that is the essence of human security.

## NOTES

1. Information on the case of Ladislas Ntaganzwa can be found at http://www.unmict.org/en/news/drc-transfers-ladislas-ntaganzwa-rwanda.

2. The reader can go to the following websites to learn about these accomplishments of the ad hoc tribunals. For the ICTY, go to http://www.icty.org/sections/AbouttheICTY. For the ICTR, go to http://www.unictr.org/en/tribunal. For the SCSL, go to http://www.rscsl.org/index.html.

3. It is important to emphasize that Karadžić and Mladić did remain outside the custody of the ICTY for many years, but for most of that period they were on the run and were not taking an active role in politics. Thus, their ability to hamper the peace was severely curtailed. Even more to the point, had these individuals been allowed to take part in politics openly and without penalty for their actions, one could imagine the kind of furor that would have erupted throughout the region.

4. I have not mentioned the case of Macedonia in the context of the ICTY because that tribunal prosecuted only two cases and has not been a visible player in that country's political development since the brief flare-up of violence in 2001.

# Bibliography

## CHAPTER 1


Akhavan, Payam. 2001. "Beyond Impunity: Can International Criminal Justice Prevent Future Atrocities?" *American Journal of International Law* 95 (1): 7–31.

Bass, Gary. 2002. *Stay the Hand of Vengeance*. Princeton, NJ: Princeton University Press.

Boas, Gideon, James Bischoff, and Natalie Reid. 2011. *Forms of Responsibility in International Criminal Law*. Cambridge: Cambridge University Press.

Bosco, David. 2014. *Rough Justice: The International Criminal Court in a World of Power Politics*. Oxford: Oxford University Press.

Clark, Janine Natalya. 2010. "The ICC, Uganda and the LRA: Re-Framing the Debate." *African Studies* 69: 141–60.

deGuzman, Margaret. 2012. "Choosing to Prosecute: Expressive Selection at the International Criminal Court." *Michigan Journal of International Law* 33: 265–320.

Drumbl, Mark A. 2007. *Atrocity, Punishment and International Law*. Cambridge: Cambridge University Press.

Grodsky, Brian. 2007. "Producing Truth: The Politics of Investigating Past Human Rights Violations in Post-Communist States." *World Affairs* 169 (3): 125–33.

Kelsall, Tim. 2009. *Culture Under Cross Examination*. Cambridge: Cambridge University Press.

Kerr, Rachel 2007. "Peace through Justice? The International Criminal Tribunal for the Former Yugoslavia." *Southeast European and Black Sea Studies* 7: 379.

Meernik, James. 2013. "Justice, Power and Peace: Conflicting Interests and the Apprehension of ICC Suspects." Special Issue of *International Criminal Law Review*, The Reality of International Criminal Justice 13: 169–90.

Mendeloff, David. 2004. "Truth-Seeking, Truth-Telling, and Postconflict Peacebuilding: Curb the Enthusiasm?" *International Studies Review* 6 (3): 355–80.

Poe, Steven C., and Neal Tate. 1994. "Repression of Human Rights to Personal Integrity in the 1980s: A Global Analysis." *American Political Science Review* 88: 853–72.

Prunier, Gerard. 1995. *The Rwanda Crisis: History of a Genocide*. New York: Columbia University Press.

Schabas, William. 2006. *The UN International Criminal Tribunals: The Former Yugoslavia, Rwanda and Sierra Leone*. Cambridge: Cambridge University Press.

Scharf, Michael. 1997. "The Case for a Permanent International Truth Commission." *Duke Journal of Comparative and International Law* 7: 375–403.

Snyder, Jack, and Wright L. Vinjamuri. 2003. "Trials and Errors: Principle and Pragmatism in Strategies of International Justice." *International Security* 283: 5–44.

## CHAPTER 2

Albonetti, Celesta A. 1997. "Sentencing Under the Federal Sentencing Guidelines." *Law and Society Review* 31 (4): 789–822.

Amstutz, Mark. 2005. *The Healing of Nations: The Promise and Limits of Political Forgiveness*. Lanham, MD: Rowman & Littlefield.

Bass, Gary. 2002. *Stay the Hand of Vengeance*. Princeton, NJ: Princeton University Press.

Biggar, Nigel. 2005. "Concluding Remarks." In *Burying the Past: Peace and Doing Justice after Conflict*, edited by N. Biggar, 270–85. Washington, DC: Georgetown University Press.

Black, Donald. 1996. *The Behavior of Law*. New York: Academic Press.

Black, Ryan, and Christina Boyd. 2012. "The Role of Law Clerks in the U.S. Supreme Court's Agenda-Setting Process." *American Politics Research* 40 (1): 147–73.

Black, Ryan, and Ryan Owens. 2012. "Consider the Source (and the Message): Supreme Court Justices and Strategic Audits of Lower Court Decisions." *Political Research Quarterly* 65 (2): 385–95.

Box-Steffensmeier, Janet M., Dino P. Christenson, and Matthew P. Hitt. 2013. "Quality Over Quantity: Amici Influence and Judicial Decision Making." *American Political Science Review* 107 (3): 446–60.

Brace, Paul, and Melinda Gann Hall. 1997. "The Interplay of Preferences, Case Facts, Context and Rules in the Politics of Judicial Choice." *Journal of Politics* 59: 1206–31.

Cassese, Antonio. 2004. "The ICTY: A Living and Vital Reality." *Journal of International Criminal Justice* 2: 585–97.

Chambliss, William J., and Robert B. Seidman. 1971. *Law, Order, and Power*. Reading, MA: Addison-Wesley.

Clark, Janine. 2009a. "Judging the ICTY: Has It Achieved Its Objectives?" *Journal of Southeast European and Black Sea Studies* 9: 123–42.

Clark, Janine. 2009b. "Plea Bargaining at the ICTY: Guilty Pleas and Reconciliation." *European Journal of International Law* 20: 415–36.

Clark, Janine. 2009c. "The Limits of Retributive Justice: Findings of an Empirical Study in Bosnia and Hercegovina." *Journal of International Criminal Justice* 7: 463–87.

Clark, Janine. 2009d. "From Negative to Positive Peace: The Case of Bosnia and Hercegovina." *Journal of Human Rights* 8: 360–84.

Clark, Janine. 2011. "Transitional Justice, Truth and Reconciliation: An Under-Explored Relationship." *International Criminal Law Review* 11: 241–61.

Clark, Janine. 2014. *International Trials and Reconciliation: Assessing the Impact of the International Criminal Tribunal for the Former Yugoslavia*. New York: Routledge.

Creta, Vincent M. 1998. "The Search for Justice in the Former Yugoslavia and Beyond: Analyzing the Rights of the Accused Under the Statute and the Rules of Procedure and Evidence of the International Criminal Tribunal for the Former Yugoslavia." *Houston Journal of International Law* 20 (2): 381–418.

Crow, Matthew S., and Marc Gertz. 2008. "Sentencing Policy and Disparity: Guidelines and the Influence of Legal and Democratic Subcultures." *Journal of Criminal Justice* 36 (4): 362–71.

Damaska, Mirjan. 2011. "The Competing Visions of Fairness: The Basic Choice for International Criminal Tribunals." *North Carolina Journal of International Law and Commercial Regulation* 362: 365–88.

Danner, Allison M. 2001. "Constructing a Hierarchy of Crimes in International Criminal Law Sentencing." *Virginia Law Review* 87 (3): 415–501.

deGuzman, Margaret. 2012. "How Serious are International Crimes? The Gravity Problem in International Criminal Law." *Columbia Journal of Transnational Law* 51: 18–68.

Digeser, Peter. 2001. *Political Forgiveness*. Ithaca, NY: Cornell University Press.

Dixon, Jo. 1995. "The Organizational Context of Criminal Sentencing." *American Journal of Sociology* 100: 1157–98.

Doerner, Jill, and Stephen Demuth. 2010. "The Independent and Joint Effects of Race/Ethnicity, Gender, and Age on Sentencing Outcomes in U.S. Federal Courts." *Justice Quarterly* 27 (1): 1–27.

Drumbl, Mark A. 2007. *Atrocity, Punishment and International Law*. Cambridge: Cambridge University Press.

Du Plessis, Max, Tiyanjana Maluwa, and Annie O'Reilly. 2013. "Africa and the International Criminal Court." *Chatham House, International Law*.

Fedorova, Mascha. 2012. *The Principle of Equality of Arms in International Criminal Proceedings*. Cambridge: Intersentia.

Fedorova, Masha, Sten Verhoeven, and Jan Wouters. 2009. *Safeguarding the Rights of Suspects and Accused Persons in International Criminal Proceedings*. Leuven: Institute for International Law (Faculty of Law), Catholic University of Leuven.

Ford, Stuart K. 2012. "A Social Psychology Model of the Perceived Legitimacy of International Criminal Courts: Implications for the Success of Transitional Justice Systems." *Vanderbilt Journal of Transnational Law* 45: 405–76.

Ford, Stuart K. 2013. "Fairness and Politics at the ICTY: Evidence from the Indictments." *North Carolina Journal of International Law and Commercial Regulation* 39: 45–113.

Franck, Thomas M. 1998. *Fairness in International Law and Institutions*. Oxford: Clarendon.

Galanter, Marc. 1974. "Why the 'Haves' Come Out Ahead: Speculations on the Limits of Legal Change." *Law and Society Review* 9 (1): 95–160.

Gallant, Kenneth S. 2003. "Politics, Theory and Institutions: Three Reasons Why International Criminal Defence Is Hard, and What Might Be Done About One of Them." *Criminal Law Forum* 14 (2): 317–34.

Gibson, James. 2004. *Overcoming Apartheid: Can Truth Reconcile a Divided Nation?* New York: Russell Sage Foundation.

Goldstone, Richard. 2000. *For Humanity: Reflections of a War Crimes Investigator*. New Haven, CT: Yale University Press.

Groome, Dermot M. 2007. "Re-Evaluating the Theoretical Basis and Methodology of International Criminal Trials." *Penn State International Law Review* 25 (4): 791–802.

Harmon, Mark, and Fergal Gaynor. 2004. "Prosecuting Massive Crimes with Primitive Tools: Three Difficulties Encountered by Prosecutors in International Criminal Proceedings." *Journal of International Criminal Justice* 2: 403–26.

Harmon, Mark, and Fergal Gaynor. 2007. "Ordinary Sentences for Extraordinary Crimes." *Journal of International Criminal Justice* 5: 683–712.

Harvard Law Review. 2001. "Fair Trials and the Role of International Criminal Defense." *Harvard Law Review* 114 (May): 1982–2006.

Haynie, Stacia L., and Kaitlyn L. Sill. 2007. "Experienced Advocates and Litigation Outcomes: Repeat Players in the South African Supreme Court of Appeal." *Political Research Quarterly* 60 (3): 443–53.

Henham, Ralph. 2003. "The Philosophical Foundations of International Sentencing." *Journal of International Criminal Justice* 1: 64–85.

Henham, Ralph. 2007. "Developing Contextualized Rationales for Sentencing in International Criminal Trials." *Journal of International Criminal Justice* 5: 757–78.

Johnson, Scott T. 1998. "On the Road to Disaster: The Rights of the Accused and the International Criminal Tribunal for the Former Yugoslavia." *International Legal Perspectives* 10 (Spring): 111–92.

Karnavas, Michael G. 2011. "The ICTY Legacy: A Defense Counsel's Perspective." *Goettingen Journal of International Law* 3 (3): 1052–92.

Khan, Karim A. A., and Anand A. Shah. 2014. "Defensive Practices: Representing Clients Before the International Criminal Court." *Law and Contemporary Problems* 76: 191–233.

King, Ryan D., Kecia R. Johnson, and Kelly McGeever. 2010. "Demography of the Legal Profession and Racial Disparities in Sentencing." *Law and Society Review* 44 (1): 1–32.

Knoops, Geert-Jan. 2004. "The Dichotomy between Judicial Economy and Equality of Arms within International and Internationalized Criminal Trials: A Defense Perspective." *Fordham International Law Journal* 28: 1595–644.

Kritzer, Herbert M., and Susan S. Silbey. 2003. *In Litigation: Do the Haves Still Come Out Ahead?* Stanford, CA: Stanford Law and Politics.

Kuersten, A. K., and Jason Jagemann. 2000. "Does the Interest Group Choir Really 'Sing with an Upper Class Accent?' Coalitions of Race and Gender Groups Before the Supreme Court." *Women and Politics* 21: 53–74.

Massa, Anne-Sophie. 2006. "NATO's Intervention in Kosovo and the Decision of the Prosecutor of the International Criminal Tribunal for the Former Yugoslavia Not to Investigate: An Abusive Exercise of Prosecutorial Discretion?" *Berkeley Journal of International Law* 24: 610–49.

McGuire, Kevin. 1995. "Repeat Players in the Supreme Court: The Role of Experienced Lawyers in Litigation Success." *Journal of Politics* 57: 187.

Mears, Daniel. 1998. "The Sociology of Sentencing: Reconceptualizing Decision-making Processes and Outcomes." *Law and Society Review* 32: 667–724.

Meernik, James. 2003. "Equality of Arms? The Individual vs. the International Community in War Crimes Tribunals." *Judicature* 86 (6): 312–19.

Meernik, James. 2011. "Sentencing Rationales and Judicial Decision-Making at the International Criminal Tribunals." *Social Science Quarterly* 92 (3): 588–608.

Meernik, James, and Rosa Aloisi. 2008. "Is Justice Delayed at the International Criminal Tribunals?" *Judicature* 91 (6): 276–87.

Meernik, James, and Raul Guerrero. 2014. "Can International Criminal Justice Advance Ethnic Reconciliation? The ICTY and Ethnic Relations in Bosnia-Hercegovina." *Journal of Southeast European and Black Sea Studies* 14: 383–407.

Meernik, James, and Kimi King. 2002. "The Effectiveness of International Law and the ICTY—Preliminary Results of an Empirical Study." *International Criminal Law Review* 1: 343–73.

Meernik, James, and Kimi King. 2003. "The Determinants of ICTY Sentencing: An Empirical and Doctrinal Analysis." *Leiden Journal of International Law* 16 (4): 717–50.

Meernik, James, and Kimi King. 2004. "Crimes and Punishment: How the International Criminal Tribunal for the Former Yugoslavia Distinguishes Among Massive Human Rights Violations." In *Understanding Human Rights Violations*, edited by Sabine Carey and Steven Poe. London: Ashgate.

Meernik, James, Kimi King, and Geoff Dancy. 2005. "Judicial Decision Making and International Tribunals: Assessing the Impact of Individual, National and International Factors." *Social Science Quarterly* 86: 683–703.

Mégret, Frédéric. 2009. "Beyond Fairness: Understanding the Determinants of International Criminal Procedure." *UCLA Journal of International Law and Foreign Affairs* 14 (1): 37–76.

Moghalu, Kingsley Chiedu. 2002. "Image and Reality of War Crimes Justice: External Perceptions of the International Tribunal for Rwanda." *The Fletcher Forum of World Affairs* 26/2 (Summer/Fall): 21–46.

Negri, Stefania. 2005. "The Principle of 'Equality of Arms' and the Evolving Law of International Criminal Procedure." *International Criminal Law Review* 54: 513–71.

Noor, Masi, Rupert Brown, Roberto Gonzalez, Jorge Manz, and Christopher Lewis. 2008. "On Positive Psychological Outcomes: What Helps Groups with a History of Conflict to Forgive and Reconcile with Each Other?" *Personality and Social Psychology Bulletin* 6: 819–32.

Olusanya, Olaoluwa. 2005. *Sentencing War Crimes and Crimes against Humanity Under the International Criminal Tribunal for the Former Yugoslavia*. Groningen: Europa Law.

Poe, Steven C., and Neal Tate. 1994. "Repression of Human Rights to Personal Integrity in the 1980s: A Global Analysis." *American Political Science Review* 88: 853–72.

Schabas, William. 2001. "Cambodia: Was It Really Genocide?" *Human Rights Quarterly* 23 (2): 470–77.

Scharf, Michael. 2004. "Trading Justice for Efficiency: Plea Bargaining and International Tribunals." *Journal of International Criminal Justice* 2: 1070–81.

Sheehan, Reginald S., William Mishler, and Donald R. Songer. 1992. "Ideology, Status, and Differential Success of Direct Parties Before the U.S. Supreme Court." *American Political Science Review* 86: 464–71.

Songer, Donald R., and Reginald S. Sheehan. 1992. "Who Wins on Appeal? Upperdogs and Underdogs in the United States Courts of Appeals." *American Journal of Political Science* 36 (1): 235–58.

Staub, Ervin. 2006. "Reconciliation after Genocide, Mass Killing, or Intractable Conflict: Understanding the Roots of Violence, Psychological Recovery, and Steps toward a General Theory." *Political Psychology* 27: 867–894.

Staub, Ervin. 2013. "Building a Peaceful Society: Origins, Prevention, and Reconciliation After Genocide and Other Group Violence." *American Psychologist* 7: 576–89.

Subasić, Haris, and Nerzuk Ćurak. 2014. "History, the ICTY's Record and the Bosnian Serb Culture of Denial." In *Prosecuting War Crimes; Lessons and Legacies of the International Criminal Tribunal for the Former Yugoslavia*, edited by James Gow, Rachel Kerr, and Zoran Pajić, 133–50. London: Routledge.

Ulmer, Sidney S. 1984. "The Supreme Court's Certiorari Decisions: Conflict as a Predictive Variable." *American Political Science Review* 78 (December): 901–11.

Van Schaack, Beth. 1999. "The Definition of Crimes Against Humanity: Resolving the Incoherence." *Columbia Journal of Transnational Law* 37 (3): 787–91.

Wilson, Richard. 2005. "Judging History: The Historical Record of the International Criminal Tribunal for the former Yugoslavia." *Human Rights Quarterly* 27: 908–42.

Zacklin, Ralph. 2004. "The Failings of Ad Hoc International Tribunals." *Journal of International Criminal Justice* 2 (2): 541–45.

Zappalà, Salvatore. 2007. "How to Ameliorate International Criminal Proceedings: Some Constructive Suggestions." *Journal of International Criminal Justice* 5: 346–47.

## CHAPTER 3

Akhavan, Payam. 2001. "Beyond Impunity: Can International Criminal Justice Prevent Future Atrocities?" *American Journal of International Law* 95 (1): 7–31.

Barria, Lilian A., and Steven D. Roper. 2005. "How Effective are International Criminal Tribunals? An Analysis of ICTY and the ICTR." *The International Journal of Human Rights* 9 (3): 349–68.

Chayes, Abram, and Antonia Handler Chayes. 1993. "On Compliance." *International Organization* 47: 175–205.

Clark, Janine N. 2009. "International War Crimes Tribunals and the Challenge of Outreach." *International Criminal Law Review* 9: 99–116.

David, Roman. 2014. "International Criminal Tribunals and the Perception of Justice: The Effect of the ICTY in Croatia." *International Journal of Transitional Justice* 8 (3): 476–95.

Drumbl, Mark A. 2007. *Atrocity, Punishment and International Law*. Cambridge: Cambridge University Press.

Dunne, J. Paul. 2006. "After the Slaughter: Reconstructing Mozambique and Rwanda." *The Economics of Peace and Security Journal* 1: 39–46.

Gilligan, Michael J. 2006. "Is Enforcement Necessary for Effectiveness? A Model of the International Criminal Regime." *International Organization* 60 (4): 935–67.

Gordy, Eric. 2003. "Accounting for a Violent Past, by Other Than Legal Means." *Southeast European and Black Sea Studies* 3: 1–24.

Jo, Hyeran, and Beth Simmons. Forthcoming. "Can the International Criminal Court Deter Atrocity?" *International Organization*.

Kim, Hunjoon, and Kathryn Sikkink. 2010. "Explaining the Deterrence Effect of Human Rights Prosecutions for Transitional Countries." *International Studies Quarterly* 54 (4): 939–63.

Ku, Julian, and Jide Nzelibe. 2006. "Do International Criminal Tribunals Deter or Exacerbate Humanitarian Atrocities?" *Washington University Law Review* 84: 777–833.

McAllister, Jacqueline. 2014. "On the Brink: Understanding When Armed Groups Might Be More Susceptible to International Criminal Tribunals' Influence." Paper presented at the 2014 Annual Meeting of the American Political Science Association.

Meernik, James. 2005. "Justice or Peace: How the International Criminal Tribunal Affects Societal Peace in Bosnia." *Journal of Peace Research* 42: 271–90.

Meernik, James, Rosa Aloisi, Angela Nichols, and Marsha Sowell. 2012. "The Impact of Human Rights Organizations on Naming and Shaming Campaigns." *Journal of Conflict Resolution* 56: 233–56.

Meernik, James, Angela Nichols, and Kimi King. 2010. "The Impact of International Tribunals and Domestic Trials on Peace and Human Rights After Civil War." *International Studies Perspectives* 11 (4): 309–34.

Minnow, Martha. 2002. *Breaking the Cycle of Hatred*. Princeton, NJ: Princeton University Press.

Neier, Aryeh. 1999. "Rethinking Truth, Justice and Guilt After Bosnia and Rwanda." In *Human Rights in Political Transitions: Gettysburg to Bosnia*, edited by Carla Hesse and Robert Post, 39–52. New York: Zone Books.

Oomen, Barbara. 2005. "Donor-Driven Justice and its Discontents: The Case of Rwanda." *Development and Change* 36 (5): 887–910.

Sloane, Robert. 2007. "Sentencing for the Crime of Crimes: The Evolving Common Law of Sentencing of the International Criminal Tribunal for Rwanda." *Journal of International Criminal Justice* 5: 713–34.

Snyder, Jack, and Leslie Vinjamuri. 2003. "Trials and Errors: Principle and Pragmatism in Strategies of International Justice." *International Security* 283: 5–44.

Stover, Eric, and Harvey Weinstein. 2004. *My Neighbor, My Enemy: Justice and Community in the Aftermath of Mass Atrocity*. Cambridge: Cambridge University Press.

Teitel, Ruti. 1999. "The Universal and Particular in International Criminal Justice." *Columbia Human Rights Law Review* 30 (2): 285–303.

Wippmann, David. 1999. "Atrocities, Deterrence and the Limits of International Justice." *Fordham International Law Journal* 23: 473–88.

## CHAPTER 4

Barria, Lilian A., and Steven D. Roper. 2005. "How Effective are International Criminal Tribunals? An Analysis of ICTY and the ICTR." *International Journal of Human Rights* 9 (3): 349–68.

Clark, Janine. 2011. "Transitional Justice, Truth and Reconciliation: An Under-Explored Relationship." *International Criminal Law Review* 11: 241–61.

Clark, Janine Natalya. 2014. *International Trials and Reconciliation: Assessing the Impact of the International Criminal Tribunal for the Former Yugoslavia*. New York: Routledge.

Cronin-Furman, Kate. 2013. "Managing Expectations: International Criminal Trials and the Prospects for Deterrence of Mass Atrocity." *International Journal of Transitional Justice* 7: 434–54.

David, Roman. 2014. "International Criminal Tribunals and the Perception of Justice: The Effect of the ICTY in Croatia." *International Journal of Transitional Justice* 8: 476–95.

Dijxhoorn, Ernst. 2014. "International Criminal Justice and Kosovo: Critical Legitimacy and Impact on a Quasi-State Entity: Critical Legitimacy and Impact on a Quasi-State Entity." In *Prosecuting War Crimes: Lessons and Legacies of the International Criminal Tribunal for the former Yugoslavia*, edited by James Gow, Rachel Kerr, and Zoran Pajić, 204–29. London: Routledge.

Drumbl, Mark A. 2007. *Atrocity, Punishment and International Law*. Cambridge: Cambridge University Press.

Ford, Stuart K. 2012. "A Social Psychology Model of the Perceived Legitimacy of International Criminal Courts: Implications for the Success of Transitional Justice Systems." *Vanderbilt Journal of Transnational Law* 45: 405–76.

Greig, Michael, and James Meernik. 2014. "To Prosecute or Not to Prosecute: Civil War Mediation and International Criminal Justice." *International Negotiation* 19: 257–84.

Hultman, Lisa. 2009. "The Power to Hurt in Civil Wars: The Strategic Aim of RENAMO Violence." *Journal of Southern African Studies* 35: 821–34.

Jo, Hyeran, and Beth Simmons. Forthcoming. "Can the International Criminal Court Deter Atrocity?" *International Organization*.
Mendeloff, David. 2004. "Truth-Seeking, Truth-Telling, and Postconflict Peacebuilding: Curb the Enthusiasm?" *International Studies Review* 6 (3): 355–80.
Neier, Aryeh. 1999. "Rethinking Truth, Justice and Guilt After Bosnia and Rwanda." In *Human Rights in Political Transitions: Gettysburg to Bosnia*, edited by Carla Hesse and Robert Post, 39–52. New York: Zone Books.
Prunier, Gerard. 2011. *Africa's World War: Congo, the Rwandan Genocide and the Making of a Continental Catastrophe*. Oxford: Oxford University Press.
Roht-Arriaza, Naomi, and Javier Mariezcurrena. 2006. *Transitional Justice in the Twenty-First Century: Beyond Truth Versus Justice*. Cambridge: Cambridge University Press.
Sloane, Robert D. 2007. "The Expressive Capacity of International Punishment: The Limits of National Law Analogy and the Potential of International Criminal Law." *Stanford Journal of International Law* 43 (Winter): 39–94.
Staub, Ervin. 2013. "Building a Peaceful Society: Origins, Prevention, and Reconciliation After Genocide and Other Group Violence." *American Psychologist* 7: 576–89.
Valentino, Benjamin, Paul Huth, and Sarah Croco. 2006. "Covenants without the Sword: International Law and the Protection of Civilians in Times of War." *World Politics* 58: 339–77.
Wilson, Richard. 2005. "Judging History: The Historical Record of the International Criminal Tribunal for the former Yugoslavia." *Human Rights Quarterly* 27: 908–42.
Wippman, David. 1999. "Atrocities, Deterrence, and the Limits of International Justice." *Fordham International Law Journal* 23 (2): 473–88.

## CHAPTER 5

Akhavan, Payam. 2013. "The Rise and Fall, and Rise of International Criminal Justice." *Journal of International Criminal Justice* 11: 527–36.
Anku Megwalu, Amaka, and Neophytos G. Loizides. 2009. "Dilemmas of Justice and Reconciliation: Rwandans and the Gacaca Courts." *African Journal of International and Comparative Law* 5: 1–33.
Arzt, Donna E. 2006. "Views on the Ground: The Local Perception of International Criminal Tribunals in the Former Yugoslavia and Sierra Leone." *The Annals of the American Academy of Political and Social Science* 603: 226–39.
Clark, Janine N. 2009. "International War Crimes Tribunals and the Challenge of Outreach." *International Criminal Law Review* 9: 99–116.
Ford, Stuart. 2012. "A Social Psychology Model of the Perceived Legitimacy of International Criminal Courts: Implications for the Success of Transitional Justice Systems." *Vanderbilt Journal of Transnational Law* 45: 405–76.
Gallup International. 2012. *Voice of the People End of the Year Survey*. Accessed online at http://www.icpsr.umich.edu/icpsrweb/ICPSR/studies/35201.

Hagan, John, and Sanja K. Ivkovic. 2006. "War Crimes, Democracy, and the Rule of Law in Belgrade, the Former Yugoslavia, and Beyond." *The Annals of the American Academy* 605 (May 2006): 130–151.

Hatay, J. 2005. "Peacebuilding and Reconciliation in Bosnia and Herzegovina, Kosovo and Macedonia 1995–2004." Accessed online at http://www.pcr.uu.se/publications/other_pub/Reconciliationreport_jacobsson_050615.pdf

Hudson, Valerie, Bonnie Ballif-Spanvill, Mary Caprioli, and Chad F. Emmett. 2012. *Sex and World Peace*. New York: Columbia University Press.

Hussain, Varda. 2005. "Sustaining Judicial Rescues: The Role of Outreach and Capacity-Building Efforts in War Crimes Tribunals." *Virginia Journal of International Law* 45: 547–63.

Kelsall, Tim. 2009. *Culture Under Cross Examination*. Cambridge: Cambridge University Press.

Kerr, Rachel, and Jessica Lincoln. 2008. *The Special Court for Sierra Leone: Outreach, Legacy and Impact*. London: King's College London.

Klarin, Mirko. 2009. "The Impact of the ICTY Trials on Public Opinion in the Former Yugoslavia." *Journal of International Criminal Justice* 7: 89–96.

Meernik, James. 2015. "Explaining Public Opinion on International Criminal Justice." *European Political Science Review* 7: 567–91.

Nettelfield, Lara. 2010. *Courting Democracy in Bosnia and Herzegovina*. Cambridge: Cambridge University Press.

No Peace Without Justice. 2012. *Making Justice Count*. Accessed online at http://www.npwj.org/content/Making-Justice-Count-Assessing-impact-and-legacy-Special-Court-Sierra-Leone-Sierra-Leone-and.

Orentlicher, Dianne. 2008. "Shrinking the Space for Denial: The Impact of the ICTY in Serbia. Open Society Justice Initiative." Accessed online at http://www.grotiuscentre.org/files/NWOOpenSocietyImpactICTY.pdf.

Organization for Security and Cooperation in Europe. 2011. *Attitudes toward War Crimes Issues, ICTY and the National Judiciary*. Accessed online at http://www.osce.org/serbia/90422?download=true.

Peskin, Victor. 2005. "Beyond Victor's Justice? The Challenge of Prosecuting the Winners at the International Criminal Tribunals for the Former Yugoslavia and Rwanda." *Journal of Human Rights* 4: 213–31.

Peskin, Victor. 2008. *International Justice in Rwanda and the Balkans: Virtual Trials and the Struggle for State Cooperation*. Cambridge: Cambridge University Press.

Pham, Phuong N., Harvey M. Weinstein, and Timothy Longman. 2004. "Trauma and PTSD Symptoms in Rwanda: Implications for Attitudes toward Justice and Reconciliation." *Journal of the American Medical Association* 292: 602–12.

Prism Research. 2013. Report for the Office of the UN Resident Coordinator in Bosnia and Herzegovina. Accessed online at http://ba.one.un.org/content/unct/bosnia_and_herzegovina/en/home/publications/public-opinion-poll.html.

Schulz, Philipp. 2014. *Outreach and the ICTR: Assessing the Impact of Outreach Activities by the International Criminal Tribunal for Rwanda (ICTR)*. Uppsala, Sweden: The Hugo Valentin Centre.

Subotic, Jelena. 2009. "Expanding the Scope of Post-Conflict Justice: Individual, State and Societal Responsibility for Mass Atrocity." *Journal of Peace Research* 48: 157–69.

Tyler, Tom. 1990. *Why People Obey the Law*. New Haven, CT: Yale University Press.

Tyler, Tom, and John Darley. 2000. "Building a Law-Abiding Society: Taking Public Views About Morality and the Legitimacy of Legal Authorities into Account When Formulating Substantive Law." *Hofstra Law Review* 28: 707–39.

UN Development Program Early Warning System Special Report. 2005. "Justice and Truth in Bosnia and Herzegovina: Public Perceptions." Accessed online at http://www.undp.ba/.

United Nations Development Program. 2012. *Perceptions on Transitional Justice*. Accessed online at http://www.undp.org/content/dam/kosovo/docs/TJ/English-Web_965257.pdf.

## CHAPTER 6

Akhavan, Payam. 2013. "The Rise and Fall, and Rise of International Criminal Justice." *Journal of International Criminal Justice* 11: 527–36.

Dunne, J. Paul. 2006. "After the Slaughter: Reconstructing Mozambique and Rwanda." *The Economics of Peace and Security Journal* 1 (2): 39–46.

Ford, Stuart. 2012. "A Social Psychology Model of the Perceived Legitimacy of International Criminal Courts: Implications for the Success of Transitional Justice Systems." *Vanderbilt Journal of Transnational Law* 45: 405–76.

Kerr, Rachel. 2007. "Peace through Justice? The International Criminal Tribunal for the Former Yugoslavia." *Southeast European and Black Sea Studies* 7 (3): 373–85.

Kerr, Rachel, and Jessica Lincoln. 2008. *The Special Court for Sierra Leone: Outreach, Legacy and Impact*. London: King's College London.

Mason, T. David, and James David Meernik. 2006. *Conflict Prevention and Peacebuilding in Post-War Societies: Sustaining the Peace*. London: Routledge.

Wu, Kristin Xueqin. 2013. "Experiences that Count: A Comparative Study of the ICTY and SCSL in Shaping the Image of Justice." *Utrecht Law Review* 9 (1): 60–77.

# Index

# About the Author

**James Meernik** is professor of political science and director of the Castleberry Peace Institute at the University of North Texas. He is also division coordinator for the social sciences in the College of Arts and Sciences. He specializes in research on international justice and international courts, post-conflict peace building, and U.S. foreign policy. Professor Meernik's research focuses on the judgments of the international criminal tribunals and the impact these decisions have on local populations. Currently, Professor Meernik is working on projects related to victim and witness testimony at international tribunals, the impact of international tribunals, and international human rights. He teaches introductory American government courses, peace studies, U.S. foreign policy, transitional justice, and international criminal law courses.

From 2003 to 2008, Meernik was associate editor of the flagship journal of the International Studies Association, *International Studies Quarterly*. He co-leads a UNT Study Abroad Program to the International Criminal Tribunal for the former Yugoslavia that won the 2007 American Political Science Association award for the most innovative course in the United States. Meernik has conducted research in The Hague, Bosnia, Rwanda, and Arusha, Tanzania, on transitional justice issues. He won a Fulbright Specialist grant to the Autonomous University of the State of Mexico (UAEM) in 2009 to teach a course on post-conflict peace building, and another Fulbright Specialist award in 2013 to lecture and develop curriculum with Soochow University in Taiwan. He has authored over sixty articles and book chapters and has authored or co-edited four books on international relations. He was formerly chair of the Department of Political Science (2002–2008), associate dean of the College of Arts and Sciences (2009), American Council on Education Fellow (2009–2010), and acting dean of the Toulouse Graduate School (2010–2012). He has taught at the University of North Texas since 1991.

Lightning Source UK Ltd.
Milton Keynes UK
UKOW01n1406260916

283846UK00001B/36/P

9 781442 269668